CONTEMPORARY APPRC
THE QUR'AN AND SUNNAH

CONTEMPORARY APPROACHES TO THE QUR'AN AND SUNNAH

EDITED BY

MAHMOUD AYOUB

THE INTERNATIONAL INSTITUTE OF ISLAMIC THOUGHT
LONDON • WASHINGTON

The International Institute of Islamic Thought
P.O. BOX 669, HERNDON, VA 20172, USA
www.iiit.org

LONDON OFFICE
P.O. BOX 126, RICHMOND, SURREY TW9 2UD, UK
www.iiituk.com

ISBN 978-1-56564-577-6 *limp*
ISBN 978-1-56564-578-3 *cased*

Typesetting and cover design by Sideek Ali
Printed in Malta by Gutenberg Press Ltd

CONTENTS

PART III

PART IV

CONTRIBUTORS

ISRAR AHMAD KHAN
Professor of Qur'an and Sunnah, International Islamic University, Malaysia.

AISHA MUSA
Professor of Islamic Studies, Department of Religious Studies, Florida International University, USA.

MAHMOUD AYOUB
Professor of Islamic Studies and Christian-Muslim Relations, Hartford Seminary, USA, and Professor Emeritus, Temple University, USA

KHALED TROUDI
Holds a Ph.D in Qur'anic Hermeneutics with Reference to Narratives: A Study in Classical Exegetical Traditions, from the University of Exeter, UK, and is Research Associate at IIIT, USA.

MOHAMMED ABU-NIMER
Associate Professor at the American University's School of International Service in International Peace and Conflict Resolution, Washington, DC, and Director of the Peacebuilding and Development Institute.

IMAD-AD-DEAN AHMAD
Adjunct Professor at Georgetown University, Washington DC, USA and President and Founder of the Minaret of Freedom Institute.

DAOUD NASSIMI
Holds a Ph.D in Islamic Studies, is the Vice-Chairman of the Council of Muslim Organizations, Washington, DC and teaches Islamic studies at Fairfax Institute in Virginia.

SAMI CATOVIC
Attorney and doctoral candidate at Temple University, USA.

MOHAMAD ADAM EL SHEIKH
Jurist and member of the Fiqh Council of North America.

KHALEEL MOHAMMED
Professor of Islamic Studies, Department of Religious Studies, San Diego State University, California, USA.

FOREWORD

Contemporary Approaches to the Qur'an and Sunnah is a collection of specially selected papers presented at the 2008 Summer Institute for Scholars convened at the IIIT headquarters in Herndon, Virginia, USA July 15 to August 15, 2008. The essays making up the collection are not random but focused discussions, divided into four parts, and comprised of diverse writings on various significant subjects relating to the Qur'an and Sunnah, of common and intellectual interest as well as relevancy.

Inaugurated in 2008 and now in its fourth year, the purpose of the Summer Institute is to bring together and engage senior and young scholars with a particular interest or expertise in Qur'anic Studies or the Sunnah in focused, organized discussions of topics related to a contemporary understanding and articulation of issues involving the Qur'an and the Sunnah. The specific objectives of the Summer Institute are to:

- Develop methods or approaches of understanding the Qur'an and Sunnah that are both authentic and relevant to contemporary realities and sensibilities in the West and the Muslim world.
- Suggest means and instruments of engaging the scholarly community, the religious community, the media and the public at large in learning processes, debates or experiences that make intelligible the wisdom of the Qur'an and the Sunnah and their relevance to contemporary human affairs.
- Broaden the scope of conversations on issues pertaining to the Qur'an and Sunnah through the inclusion of social and physical scientists beside the scholars of the traditional Islamic disciplines.

We hope that both general and specialist readers benefit from the perspectives offered and the overall issues examined in the book.

Where dates are cited according to the Islamic calendar (hijrah) they are labelled AH. Otherwise they follow the Gregorian calendar and labelled CE where necessary. Arabic words are italicized except for those which have entered common usage. Diacritical marks have been added only to those Arabic names not considered modern. English translations taken from Arabic references are those of the author.

The IIIT, established in 1981, has served as a major center to facilitate serious scholarly efforts based on Islamic vision, values and principles. The Institute's programs of research, seminars and conferences during the last thirty years have resulted in the publication of more than four hundred titles in English and Arabic, many of which have been translated into other major languages.

We express our thanks and gratitude to the contributors for their cooperation throughout the various stages of production. We would also like to thank the editorial and production team at the IIIT London Office and all those who were directly or indirectly involved in the completion of this book including, Shiraz Khan, Dr. Maryam Mahmood, Tahira Hadi, Sara Mirza and Salma Mirza. May God reward them for all their efforts.

IIIT LONDON OFFICE
January 2012

EDITOR'S INTRODUCTION

THE QUR'AN AND SUNNAH are the two primary sources of Muslim faith, life, law and morality. They are as well the framework of the Islamic worldview and civilization. The Qur'an is believed by all faithful Muslims to be literally the Book of God, and the Sunnah, or life-example of the Prophet Muhammad (ṢAAS),* is the key to the understanding and interiorization of the Qur'an.

The Qur'an is for Muslims the foundation of their faith and the Sunnah is the framework of their morality. Together they constitute the two sources of the law (Shariᶜah) of God, which is humanity's guide to prosperity and happiness in this life and to the bliss of the hereafter. Both the Qur'an and Sunnah were revealed by God. The Qur'an, being the divine communication or revelation (*waḥy*), was sent down to the Prophet through Gabriel, the angel of revelation. The Sunnah, being divine inspiration (*ilhām*), was taught and instituted by the Prophet Muhammad. God says, "He it is who sent a messenger to the unlettered people from among themselves to recite to them His revelations, purify them and teach them the Book and Wisdom..." (62:2). The Qur'an is the Book (*Kitāb*) and the Sunnah is the wisdom (*ḥikmah*) with which Muhammad, the last prophet of God was sent to guide humankind to the straight way (*al-ṣirāṭ al-mustaqīm*), which leads to God.

After the Prophet's death, ᶜĀ'ishah, the "mother of the faithful" was asked to describe the Prophet's character, or moral conduct (*khulq*). She replied, "His character was the Qur'an." During his life, the Prophet Muhammad was the living embodiment of the Qur'an. After his death, his Sunnah continued and will continue to live in the life of the Muslim Ummah till the day of Resurrection.

---

*ṢAAS – *Ṣallā Allāhu ᶜalayhi wa sallam*: May the peace and blessings of God be upon him. Said whenever the name of the Prophet Muhammed is mentioned.

Although the Qur'an and Sunnah are materially and formally two independent sources, they are inextricably bound in a dynamic relationship. The rulings and precepts (*aḥkām*) of the Qur'an constitute the law (*sharᶜ*) of God. They were supplemented by the precepts of the Sunnah, which possess equal authority with the precepts of the Qur'an. The authority of the Prophet's Sunnah is legislated in the Qur'an, as God says: "He who obeys the Messenger would in fact obey God..." (4:80). Even more emphatically God commands all Muslims, "Whatever the Messenger gives you, that you must take, and whatever he forbids you, you must desist therefrom...." (59:7).

In answer to this divine command, and realizing the need to remind others of it, the IIIT resolved to convene an annual Summer Institute for scholars and students to study the Book of God and Sunnah of His Prophet. To date, the Summer Institute has met twice: in July and August of 2008 and 2009. The eleven papers included in this volume constitute some of the proceedings of the first Summer Institute, 2008. Proceedings of future colloquiums will also be published. We hope that these annual volumes will serve as a reminder to Muslims and non-Muslims of the place of the Qur'an and Sunnah in the life of Muslim societies around the world, despite their cultural, racial and linguistic diversity.

The eleven papers comprising this volume deal with a variety of subjects. While most of them treat in one way or another the Qur'an and Sunnah, one as we shall see, in reality is not related to the main subject of this book. Yet included for reasons that will be explained below.

Since there is no clear continuity among the articles under discussion, I arranged them in terms of their specific approach or subject. I therefore placed the first two papers which concentrate on a Qur'anic science or concept together. The next five papers deal with the Qur'an in relation to non-Qur'anic disciplines. These are followed by three papers specifically dealing with the Sunnah and its juridical application, and one unrelated final paper which closes this volume.

Therefore, this book comprises four parts. The first part consists of two papers: Israr Ahmad Khan's essay examining the important issue of abrogation (*naskh*) in the Qur'an, and Aisha Musa's dealing with issues of just war, jihad, and fighting (*qitāl*) in the Qur'an.

The next five papers forming part two deal with the Qur'an in relation to other disciplines, such as theology, broadly speaking, inter-scriptural relations and natural and social sciences: "Religious Pluralism and the Qur'an" by the editor of this work; Dr. Khaled Troudi's examination of the relationship of the Qur'an with the earlier Abrahamic Scriptures; Professor Mohammed Abu-Nimer's, "Exegesis, Social Science and the Place of the Jews in the Qur'an" in which he relies on both classical Qur'an commentaries and contemporary non-exegetical sources; Imad-ad-Dean Ahmad's "Qur'an and Science," in he which studies in some depth the relationship of the Qur'an to science; and finally Daoud Nassimi's study of the English translations of certain Qur'anic verses containing particular rulings and injunctions. The themes he analyzes are the Friday prayer and the veil or *ḥijāb*.

The next two papers forming part three constitute a somewhat coherent unit. Sami Catovic examines the significance of the actual text (*matn*) analysis of the Prophetic Hadith traditions, and Mohamad Adam El Sheikh discusses the social and juridical status of divorced women and their right to "Post-Divorce Financial Support."

The last paper of this volume by Khaleel Mohammed forming part four is simply an independent study of an important subject. It is an appeal to Muslim scholars to evolve a coherent Muslim approach to western studies of Islam. Our reason for including it is not dependent on its subjects or themes, but on the fact that in its own right, it is a good contribution to Islamic studies. Moreover, it touches on the Qur'an from the perspectives of western Orientalist and modern scholars. Finally, in its own way, it also touches on interfaith dialogue, whose significance to the life of Muslims in the West is undeniable.

The Qur'an is an inexhaustible source of study and it is clear that our relationship with the Book, meaning its message, should always be one of depth and wise discernment, carefully observed and constantly maintained. The Sunnah of our Prophet Muhammad, is not in essence a body of religious literature, but a living and dynamic force which all Muslims ought to use as the model for their own lives. Prophet Muhammad was a loving father, a just and loving husband, a political leader, but above all "the Messenger of God to all of humankind..." (7:158). He is the Imam and role model for all Muslims. Following his noble example, or Sunnah, is the Islamic quest for achieving prophetic existence. We offer this humble effort as a little candle to illuminate our way to this noble quest.

MAHMOUD AYOUB
December 20th, 2009

PART I

I

Arguments for Abrogation in the Qur'an: A Critique

ISRAR AHMAD KHAN

INTRODUCTION

THE Qur'an is perhaps the most widely consulted scripture in the world, and also perhaps the most manipulated with regards to source of law. *Fuqahā'* and *mufassirūn* have provocatively subjected the Qur'an to progressively more complex interpretative and legislative contemplation. One group of scholars uses the Qur'an to substantiate its own set of views and rebut others whilst another uses the Qur'an to authenticate its particular thoughts and condemn the approach of rivals. Theological and legislative debates revolving around the Qur'an have caused the once united Muslim Ummah to divide into various camps which most of the time have been at odds with each other over most issues.

One such issue related to the Qur'an is that of abrogation. Muslim scholars in general, and *fuqahā'* and *mufassirūn* in particular, have been fairly aggressive and hostile towards one another over the question of abrogation in the Qur'an. The opinion of the *ʿulamā'* can be predominantly divided into two camps, those favoring abrogation and those negating it, with both insisting upon the validity of their own respective opinion on the subject. Fifteen hundred years later (that is since the revelation of the Qur'an) the dispute over the issue of abrogation is as fresh as it might have been during its early stage.

Logically speaking, only two probabilities can exist concerning the claim of the two groups: either both groups of scholars have mistaken the issue of abrogation or only one of them stands for the truth. In no way can both be right. Innumerable books have been written on this subject. Yet, the matter remains unsettled. The basic factor for this lies in the traditional approach of scholars who almost abhor a rational and critical approach on anything pertaining to the Qur'an. This study takes a rational and critical look at the arguments for or against the doctrine of abrogation in the Qur'an.

ABROGATION IN THE QUR'AN: DEFINITION

The original Arabic term for abrogation is *al-naskh*. In defining this term, Muslim scholars have stated so many things, leaving the term undefined in a categorical manner. Anyone who reads the works of Abū ᶜUbayd (d. 224 AH), al-Naḥḥās (d. 377 AH), Makkī (d. 437 AH), Ibn al-ᶜArabī (d. 543 AH), Ibn al-Jawzī (d. 597 AH), al-Zarkashī (d. 794 AH), al-Suyūṭī (d. 911 AH), and al-Dehlawī (d. 1176 AH) on the issue of abrogation issue will be left confused regarding its definition. Ibn al-Jawzī, to some extent, may be considered the first to offer a clear definition of abrogation in the Qur'an:

> *Al-naskh* literally signifies two things: (1) removal and lifting up; for example, the sun removes (carries *naskh*) the shadow because with the light of the sunrise the shadow recedes; one such example is also in the Qur'an – 'Allah removes (applies *naskh*) what Satan casts in' and (2) copying a document in another place, for example, they say that the book was copied; a Qur'anic example of this import is 'We had been documenting what you had been doing.' As for the application of *al-naskh* in Shari'ah (Islamic law), it signifies in the first sense because the lifting up of a command which was initially obligatory for the people denotes its removal with or without its replacement.[1]

Al-Zurqānī was uncomfortable with the complicated approach of scholars in defining *al-naskh*. He found discussions on its meaning in sources of various nature (i.e. *tafsīr*, works on *al-naskh* etc.), and hence saw no wisdom in referring to them. He coined a definition of abrogation that he claimed more reasonable and closer to reality: "Removal of an Islamic command by a legally valid argument" (*rafᶜ al-ḥukm al-sharᶜī bi dalīl sharᶜī*).[2] Subhi Salih deemed this definition the most precise, and was not content with the controversies of Muslim scholars over the definition of abrogation.[3]

Ibn al-Jawzī has suggested five conditions for the occurrence of abrogation. First, the ruling in the abrogating verse and the abrogated verse should contradict each other. Second, the abrogated ruling should chronologically precede its abrogating ruling. This could be known either through divine statement or through historical information. Third, the abrogated ruling should have been initially part of Islamic law. Fourth, the abrogating ruling should also be a confirmed part of Islamic law. Fifth, the justification for an abrogating ruling should be either as strong as that of its abrogated ruling or stronger than that of the abrogated one. Where the strength of the abrogating in comparison to the abrogated one is tenuous, the abrogation will not occur.[4]

ARGUMENTS FOR ABROGATION IN THE QUR'AN

The proponents of abrogation do not seem to be very clear as to the arguments confirming the theory of abrogation in the Qur'an. The reason is very simple. A controversial approach to abrogation makes the proposed arguments controversial hence not altogether valid. Arguments advanced for abrogation are numerous due to the classification of abrogation into various categories. All these arguments are of two kinds, those strengthening the concept of abrogation in general, and those reinforcing the occurrence of abrogation in the Qur'an itself.

Regarding the validity of abrogation in normal life and in Islamic law, there is actually no controversy among Muslim scholars. Ironically, the advocates of abrogation focus more and more on this dimension of the issue, stressing the message that the Qur'an is not excepted from this general rule. This category of arguments is not within the purview of this study. The scope of this study is confined to the arguments for abrogation in the Qur'an. Ibn al-Jawzī and al-Zurqānī have both categorically mentioned all the probable arguments for abrogation in the Qur'an based on the Qur'anic verses, the opinions of the *Ṣaḥābah*, the views of the *Tābiʿūn*, and the claim of consensus.[5]

ARGUMENTS BASED ON QUR'ANIC VERSES

The verses quoted to corroborate the occurrence of abrogation in the Qur'an are (2:106), (2:269), (3:7), (4:160), (5:48), (13:39), (16:101), (17: 86), and (22:53). (2:106) reads: "We do not abrogate any verse or cause it to be forgotten but We bring another verse either similar to it or better than that...." This verse clearly states the occurrence or possibility of abrogation effected by God Himself. Undoubtedly, this verse forms a substantial evidence for abrogation. However, the question is whether this statement talks about abrogation within the Qur'an.

Does the word "*āyah*" invariably connote a verse of the Qur'an? To the defenders of abrogation, "*āyah*" does signify a verse of the Qur'an. The answer to this question is found in the Qur'an. In Qur'anic usage the word "*āyah*," its dual variant, and its plural form "*āyāt*" have been used 86 times, only once, and 296 times respectively. These usages do not signify just the simple meaning of "verse" of the Qur'an. The Qur'an uses "*ayah*" in the following shades of meaning: message of Allah (SWT),* (2:129), (2:252); mark (3:97); symptom (19:10); masterpiece (30:21), (36:33); lesson (10:92); miracle (20:22), (23:50); Qur'anic statement (3:7); revelation in the previous Scriptures (3:113); and irrefutable proof (30:22).

Verse 2:115 states, "And God's is the east and the west: and wherever you turn, there is God's Countenance...." Maintaining that the Prophet's facing toward Jerusalem in his prayers was in the light of this revelation seems a far-fetched idea. Ibn ʿAbbās (RAA)** believed the verse came in response to the Jewish objection to the change of direction in prayer from Jerusalem to Makkah.[6] The Prophet faced Jerusalem not only for around two years in Madinah but also in Makkah, right from the beginning of his mission, whereas (2:115) is a *Madanī* revelation.

---

*SWT – *Subḥānahu wa Taʿālā*: May He be praised and may His transcendence be affirmed. Said when referring to God.

**RAA – *Raḍiyā Allāhu ʿanhu* (May God be pleased with him).

(2:269) reads, "He who was granted wisdom was granted indeed an overflowing good...." This verse is used as argument for abrogation in the Qur'an based on Ibn ʿAbbās's interpretation of it as follows: "Wisdom (*ḥikmah*) here signifies the understanding of the Qur'an's abrogating and abrogated rulings, that of its clear (*muḥkam*) and unclear (*mutashābih*) verses, that of its beginning and its ends, that of its lawful and unlawful, and its parables."7 The report through which this statement is attributed to Ibn ʿAbbās contains a defective chain of reporters. The narrator who reports from Ibn ʿAbbās is ʿAlī ibn Abī Ṭalḥah who never met Ibn ʿAbbās. A weak report cannot be used as an argument. It should be checked whether *ḥikmah* denotes knowledge of abrogation in the Qur'an. *Ḥikmah* literally connotes practical and methodological understanding of knowledge.

The Qur'an articulates the duties of the Last Prophet. One of his various tasks was to teach the Book and wisdom. If, as Ibn ʿAbbās interprets, *ḥikmah* refers to, among other things, knowledge of abrogation in the Qur'an, the Prophet must have taught his followers which verses of the Qur'an were abrogating and which ones were abrogated. However, all the sources lack any such information on the Prophet's teaching his Companions about abrogated and abrogating verses in the Qur'an.

To attain the import of the word *ḥikmah* in the verse just cited (2:269), one has to read the entire context spread across verses (2:267-283). In these seventeen verses, three main messages are apparent: charity work is of great benefit for believers; usury-based monetary transaction is baneful for man; and monetary loans are to be properly documented and reliably testified. All these matters are financial. (2:269) is a part of that context. This particular verse communicates that understanding the objectives and advantages of these wealth-related acts is wisdom; one who understands it is ever prepared to be generous for the sake of Allah.

If those scholars who claim to have knowledge of abrogated verses in the Qur'an are indeed blessed with wisdom, they should have irrefutable arguments at their disposal. Conversely, proponents of abrogation in the Qur'an stand confused over how to surely identify and then justify abrogation in the Qur'an.

(3:7) reads, "He it is who bestowed upon you from on high this divine writ, containing *āyāt muḥkamāt* that are the essence of the divine writ, and others that are *mutashībihāt....*" This verse refers to the two categories of the Qur'anic verses, *muḥkamāt* and *mutashābihāt*. Aside from the original and allegorical imports of these two terms, Ibn ʿAbbās, al-Ḍaḥḥāk Ibn Muzāḥim, and others insist that the word *mutashābihāt* signifies abrogated *āyāt* in the Qur'an.[8]

This suggestion is difficult to accept and results in several problems. Allah makes clear that these two categories of *āyāt* are of a permanent nature; the *muḥkamāt* will forever remain *muḥkamāt* and the *mutashābihāt* will not change at any stage of time into non-*mutashābihāt*. Yet here in the abrogation system, the scholars keep changing their stand on the abrogated verses of the Qur'an. Does it, then, mean that *mutashābihāt* will keep changing its position to *muḥkamāt*? Is it fair to supersede the statement of Allah? An example may suffice to illustrate the point.

According to Ibn ʿAbbās, the following command in (2:180) is abrogated: "It is ordained for you, when death approaches any of you and he is leaving behind much wealth, to make bequests in favor of his parents and near of kin in accordance with what is fair: this is binding on all who are conscious of God." Hence, this statement of the Qur'an must be considered as *mutashābih*. Yet to ʿAlī, 'Ā'ishah, al-Shaʿbī, and al-Nakhaʿī, the same command (2:180) is not abrogated and hence is *muḥkam*.[9] One should not refer to the same verse as *muḥkam* as well as *mutashābih*.

What is attributed to Ibn ʿAbbās concerning the meaning of *mutashābihāt* as abrogated verses of the Qur'an is doubtful. Al-Ṭabarī has recorded Ibn ʿAbbās's view through four chains of narrators (*sanad*). Two of these chains contain anonymous reporters and hence, these reports are weak. The two other chains are also defective due to the availability of weak reporters therein. In one chain the reporter reporting the view of Ibn ʿAbbās is ʿAlī ibn Abī Ṭalḥah, who did not learn anything from Ibn ʿAbbās. Therefore, his report from Ibn ʿAbbās may not be considered reliable. The other chain has two unreliable reporters, Asbāṭ ibn Naṣr and Ismāʿīl al-Suddī. The view ascribed to al-Ḍaḥḥāk ibn Muzāḥim is also not based on reliable chains. Al-Ṭabarī has used five chains. All of them are weak due to the names of

Juwaybir, Salmah ibn Nubayt, Juwaybir, al-Ḥuṣayn ibn al-Farj, and Salmah ibn Nubayt respectively.

The word *mutashābihāt* means illustrative. In the Qur'an one finds mention of the life hereafter and many other things unseen to man. To describe such unseen elements God has used metaphoric language to bring the picture of the unseen close to human perception. All places in the Qur'an where unseen items, creations, and phenomena have been mentioned constitute *mutashābihāt.*[10]

(4:160) reads: "For the iniquity of [the Israelites] We made unlawful for them certain good things which had been lawful for them...." None but al-Zurqānī claims this verse speaks about the existence of abrogation in the Qur'an. He takes this position based on the phrase "which had been made lawful for them." For al-Zurqānī, the making of lawful into unlawful signifies abrogation.[11] It is certainly an occurrence of abrogation. But where did it occur, in the Qur'an or the Torah? There should not be any confusion over the meaning of verse (4:160). It indicates how the Israelites were punished due to their belligerent approach to their religion. In one such punishment, they were barred from utilizing certain things already lawful. Ibn ʿAbbās states this verse (4:160) reminds us of the fact that the Israelites carried out some changes in the Torah, making certain things unlawful on their own.

The part in question of verse (5:48) reads: "...For every one of you We made a law and a way...." Does this verse in any way indicate the occurrence of abrogation in the Qur'an? For a vivid picture of this divine statement it is desirable to read not only the whole verse but also its preceding and succeeding verses. The translation of the whole verse is as follows:

> And We revealed to you the Book with truth which confirms the Book before it and serves as its guardian: so judge between them by what Allah has revealed, and follow not their vain desires diverging from the truth that has come to you. For every one of you We made a law and a way. If Allah had so willed, He would have made you a single people but [His plan is] to test you in what He has given you: so strive as in a race in all virtues. The goal of you all is to Allah; it is He who will show you the truth of the matters in which you dispute.

This verse relays three main messages: the Qur'an represents the truth; the Qur'an is the only source of law for the people; and decision of any dispute is to be made in the light of the Qur'an, and not based on what exists in the previous scriptures. The occurrence of the word "truth" as the attribute of the Qur'an in the verse sends a message beyond any doubt that the Qur'an contains truth from every angle and in every single verse. To say that certain verses of the Qur'an are abrogated as to their practicability is tantamount to not accepting the Qur'an as the truth. This verse (5:48) and its preceding and succeeding verses give a repeated call to reject the stand of the Jews on the scriptures of God and to follow the last revealed scripture of Allah. The above clause of the verse, "For every one of you We made a law and a way" rather confirms that the previous laws revealed in the previous scriptures are no longer valid; and that the laws revealed in the Qur'an are the only valid provisions of law. Makkī ibn Abī Ṭālib stressed that this verse refers to the abrogation of the previous prophets' laws and not to the laws in the Qur'an.[12]

(13:39) reads, "Allah annuls or confirms whatever He wills, for with Him is the source of all revelation," and is used as an argument for abrogation on the basis of a statement attributed to Ibn ʿAbbās: "Allah replaces in the Qur'an whatever He wills to abrogate and retains whatever He wills not to abrogate. Both the abrogated and the abrogating are in the mother of the Book. All that are replaced as well as retained are in the Book."[13] Qatādah ibn Diʿāmah claims this verse conveys the same idea as (2:106) and talks about abrogation in the Qur'an, and that (13:39) also substantiates the theory of abrogation in the Qur'an.[14] The chain through which Ibn ʿAbbās's view has been reported seems to be defective due to the inclusion of ʿAlī ibn Abī Ṭalḥah, who never benefited from Ibn ʿAbbās. Qatādah probably based his opinion on Ibn ʿAbbās's statement. This verse uses the word *maḥū*, which means effacement and total removal; wherever the *maḥū* takes place, nothing remains in place. Abrogation theory emphasizes that both the abrogating and the abrogated verse remain in the Qur'an. In that case, (13:39) should not speak about abrogation in the Qur'an.

If we read the whole of *Sūrah al-Raʿd* (13), we can see that the surah consoles the Prophet and his followers, and also rebuts various suppositions developed by the opponents; i.e., the Quraysh. The above verse (13:39) forms an answer to the objection raised by the Quraysh that due to the presence of previous divine scriptures revealed to previous prophets, there did not arise any need for the new scripture. In answer it was stressed that God willed to efface the previous scriptures as the sources of law and send a new scripture, that is the Qur'an.[15]

"...Every fixed term (*ajal*) has had its *Kitāb*," is the last statement of the preceding verse (13:38). The statement in (13:39) connects to the previous one. In this way, (13:39) is not advocating the theory of abrogation but rather the prerogative of God to annul previous scripture and replace it with the Qur'an. Apart from this, the verse is a *Makkī* revelation; it is, then, wonderfully strange to suggest that this verse alludes to abrogation theory. The concept of abrogation surfaced only in Madinah where a new society based on Islamic laws was being developed.

(16:101) reads: "And when We substitute one revelation for another – and Allah knows best what He reveals (in stages) – they say: 'You are but a forger': Nay, but most of them do not understand it!" This verse is taken as an argument for the progression in the commands of Allah through revelation in the Qur'an. This stand is untenable. This verse is a *Makkī* revelation. In *Makkī* revelations one may not find such progression in the laws. (16:101) itself refers to the observation of the Quraysh that Muhammad himself fabricated the messages in different ways and presented them in stages in the name of God. The Quraysh could not have raised the question of abrogation of laws in Makkah. This verse reminded the Quraysh that it was not Muhammad who revealed the Qur'an in stages but God Who knew very well what to reveal where and when in the Qur'an. Seyyed Mawdudi, while interpreting (16:101), observed that in *Makkī* revelations one could see the same message in different styles and arguments scattered at various places in the Qur'an. It was this revelation in stages which made the Quraysh assume that the Qur'an was Muhammad's own work; had it been from God, it would have been revealed all at once. He maintained that the *Makkī* revelations do not have the progression in Islamic laws.[16]

(17:86) reads: "If it were Our will, We could take away that which We have revealed to you: then would you find none to plead your case against Us." Undoubtedly, this verse refers to the power of God to remove His own command, but it does not prove that God sent a revelation in the Qur'an and then lifted it away. The verse after it, "Except for mercy from your Lord; for His bounty on you is great" (17:87), reasserts that Allah out of His bounty on the Last Prophet would never take away what He had revealed to him. This verse speaks only of the possibility of abrogation and not the occurrence of abrogation in the Qur'an. In fact (17:86) forms part of an answer to a question raised by the Quraysh on behalf of the Jews in Madinah concerning the meaning of the "spirit." The answer begins from verse (17:85): "They ask you concerning the Spirit. Say: 'The Spirit is of the command of my Lord. And you were not granted of this knowledge but very little,'" and ends with (17:87). The Spirit is actually revelation entirely at the discretion of Allah as to where, when, what, and to whom to send it down to. Makkī used (17:86) as the basis to claim that God had erased certain revelations of the Qur'an from the hearts and documents,[17] which is gross speculation, and speculation or "conjecture can never be a substitute for truth" (10:36).

(22:52) reads: "Never did We send a messenger or a prophet before you, but, when he framed a desire, Satan cast something into his desire: but Allah cancels what Satan casts in, and He confirms His messages. Allah is full of knowledge and wisdom." It is obvious, even to a layman, that this verse refers to abrogation of something cast in the hearts of prophets by Satan, and not the abrogation of Qur'anic verses. Nevertheless, certain *mufassirūn*, while interpreting this verse, decided to do so in light of a story widely considered a forgery concerning the infamous satanic verses (which mentions Satan having put into the mouth of the Prophet some of his own verses admiring the Makkan gods of the Quraysh) as proof of how God had deleted these satanic insertions into revelation. These *Mufassirūn* it would seem forgot the assurance of God in verse 15:9 that, "We [without doubt] sent the Message to you step by step and We are responsible to safeguard it." God's promise to protect the Qur'an does not merely signify after it had been revealed but also before and during its revelation. In other words to claim that Satan had somehow managed to interfere in the process of the revelation of *Sūrah al-Najm* (53) is to falsify the divine guarantee made in (15:9) that the revelation would be safe from any corruption whatsoever.

ARGUMENTS BASED ON THE VIEWS OF THE *ṢAHĀBAH* AND *TĀBIᶜŪN* SCHOLARS

While discussing the significance of abrogation in the Qur'an, advocates of abrogation quote the following three statements attributed to three *Ṣaḥābah*: ᶜUmar ibn al-Khaṭṭab, ᶜAlī ibn Abī Ṭālib, and ᶜAbd Allāh ibn ᶜAbbās.

Statement 1: ᶜUmar said, "Ubay ibn Kaᶜb is the most knowledgeable among us on abrogation."[18] Ibn al-Jawzī did not give the chain of narrators of this report, so its reliability cannot be ascertained. Apart from the problem of its authenticity, one need not construe into ᶜUmar's statement a reference to abrogation in the Qur'an. He simply praises Ubay's knowledge on the issue of abrogation but crucially does not state that Ubay was the most knowledgeable concerning abrogation *in the Qur'an*. Ubay ibn Kaᶜb in fact had knowledge of previous scriptures, and hence knew very well which commands of the Torah had been annulled by the Qur'an.

Statement 2: ᶜAlī's view is advanced in the form of a dialogue between him and a storyteller. ᶜAlī asks the latter whether he was aware of the abrogating (*al-nāsikh*) and the abrogated (*al-mansūkh*). When he answers in the negative, ᶜAlī warns him: "You destroyed yourself as well as others."[19] In what way does this report constitute an argument in favor of abrogation in the Qur'an? Was the storyteller a teacher of the Qur'an whom ᶜAlī warned of the serious consequences of his ignorance of abrogation in the Qur'an? Was there any reference in ᶜAlī's question to abrogation in the Qur'an? Indeed, the storyteller was not a teacher of the Qur'an but, as his title 'storyteller' conveys, very clearly just that, a storyteller. Had he been a teacher of the Qur'an, he would never have been mentioned as a storyteller. It seems from the report that the storyteller would narrate stories of all sorts, including stories of previous people and prophets based on his understanding of previous scriptures. When ʿAlī asks him with regards to his knowledge of the abrogating and the abrogated, he might have have been asking him about the abrogating revelations in the Qur'an and the abrogated verses in previous scriptures.

Statement 3: Ibn ʿAbbās's view has been discussed above. His interpretation of verses such as (2:106), (3:7), etc. confirms his view on abrogation in the Qur'an. These verses have been discussed thoroughly as to their import. They do not speak about abrogation in the Qur'an but about abrogation by the Qur'an of the previous scriptures. The name of Ibn ʿAbbās has been misused and abused by those with vested interests. If all the reports attributed to Ibn ʿAbbās are critically checked, they might prove either their weakness or unreliability. For instance, the *tafsīr* work *Tanwīr al-Miqbās* is attributed to Ibn ʿAbbās. Yet, scholars have proven beyond any doubt that the two reporters who report the *tafsīrī* views of Ibn ʿAbbās are liars and hence unreliable. Ibn ʿAbbās should not be blamed, but rather the reporters who attribute the statements to him are to be condemned as unreliable.

Among *tābiʿūn* scholars, the most prominent supporters of abrogation are Saʿīd ibn al-Musayyab, Mujāhid ibn Jabr, Qatādah ibn Diʿāmah, and al-Ḍaḥḥāk ibn Muzāḥim. One can find their declaration of this or that verse as abrogated in the sources. Since they consider certain verses of the Qur'an abrogated, the theory of abrogation in the Qur'an is taken as justified. There is no doubt that they declared certain verses as abrogated, but we have to investigate what they meant by declaring a verse abrogated. Some examples may suffice to crystallize the matter.

First, when Anas ibn Mālik grew old and unable to fast in the month of Ramadan, he would feed the poor instead, everyday as compensation for the missed fasts. This he used to do in light of the concession granted in the Qur'an: "...and [in such cases] it is incumbent upon those who can afford it to make sacrifice by feeding a needy person...." (2:184).[20] Anas ibn Mālik, like others, also considered that facility as abrogated. Why did he then practice it? To him, abrogation of a ruling in the Qur'an never signified permanent invalidity of the Qur'anic command. Second, Ibn ʿAbbās decreed that after a woman gave birth she was allowed to pay ransom in place of fasting.[21] Ibn ʿAbbās said time and again that the permission to pay ransom for fasting (2:184) was abrogated. If he meant permanent abrogation of the verse, why did he, then, allow women to do this? Certainly, to him, abrogation in the Qur'an meant impracticability of certain rulings of the Qur'an in certain given situations. Third, ʿAbd Allāh ibn ʿUmar was once asked about the position of a pregnant woman who fasted in Ramadan but suffered from dehydration. He advised the woman to break the fasting and pay the ransom every day.[22] He did consider that concession abrogated for healthy, normal women and men, but for the pregnant and the sick, he did not find the ruling abrogated. Fourth, Abū al-ʿĀliyah did not fast in the month of Ramadan in his old age, and paid the ransom instead.[23]

ARGUMENT BASED ON THE EXISTENCE OF ABROGATED RULINGS IN THE QUR'AN

Al-Zurqānī advanced an argument in favor of abrogation in the Qur'an, stating there existed certain verses in the Qur'an that can never be practiced.[24] Are we to take this as an argument? Where is the evidence? Who decided this or that verse was abrogated? Did God clearly indicate the abrogated revelation in the Qur'an? Certainly, there is no statement in the Qur'an referring to the abrogated rulings. Did, then, the Prophet identify the practically invalid commands in the Qur'an? There is no such tradition in the hadith literature. Al-Zurqānī's statement is simply supposition, meaning that he and others from the community of Muslim scholars invented suppositions on their own that some verses of the Qur'an were practically invalid forever. Ironically, the identification of abrogated rulings in the Qur'an was in the past and still is an act of personally motivated manipulation of the Qur'an.

Scholars of abrogation, *fuqahā'* and *mufassirūn*, have miserably failed to refine the principles of abrogation so as to give them universal shape. Different scholars developed their own standards of abrogation in the Qur'an, which is why they could not unanimously agree as to which verses are abrogated.

Behind this declaration there is a hypothesis that the number of abrogated verses might be reduced further. Probably, Shāh Walī Allāh al-Dehlawī took up this challenge and decreased the number of abrogated verses from twenty-one to only five. This narrowing down of the abrogated verses took place based on interpretation of the verses concerned. According to al-Dehlawī, the only abrogated verses in the Qur'an are (2:180), (2:240), (8:65), (33:52), and (58:12).[25] Interestingly, these five verses have been declared by others from the proponents of abrogation as non-abrogated.[26] Therefore, no verse of the Qur'an stands abrogated. In this case, the stance of al-Zurqānī regarding the existence of abrogated verses in the Qur'an turns out to be untenable.

ARGUMENT BASED ON THE CLAIM OF CONSENSUS

Some commentators of the Qur'an and scholars of Qur'anic studies claim there is a consensus amongst the Muslim Ummah over abrogation in the Qur'an. Ibn al-Jawzī states that *ʿulamā'* have consensus over the occurrence of abrogation in the Qur'an but some did not agree to it.[27] Al-Naḥḥās states that some people rejected the existence of abrogating and abrogated verses in the Qur'an; their approach is not reasonable because they oppose the consensus of the Muslim Ummah and also the Qur'anic stipulation on the matter.[28] Al-Suyūṭī claims that there exists consensus amongst Muslims concerning abrogation in the Qur'an.[29] Al-Zurqānī slightly changes his statement: "Early generations of Muslim scholars (*salaf al-ummah*) had consensus of opinion over the fact that there occurred abrogation in the Islamic law."[30]

In the statements of al-Naḥḥās and Ibn al-Jawzī there is a very clear recognition of controversy among scholars over abrogation in the Qur'an. Both accept the existence of some who rejected the abrogation theory. Does this situation refer to consensus? They have themselves disputed their own stance. Consensus occurs only when all the scholars, without any exception, agree to the issue concerned; even the dissent of one single scholar makes the matter controversial. Al-Suyūṭī avoided mention of the difference of opinion on abrogation, although he knew very well the nature of the situation. He frequently borrowed ideas and information from al-Zarkashī's work, *ʿUlūm al-Qur'ān*. This being the case why did he not, then, also take from al-Zarkashī the statement concerning Muslim scholars' controversy over the issue of abrogation?

Al-Zarkashī referred to the views of some other scholars who considered the Qur'an as abrogator of the previous scriptures, and not of its own revelations. Al-Zarkashī seems to have supported the idea of the Qur'an being protected from all kinds of contradictions. To substantiate his understanding, he quotes (15:9): "Verily, We sent the Message (Qur'an) down step by step and We shall safeguard it."[31] Al-Zurqānī suggests Muslim scholars' consensus over abrogation in Islamic law and describes disagreement of other scholars from early to modern times.[32]

There is actually no consensus on abrogation in the Qur'an among Muslim scholars; scholars are divided into groups, one supporting it and the other negating it. In addition, the claim of consensus controverts the reality in history today. Al-Rāzī stated that a consensus amongst Muslim scholars is not a sufficient basis to cancel the practical validity of Qur'anic rulings.[33]

ĀYAT AL-SAYF AND *ĀYAT AL-QITĀL* VERSUS GENEROSITY AND JUSTICE TOWARDS NON-MUSLIMS

A number of verses in the Qur'an exhort believers to uphold justice and treat non-believers generously. For example, (4:90): "So if they [non-Muslim fighters] withdraw from you, and fight not against you, and offer peace to you, then Allah has opened no way for you (to war against them)." Part of (5:2) reads: "And let not the hatred of some people in shutting you out of the Sacred Mosque lead you to transgression. Help you one another in righteousness and piety, but help you not one another in sin and rancor." The starting phrase of (20:130) reads: "So be patient with what they (non-believers) say," while (33:48) reads: "And obey not the unbelievers and hypocrites, and disregard their insolence; but put your trust in Allah, for enough is Allah as a Disposer of affairs."

These verses and many others advise the Prophet and his followers to be patient with the insolent approach of the enemies, to be generous towards non-believers, and to be just towards non-Muslims. Yet the staunch supporters of abrogation have dared to declare all such commands of the Most Merciful to be null and void, based on two statements: (9:5) "Kill the polytheists wherever you find them, capture them and besiege them, and lie in wait for them in each and every ambush;..." and (9:29) "Fight against those who believe not in Allah, nor in the Last Day, nor forbid that which has been forbidden by Allah and His Messenger, and those who acknowledge not the religion of truth among the people of scripture, until they pay the *jizyah* with willing submission and feel themselves subdued." These two verses are known in legal terminology as *āyat al-sayf* and *āyat al-qitāl*.

Qatādah ibn Diʿāmah observed: "Everything in the Qur'an advising avoidance of conflict with the disbelievers stands abrogated by the *āyat al-sayf* and *āyat al-qitāl*."[34] As per the calculation of Ibn al-Jawzī, around one hundred and ten verses that promote leniency, kindness, patience, and generosity towards non-believers are considered abrogated by *āyat al-sayf* and *āyat al-qitāl*. He did not agree with this number but supported the abrogation of only twelve of them. *Āyat al-sayf* and *āyat al-qitāl* were revealed in connection with the situation of war. When the situation is normal (that is, not one of war), these two verses remain unexecuted. The Prophet's agreements with the Jews and Arabs, particularly the Quraysh, and other warring parties for peace serve as enough evidence for the peaceful coexistence policy of Islam. It seems that the image of Muslims in the West as terrorists is consequent upon the abrogation of generosity towards non-Muslims.

ARGUMENTS AGAINST ABROGATION IN THE QUR'AN

At the forefront of the movement against abrogation theory was Abū Muslim al-Aṣfahānī. His arguments to rebut the claim of abrogation in the Qur'an are of two kinds: the statement of the Qur'an; and the interpretation of the Qur'an.

According to al-Aṣfahānī, the statement of the Qur'an that negates the existence of abrogation in the Qur'an is, "No falsehood can approach it from before or behind it: it is sent down by One Full of Wisdom, Worthy of all Praise" (41:42). He declared abrogation theory a falsehood (*bāṭil*).[35] Is his stance correct? Al-Zurqānī rebuts al-Aṣfahānī's observation with his conviction that abrogation in the Qur'an is the truth (*al-ḥaqq*), and not falsehood (*bāṭil*). Yet, al-Zurqānī provides no evidence to substantiate his claim other than verse (2:106), which as we have seen earlier states that God carries out abrogation, not in the Qur'an but in previous scriptures by the Qur'an. It is difficult to accept the theory of abrogation in the Qur'an as being the truth (*al-ḥaqq*) because abrogation insists on the existence of conflict (*taʿāruḍ* and *tanāqud*). The notion of conflict between one revelation of the Qur'an and another is false. Al-Zurqānī maintained that abrogation denotes permanent suspension of the practical validity of a verse but retains the position of the verse concerned as being a Qur'anic revelation.[36]

Al-Zurqānī forgets that to recite a Qur'anic verse and to believe in its authenticity as part of the Qur'an necessitates its imperativeness. Every command of the Qur'an represents the truth from every possible angle: it is a revelation from on high; it is a part of the Qur'an; it is to be believed as the most sacred; it is to be recited as a command of God; and it is to be acted upon wherever it is relevant. Yet abrogation theory throws aside the verse's validity in terms of practical purpose. This is certainly tantamount to considering it invalid. Invalidity of a Qur'anic command renders it false. The argument of al-Aṣfahānī therefore seems to be logical.

Al-Aṣfahānī proposed that the Qur'anic verses should be interpreted rather than abrogated. Supporters of abrogation, for instance, declare (2:180) to be abrogated: "It is prescribed for you, when death approaches any of you, if he leaves wealth, that he makes bequest to parents and next of kin according to reasonable usage. This is a duty upon the pious." Al-Aṣfahānī interpreted it to remain practically valid, saying that the bequest, as the verse suggests, should be as per a reasonable manner (*bi al-maʿrūf*). He explained that *al-maʿrūf* here meant in accordance with the command of God as stated in the inheritance verses (*āyat al-mīrāth*) (4:7-14). *Al-maʿrūf* certainly does not mean according to the prevalent custom in the society, but means "what is good." Furthermore, the good is only what God declares as good. There is nothing wrong in this interpretative approach of al-Aṣfahānī, his suggestion seems quite rational. With this method of interpreting the Qur'an, the practical validity of the so-called abrogated verses can be traced. The stance of Abū Muslim is sufficiently substantiated by the Qur'an. Verses such as (2:185), (4:82), (5:3), (11:1), (17:82), (36:2), and (39:28) unequivocally spell out that the Qur'an in its entirety is ever relevant in human life.

(2:185) reads: "Ramadan is the month in which was sent down the Qur'an as a guide to mankind, and as clear proofs for guidance, and as the criterion (for right and wrong)...." This verse speaks about three attributes of the Qur'an: a source of guidance, proofs of guidance, and a standard for right and wrong. These three qualities apply to the entire Qur'an. If abrogation in the Qur'an is taken for granted, then this means that a certain part of the scripture is deprived of these attributes. Abrogation has created confusion and irreconcilable controversy among *ʿulamā'* and the Muslim masses. This is not a situation of guidance. Thus, anything curtailing the position of the Qur'an as guidance is not sustainable.

(4:82) reads: "Do they not ponder on the Qur'an? Had it been from any other than Allah, they would surely have found therein many discrepancies." According to this statement, the Qur'an is free from any kind of discrepancy, yet the supporters of abrogation theory insist that there are legal rulings that are contradictory to each other. Now, we have a matter of choice between the two statements, one from Allah and the other from man. Of course the right choice is that of Allah's declaration because belief in abrogation theory amounts to the existence of contradiction among verses of the Qur'an. If there exists no conflict between the commands of Allah, as (4:82) informs us, then we can conclude there is no abrogation in the Qur'an at all.

(5:3) highlights the lawful and unlawful for the believers: "...This day have I perfected your religion, completed My favor upon you, and have chosen for you Islam as your way of life...." With the revelation of this message, the Prophet and his followers were assured of the perfection of the Qur'an. Abrogation theory negates this and thrusts by force an idea that the Qur'an is still imperfect.

(11:1) reads: "*Alif Lām Rā'*. This is a Book the verses whereof were perfected (*uḥkimat*) and then explained in detail from One Who is All-Wise, Well-Aware." The message of this verse is very clear. Both the categories of verses in the Qur'an – *muḥkamāt* and *mutashābihāt* – are full of wisdom. No lacuna remains in either of the two kinds of verses whereby imperfection of any nature can penetrate into the Qur'an. This verse refers to two qualities of Qur'anic verses: perfected and explained in detail. Do these two attributes of Qur'anic revelations give way to abrogation? Abrogation lies in stark contrast to these two features of the Qur'an.

(17:82) reads: "We send down of the Qur'an that which is a cure and mercy for the believers...." Whatever has been revealed in the Qur'an serves as a cure for the suffering of man in this life. By regarding some Qur'anic revelations as poison for practical life abrogation in effect prevents believers from benefiting from some of this Qur'anic panacea. In other words, the Qur'an is remedy in its entirety but abrogation theory renders some part thereof as malady. Every piece of the Qur'an is indisputably a cure, as opposed to what the champions of abrogation would proclaim.

(36:2) reads: "By the Qur'an, full of wisdom." This verse refers to the Qur'an as *ḥakīm* (wise). This is also one of the attributes of Allah. The Qur'an is wise because it originates from the Wise. This attribute of the Qur'an speaks volumes of its great position: each and every single command of Allah is relevant. If any verse of the Qur'an is relegated as irrelevant for man, the Qur'an, then, cannot remain as wise. Abrogation theory serves as the antithesis of this Qur'anic position.

(39:28) reads: "This is a Qur'an in Arabic without any crookedness therein...." Yet, abrogation theorists indirectly and in effect utter the opposite: "Beware, there is crookedness in some places in the Qur'an." Is abrogation theory anything other than crookedness itself? Abrogation theory and the declaration in (39:28) stand in direct contradiction to each other. Which one is, then, to be accepted and which one to be rejected? Naturally, the information conveyed in (39:28) represents the truth.

ABROGATION IN THE QUR'AN AND THE PROPHET

The Qur'an was revealed to the Prophet. He was also granted by Allah the *bayān* (explanation) of the Qur'an. Since he taught the Qur'an to his followers, he must have given them all that which was necessary for them. One does not find any direct statement of the Prophet indicating any verse of the Qur'an to be practically invalid. If he remained silent over this matter, this means no verse has been abrogated. Abrogation theory adversely affects the integrity of the Qur'an. Anything causing the Qur'an to lose its original position stands logically rejected.

CONCLUSION

The arguments for abrogation in the Qur'an are based on some Qur'anic verses, views of early generations of scholars, claims about the existence of abrogated verses in the Qur'an, and claims of consensus. In most cases, the Qur'anic verses used as arguments in favor of abrogation theory are misquoted. They are read either outside of their context or are advanced only in part. When reading those verses in full and also in context, a totally different message emerges. Reading the Qur'an halfheartedly is manipulation and not interpretation. The concept of abrogation in the eyes of early generations of scholars was not what was construed later. To them, abrogation never denoted permanent suspension of the Qur'anic commands. Claims of consensus are a misrepresentation of the situation. There has always been controversy over this matter. To claim that some verses of the Qur'an are abrogated is to cast doubt on the authenticity of the Qur'an.

Neither God nor His Prophet ever guided man in a categorical manner stating this verse or that verse to be practically invalid. There are many verses in the Qur'an that spell out various attributes of the Qur'an (e.g., a guide, wise, a cure, etc), which necessitate the practical relevance of the Qur'an in its entirety. There is no authentic statement of the Prophet referring to the abrogated verses of the Qur'an. The only viable way to resolve the abrogation-related controversy is to endeavor to interpret the verses concerned. Sincere effort to understand the practical relevance of the verses in dispute will certainly bring results.

REFERENCES

Abū ʿUbayd, Al-Qāsim ibn Salām, *Al-Nāsikh wa al-Mansūkh fī al-Qur'ān al-ʿAzīz* (Riyādh: Maktabah al-Rushd, 1990).

Al-Dehlawī, Shāh Walī Allāh, *Al-Fawz al-Kabīr*, translated into Urdu by Khurshid Anwar (Deoband, India: Kutub Khana Husayniyah, n.d.).

Islahi, Amin Ahsan, *Tadabbur-i-Qur'ān* (Delhi: Taj Company, 1997).

Al-Jawzī, ʿAbd al-Raḥmān Ibn, *Nawāsikh al-Qur'ān* (Beirut: Dār-al-Kutub al-ʿIlmiyyah, n.d.).

Khan, Israr Ahmad, *Qur'anic Studies: An Introduction* (Kuala Lumpur: Zaman Islam Media, 2000).

Makkī, Ibn Abī Ṭālib, *Al-'Īḍāḥ li Nāsikh al-Qur'ān wa Mansūkhihi* (Jeddah: Dār al-Manārah, 1986).

Mawdudi, Seyyed, *Tafhīm al-Qur'ān* (Lahore: Idara Tarjuman al-Qur'an, 1997).

Al-Rāzī, Fakhr al-Dīn, *Mafātīḥ al-Ghayb* (Beirut: Dār Iḥyā' al-Turāth al-ʿArabī, 1997), vol. 2.

Subhi, Salih, *Mabāḥith fī ʿUlūm al-Qur'ān* (Beirut: Dār al-ʿIlm li al-Malāyīn, 2000).

Al-Suyūṭī, Jalāl al-Dīn, *Al-Itqān fī ʿUlūm al-Qur'ān* (Beirut: Dār al-Kutub al-ʿIlmiyyah, 2000).

Al-Ṭabarī, Muḥammad ibn Jarīr, *Jāmiʿ al-Bayān fī Ta'wīl al-Qur'ān* (Beirut: Dār al-Kutub al-ʿIlmiyyah, 1997).

Al-Zarkashī, Badr al-Dīn, *Al-Burhān fī ʿUlūm al-Qur'ān* (Beirut: Dār-al-Maʿrifah, 1994).

Al-Zurqani, Muhammad Abd Azim, *Manāhil al-ʿIrfān fī ʿUlūm al-Qur'ān* (Beirut: Dār Iḥyā' al-ʿArabī, 1998).

NOTES

1 (22:52) and (45:29); ʿAbd al-Raḥmān ibn al-Jawzī, *Nawāsikh al-Qur'ān* (Beirut: Dār al-Kutub al-ʿIlmiyyah, n.d.), p.20.

2 Al-Zurqani, Muhammad Abd Azim, *Manāhil al-ʿIrfān fī ʿUlūm al-Qur'ān* (Beirut: Dār Iḥyā' al-ʿArabī, 1998), vol. 2, p.460.

3 Subhi Salih, *Mabāḥith fī ʿUlūm al-Qur'ān* (Beirut: Dār al-ʿIlm li al-Malāyīn, 2000), pp.260-261.

4 Ibn al-Jawzī, *Nawāsikh*, pp.23-24.

5 Ibid., pp.17-19; al-Zurqānī, *Manāhil*, vol. 2, pp.468-472.

6 Muḥammad ibn Jarīr al-Ṭabarī, *Jāmiʿ al-Bayān fī Ta'wīl al-Qur'ān* (Beirut: Dār al-Kutub al-ʿIlmiyyah, 1997), vol. 1, p.549, report no.1835.

7 Ibn al-Jawzī, *Nawāsikh*, p.32.

8 Al-Ṭabarī, *Jāmiʿ*, vol. 3, pp.172-173.

9 Ibn al-Jawzī, *Nawāsikh*, p.58; Al-Zarkashī, *Al-Burhān fī ʿUlūm al-Qur'ān* (Beirut: Dār-al-Maʿrifah, 1994), vol. 2, pp.221-222.

10 Seyyed Mawdudi, *Tafhīm al-Qur'ān* (Lahore: Idara Tarjuman al-Qur'an, 1997), vol. 1, p.234; Amin Ahsan Islahi, *Tadabbur-al-Qur'ān* (Delhi: Taj Company, 1997), vol. 2, pp.27-28.

11 Al-Zurqani, p.472.

12 Makkī, Ibn Abī Ṭālib, *Al-'Īḍāḥ li Nāsikh al-Qur'ān wa Mansūkhihi* (Jeddah: Dār al-Manārah, 1986), p.63.

13 Al-Ṭabarī, *Jāmiʿ*, vol. 7, p.402, report no.20489.

14 Ibid.

15 Seyyed Mawdudi, *Tafhīm*, vol. 2, p.465.

16 Ibid., vol. 2, p.572.

17 Makkī, *Al-'Īḍāḥ*, p.64.

18 Ibn al-Jawzī, *Nawāsikh*, p.19.

19 Ibid. pp.29-31.

20 Abū ʿUbayd al-Qāsim ibn Salām, *Al-Nāsikh wa al-Mansūkh fī al-Qur'ān al-ʿAzīz* (Riyadh: Maktabah al-Rushd, 1990), p.55.

21 Ibid., p.65.

22 Ibid., p.63.

23 Ibid., p.57.

24 Al-Zurqani, *Manāhil*, vol. 2, p.472.

25 Shāh Walī Allāh al-Dehlawī, *Al-Fawz al-Kabīr*, Khurshid Anwar, Urdu trans. (Deoband, India: Kutub Khana Husayniyah, n.d.), pp.252-312.

26 Israr Ahmad Khan, *Qur'anic Studies: An Introduction* (Kuala Lumpur: Zaman Islam Media, 2000), pp.223-226.

27 Ibn al-Jawzī, *Nawāsikh*, p.17.

28 Ibid.

29 Jalāl al-Dīn al-Suyūṭī, *Al-Itqān fī ʿUlūm al-Qur'ān* (Beirut: Dār al-Kutub al-ʿIlmiyyah, 2000), vol. 2, p.40.

30 Al-Zurqani, *Manāhil*, vol. 2, p.472

31 Al-Zarkashī, *Al-Burhān*, vol. 2, pp.174-175.

32 Al-Zurqani, *Manāhil*, p.483.

33 Fakhr al-Dīn al-Rāzī, *Mafātīḥ al-Ghayb* (Beirut: Dār Iḥyā' al-Turāth al-ʿArabī, 1997), vol. 2, p.234.

34 Ibn al-Jawzī, *Nawāsikh*, p.208.

35 Al-Rāzī, *Mafātīḥ*, vol. 1, p.640.

36 Ibid.

2

Towards a Qur'anically-Based Articulation of the Concept of "Just War"

AISHA Y. MUSA

Fight in the way of God those who fight you, but do not commit aggression (QUR'AN 2:190)

INTRODUCTION

TODAY, the word jihad has become a very conspicuous part of the English lexicon. A search of the word "jihad" on Amazon.com in the category of "Islam" finds more than 1,000 books listed, ranging from scholarly and academic works to vitriolic anti-Muslim propaganda. In the process of entering popular English usage, however, there are connotations being imposed on the word that Qur'anic usage does not support. The most insidious of these is the common rendition of the word jihad as "holy war." Both Muslims and non-Muslims now often translate the word jihad as "holy war." Often people take verses or parts of verses from the Qur'an, ignoring context and related verses, to make Islam appear warlike and violent, or to justify hostility and aggression.

Among non-Muslims, this stems both from widespread, general ignorance about Islam and a tendency to view the violent behavior of groups and individuals who identify themselves as Muslims and claim an Islamic agenda as generally representative of Islam. The popular conception of jihad as "holy war" is also fostered by a rising tide of anti-Islam propaganda from a variety of pseudo-scholars.[1]

Unfortunately, misunderstanding of this issue is not found only among non-Muslims. Some who identify themselves as Muslims help perpetuate this misunderstanding by actively encouraging acts of terrorism and violence in the name of Islam. The former and the latter stimulate and benefit from each other's propaganda, and each provides the other with arguments and justifications for their beliefs and behavior. The propagandists portray Islam as inherently violent, and the militants react with violence to what they see as attacks against Islam. What gets lost between the deeds of militants and the words of propagandists is any sense of the Qur'anic usage of the word jihad and how it may or may not relate to armed conflict. The challenge facing us today is to derive an authentic Qur'an-based understanding of jihad and determine how that understanding governs its relationship to armed conflict, in order to articulate Qur'an-based principles of what may be called 'just war.' The principles fall into two categories: justification *for* war (*jus ad bellum*), and just conduct *in* war (*jus in bello*).

This paper proposes a literal and holistic analysis of the text from a contemporary perspective and applying the exegetical principle of *tafsīr al-qur'ān bi al-qur'ān* (explaining the Qur'an with the Qur'an)[2] and the jurisprudential principle *al-aṣl fī al-kalām al-ḥaqīqah* (the fundamental rule of speech is literalness),[3] without refracting that Qur'anic usage through the lens of history and tradition. This paper will analyze the Qur'an's usage of the word jihad together with related words of the same root (*j-h-d*) and other words that bear on an understanding of that usage, such as *qitāl* (fighting) and *ḥarb* (war), in order to discover an understanding of the Qur'an's articulation of principles of "just war" that is both contemporary and authentic. A holistic reading is a reading in which the text is read as an integral whole whose verses are understood in light of each other. A literal and holistic reading is one that proceeds from the literal meaning of the Arabic text and considers the semantic field of the root and the various morphological and syntactic aspects that contribute to meaning, together with the ways in which words of the root are used throughout the Qur'an and the context in which specific words are used. The proposed approach begins from the assumption that there is, as Fazlur Rahman has shown, an underlying unity in the Qur'an and that its words and verses should not be understood in isolation.[4]

The examination will begin by identifying each of the instances where these words and related terms from the same Arabic root are used in the Qur'an. Once all the relevant terms have been identified, the context in which they are used will be scrutinized.

Why is it important to seek a Qur'anic perspective on the question of jihad? First, because Muslims believe that the Qur'an is the Book of God and the ultimate authority that defines the beliefs and practices of Islam. All other sources are informed by it and are subordinate to it. Whether or not something is "Islamic" or "un-Islamic" is first asked of the Qur'an. Generally after consulting the text, Muslims turn to other sources of authority for clarification and elaboration. Interpretation and explanation of the Qur'an, therefore, begins with the Qur'an itself, proceeding from the idea that some parts of the Qur'an explain others (*yufassiru al-Qur'ān baʿḍuhu baʿḍan*), or of explaining the Qur'an with the Qur'an (*tafsīr al-Qur'ān bi al-Qur'ān*). Principles elaborated through such a holistic analysis can be used in conjunction with information from other sources such as the prophetic traditions (hadith) and biographical literature (*sīrah*) to formulate viable Islamic responses to contemporary situations.

TERMINOLOGY RELATED TO WAR IN THE QUR'AN

Perhaps no subject is as misunderstood and misconstrued as the Qur'an's position on fighting and warfare. In order to examine the text to determine its position on this, or any issue, one must begin by examining terminology. Exactly what does the text say, and how does it say it? When the Qur'an addresses fighting, it does not use the word jihad. It uses the word *qitāl*. There is no concept of holy war (*al-ḥarb al-muqaddasah*) in the Qur'an. Although the term jihad is often understood to refer to war, the Qur'an always uses it in a much broader context. When the Qur'an refers directly to war, the term it uses most often is *qitāl*. Let us now examine the Qur'an's use of each of these terms, applying the principle of *yufassiru al-Qur'ān baʿḍuhu baʿḍan*.

JIHAD

The noun jihad occurs only four times in the Qur'an. The verb *jāhada* (to struggle, strive) in various forms appears 31 times.[5] None of these refer directly to fighting, let alone specifically to military action. In 14 of the 31 occurrences the verb *jāhada* appears in the Qur'an, striving in the cause of God is used in a very general context as a quality of those who believe. Many of these verses have nearly identical wording: *alladhīna āmanū wa alladhīna hājarū wa jāhadū fī sabīli Allāh* (those who believe and emigrate and strive in the cause of God with their wealth and their selves).[6] Two instances tell how hypocrites hate to strive in God's cause and try to avoid it.[7] Where the Qur'an specifically commands striving, there is no reference to warfare.[8] Verses (29:8) and (31:15) give believers permission to disobey parents who strive (*jāhada*) to make them associate partners with God. Even under such circumstances, the believer is ordered to be considerate and just toward the parents. Taken together, these verses show us that believers must be willing to exert great efforts in the cause of God, using our wealth and ourselves. These efforts (jihad) may or may not include fighting.

The broad, general usage of *jāhada* in the Qur'an led classical Muslim jurists to recognize four kinds of jihad: jihad of the heart, jihad of the tongue, jihad of the hand, and jihad of the sword. The first of these, the effort to purify one's heart from the influences of the devil, is considered the greater jihad. Jihad of the tongue and hand are understood to refer to persuasive missionary efforts and doing good deeds, and jihad of the sword refers specifically to the use of just and necessary violence.[9]

Like the classical scholars before them, modern Muslim scholars also recognize the generality and breadth of the term jihad. The late Egyptian scholar, Shaykh Muhammad al-Ghazali, writes in his *Thematic Commentary on the Qur'an*:

> Jihad in our time encompasses a whole range of activities including inventiveness, development, and construction on land, in the sea, and in outer space. It implies research in all fields to gain wider and deeper understanding of the world and all of the phenomena associated with it.[10]

Thus, while the use of just and necessary violence is one particular form of jihad, the term jihad is not synonymous with fighting. Fighting that is carried out according to Islamic values and ideals is only one of the ways in which individuals and the community can struggle with their properties and persons in the cause of God. Such fighting is one of the recognized types of jihad. However, when the Qur'an addresses fighting, the word *qitāl*, rather than jihad, is used.

QITĀL IN THE QUR'AN

Like the word jihad, the word *qitāl*, is a form III verbal noun. Its root is *q-t-l*, which carries the basic meaning of "to cause death/kill."[11] Form III adds the meaning of "to attempt." Hence, "to attempt to cause death/kill" is "to fight" (*qātala/yuqātilu*).[12] While the Qur'an's usage of jihad and its affiliated terms is quite general, its usage of *qitāl* is far more specific. The amount of attention the Qur'an gives to the topic is an indication of just how serious the taking, or potential taking, of life is in Islam.

The root *q-t-l* appears 170 times in 122 verses of the Qur'an.[13] Of these occurrences, the word *qitāl* (fighting), itself, appears 13 times in 10 verses, while its corresponding noun *qātala/yuqātilu* appears 52 times. The word *qātala* (kill) in its various conjugations and together with its verbal noun (*qatl*) appears 98 times in 77 verses. In some verses both words occur. The frequency with which the root occurs in the Qur'an is a measure of the seriousness of taking or attempting to take human life. The general Qur'anic ruling about killing is articulated in (17:33): "And do not take any human being's life - [the life] which God has willed to be, sacred - otherwise than in [the pursuit of] justice. Hence, if anyone has been slain wrongfully, We have empowered the defender of his rights [guardian] [to exact a just retribution]; but even so, let him not exceed the bounds of equity in [retributive] killing. [And as for him who has been slain wrongfully -] behold, he is indeed succoured [by God]!"

The extreme seriousness of taking human life is further emphasized in (5:32), which describes God's response to the first murder committed by a human being, Cain's killing of Abel:

> Because of this did We ordain unto the children of Israel that if anyone

> slays a human being-unless it be [in punishment] for murder or for spreading corruption on earth-it shall be as though he had slain all mankind; whereas, if anyone saves a life, it shall be as though he had saved the lives of all mankind. And, indeed, there came unto them Our apostles with all evidence of the truth: yet, behold, notwithstanding all this, many of them go on committing all manner of excesses on earth.

By equating the unjust taking of a single human life with killing all of humanity and the saving of a single life with saving all of humanity, this verse leaves no uncertainty about the value of human life. It also indicates the conditions that justify taking of a human life: murder or the commission of heinous crimes in the land. Taking a single life, in the absence of one of these conditions, is morally equal to killing the human race in its entirety, according to the Qur'an. This idea has extremely serious implications for warfare and fighting.

Let us now turn to the Qur'anic discussion of fighting. The Qur'an indicates that fighting is called for under certain circumstances: "Fighting is prescribed for you while it is hateful to you. It is possible that you hate a thing that is good for you, and that you love a thing that is bad for you. God knows and you do not know"(2:216).

The Qur'an also specifies when, where, why, how, and with whom fighting is allowed:

> Fight in the way of God those who fight you. But do not commit aggression. Certainly, God does not love the aggressors. And kill them wherever you encounter them. And expel them from where they expelled you; for sedition (*fitnah*) is more grievous than killing. Do not fight them at the sacred mosque, unless they fight you therein. But if they fight you, kill them. Such is the reward of the disbelievers. (2:190-191)

(8:30) offers more specific information about the behaviors that justify fighting an enemy: "the unbelievers plot to disable you, or kill you or, expel you...." Verse 56 of the same chapter adds breaking treaties to the list of behaviors "they are those with whom you made a treaty, but they break their treaty every time": 22:39-40 offers further elucidation:

> Permission [to fight] is given to those who are being fought, because they have been oppressed. Certainly, God is able to help them. Those who have been expelled from their homes without justice only because they say: "Our Lord is God." If God did not repel some people with others, monasteries, churches, synagogues and mosques in which God's name is commemorated frequently would be destroyed, and God will surely help those who help Him; surely, God is Powerful, Mighty. (22:39-40)

Together, these verses establish an overall principle of fighting in response to aggression, together with a clear prohibition of aggression on the part of Muslims: *yuqātilūnakum wa lā taᶜtadū inna Allāha lā yuḥibbu al-muᶜtadīna* (But do not commit aggression. Certainly, God does not love the aggressors). This is supported by the verses immediately following: "But if they desist, God is Forgiving, Merciful; and fight them until there is no more unrest and oppression and religion is for God. But if they desist, let there be no hostility except against oppressors" (2:192-193).

Fighting is not limited to self-defense, however, but also includes defense of others, as indicated in (4:75): "Why would you not fight in the way of God and the weak and oppressed among men, women, and children, who say, "Our Lord save us from this place whose people are oppressors, and give us from You, a protector, and give us from You, a helper?"

Thus, the Qur'an indicates whom to fight and details specific behaviors in which they engage that justify fighting them. These same conditions are reiterated throughout the Qur'an in all its discussions of *qitāl.* These verses clearly demonstrate that the purpose of fighting, from a Qur'anic perspective, is not to conquer and convert people, but to defend the Muslim community against aggression on the part of others who attack first and, when they enter treaties, violate them and attack Muslims because of their religion. This understanding is further supported by (60:9), which states: " God only forbids you from allying with those who fight you on account of religion and expel you or support expelling you. Whoever allies with them, these are the unjust."

Taken together, the verses discussed so far lay the foundation for a principled view of war in which violence is only used in response to aggression or oppression, and hostilities are ended as soon as the aggression or oppression ends: "fight them until there is no more unrest and oppression, and religion is for God..." "But if they lean toward peace, you lean toward peace and trust in God. He is the Hearer, the Knower."[14] A popular argument against such a reading of the text is based on the claim that verses such as (22:39-40) and (2:190) have been abrogated by the so-called "verse of the sword," (9:5). Proponents of this argument generally cite the portion of the verse, which says, "then kill the polytheists wherever you find them," claiming that this abrogates any previous verses that seem to restrict fighting and killing non-Muslims. However, this argument is problematic for two very important reasons.

First, as John Burton has clearly demonstrated, there is no agreement among Muslim scholars, past or present, on the nature of abrogation, or on the specifics of the abrogating and the abrogated.[15] More important to the present discussion, however, is the fact that a literal reading of (9:5) in the surrounding context demonstrates that its message is the same as that found throughout the Qur'an.

Chapter 9 opens with an extended discussion of fighting and treaties. The first verse gives notice to the polytheists of dissolution of their treaties with the Muslims: "a notice of dissolution from God and His messenger to those among the polytheists with whom you made a covenant" (9:1). Verse 4, however, clarifies that the dissolution does not apply to all those polytheists who had treaties with the Muslims: "Except those among the polytheists with whom you have made a treaty and who have not failed you in anything or aided anyone against you, fulfill their treaty to their fullest extent. Certainly, God loves the God-fearing" (9:4).

The above is the verse that immediately precedes the so-called "verse of the sword," which some claim has abrogated other verses and calls on Muslims to kill all disbelievers wherever they may be. The dissolution of treaties mentioned in the first verse of chapter 9 may seem to support such a claim. However, verse 4 makes a clear exception. Treaties are not dissolved with the polytheists who have not failed to uphold their treaties. Verse 6 also throws doubt on the claims made about the import of the so-called "verse of the sword."

Verse 6 commands: "If one of the polytheists seeks asylum with you, give him asylum until he has heard the word of God, and after that escort him to his place of safety" (9:6). Thus, both the verse immediately preceding and the verse immediately following the verse that allegedly abrogates any moderation of fighting and killing disbelievers suggest something entirely different. Moreover, these are not the end of the discussion. Verse 7 returns to the topic of keeping treaties: "as long as they stand true to you, you stand true to them; certainly God loves the God-fearing" (9:7). The real issue is made clear in (9:12–13): If they violate their treaties after making them, fight the leaders of disbelief; certainly they have no treaties. Perhaps they will desist (9:12). Will you not fight people who violated their treaties, plotted to expel the messenger, and started the war in the first place? (9:13)

These verses reiterate and elaborate on the sentiments expressed in (2:190): "Fight in the way of God those who fight you, but do not commit aggression. Certainly, God does not love the aggressors." Therefore, rather than being abrogated, this concept is confirmed and elaborated in chapter 9, as well as elsewhere throughout the text.

Using some parts of the Qur'an to explain others on the question of struggle (jihad) and fighting (*qitāl*), four general principles become clear. The first is that fighting is sometimes necessary, even though human beings may dislike it (2:216). While fighting is necessary, it is also strictly regulated. This leads to the second principle: that aggression is intolerable. The command to fight those who fight you in (2:190) is followed immediately by the command not to aggress; the importance of non-aggression is further emphasized by the declaration that God does not love the aggressors.

In addition to the unambiguous prohibition of aggression on the part of Muslims, the Qur'an also stipulates specific actions that justify the use of violence by Muslims. These are elaborated and reiterated throughout the text, from the earliest verses believed to have been revealed on the issue of fighting in chapter 22 to the last believed to have been revealed in chapter 9, and they form the basis of the third principle: that violence is justified as a response to specific acts of

injustice such as people being attacked and persecuted because of their faith, the breaking of treaties, and the eviction of people from their homes without just cause. Verses 4:74-75 also indicates that Muslims may fight not only on their own behalf, but also on behalf of others who seek assistance against injustice and persecution. A fourth key principle is that when those who have committed acts of aggression and injustice stop doing so and seek peace, fighting against them is to cease.[16]

The four key principles outlined that:

i) fighting is sometimes necessary,
ii) aggression is forbidden,
iii) fighting is a response to specific types of aggression and injustice,
iv) fighting ceases when the causes cease and the aggressors seek peace.

These principles would form a Qur'an-based framework in which Muslim scholars can elaborate a detailed theory of justifications for war and just conduct of war in the contemporary period, which takes into account details from the prophetic Sunnah as well as contemporary political and social realities.

NOTES

1 For example, Andrew Bostom's, ed., *The Legacy of Jihad: Islamic Holy War and the Fate of Non-Muslims* (New York: Prometheus Books, 2008); and Robert Spencer's, *Onward Muslim Soldiers: How Jihad Still Threatens America and the West* (Washington: Regnery Publishing Inc., 2003).

2 Muhammad Ali al-Sabuni, *Mukhtaṣar Tafsīr Ibn Kathīr*,.1, 28, Al-Muhaddith Program.11.36 available at http://www.muhaddith.org/quran.html# Download.

3 Ibn Nujaym, *al-Baḥr al-Rā'iq*, v.1.02, Al-Muhaddith Program. 11.36 (CD).

4 Fazlur Rahman, *Islam and Modernity: Transformation of an Intellectual Tradition* (Chicago: University of Chicago Press, 1984), pp.2-3.

5 *The Holy Qur'an* (CD) (Harf Information Technology, 2002), ver. 8.0. Qur'an search on j-h-d.

6 (2:218); (3:142); (5:54); (8:72, 74, 75); (9:16, 20, 44, 88); (16:110); (29:6, 69); and (49:15).

7 (9:81, 86).

8 (5:35); (9:41, 73); (22:78); (25:52); and (66:9).

9 Majid Khadduri, *War and Peace in the Law of Islam* (Baltimore: The Johns Hopkins Press, 1955), pp.56-57.

10 Shaykh Muhammad al-Ghazali, *A Thematic Commentary on the Qur'an* (Herndon, VA: The International Institute for Islamic Thought, 2000), p.263.

11 Ibn Manẓūr, *Lisān al-ʿArab*, entry *qātala*,available, at http://www.alwaraq.net/Core/AlwaraqSrv/LisanSrchOneUtf8.

12 W. Wright, *A Grammar of the Arabic Language* (Beirut: Librairie du Liban, 1996), vol. 1, p.32D.

13 *The Holy Qur'an* (Harf Information Technology). Qur'an search on the root q-t-l.

14 (8:39, 61).

15 John Burton, *The Sources of Islamic Law: Islamic Theories of Abrogation* (Edinburgh: University of Edinburgh Press, 1990).

16 (2:193); and (8:61).

PART II

3

Religious Pluralism and the Qur'an

MAHMOUD AYOUB[1]

INTRODUCTORY REMARKS

RELIGIOUS diversity is as old as human history. From ancient cave dwellers to the societies of the great empires of China, India, Iran, Egypt and Babylon, religion as the human quest for the divine manifested itself in a variety of languages, devotional practices, myths and rituals. In reality, in these and myriad other cultures, religion has been the fountainhead of civilization.[2]

Religion may also be regarded, at least in its literary, artistic and philosophical manifestations, as the product of culture. Thus the plurality and diversity of religions is a reflection of the plurality and diversity of cultures and civilizations. In this paper, I will first define pluralism religiously and philosophically. I will then attempt to contextualize it within the history of the civilizations of the Middle East. I will finally discuss religious pluralism in the Qur'an. I am convinced that the Qur'anic worldview, with its emphasis on the diversity of human racial and cultural identities and man's innate capacity to know and have faith in God, recognizes the diverse religions of humankind as divinely preordained ways to this ultimate goal.[3]

WHAT IS PLURALISM?

In its lexical usage, pluralism signifies plurality, as opposed to singularity. Plurality, moreover, implies difference, and hence diversity. Theologically, the expression religious pluralism must be distinguished from religious exclusivism on the one hand, and religious inclusivism on the other. While the proponents of these two rival ideologies to religious pluralism affirm it as a religious phenomenon, they in fact negate, or at least, seek to render it theologically meaningless.

Exclusivism denotes the view that the truth, and consequently the way to salvation, is only one. It is furthermore limited to only one true religion, and is the prerogative of one, and only one, faith-community. Exclusivism has moral, theological and philosophical implications. Philosophically, it confines the truth to one belief and value system; while morally and theologically, it ultimately condemns all other faith-communities to manifest error in this world and to perdition in the world to come.

In the three Middle Eastern, or so-called Abrahamic religious traditions, exclusivism, in one form or another, remains a fundamental tenet. In the Jewish tradition it is expressed in the doctrine of the chosen people, with its moral, political and theological implications. To be sure, ancient prophets spoke against an exclusivist nationalism that abhorred other nations and condemned them to a state of total insignificance in the sight of God. Jewish exclusivism has remained largely an exclusivism of indifference to what may be termed gentile religions and belief-systems.

The well-known exclusivist Christian doctrine formulated by the North African theologian Cyprian in the third century, "salus extra ecclesiam non est" (outside the Church there is no salvation)[4] characterized the theology of the Catholic Church at least until the Second Vatican Council. However, the Vatican Council adopted an inclusivist theology which denied real validity to religions other than Christianity, as we shall presently see.

The Qur'anic assertion, "Anyone who desires a faith other than Islam, it shall not be accepted of him; and in the hereafter he shall be among the losers," (3:85)[5] expresses an exclusivist view of religion, but only if the term Islam is taken narrowly to refer to Islam as an institutionalized religion. If, however, it is taken to signify a human attitude of total submission (Islam) to God, then we are talking not about religious institutions, but about an ideal relationship between God and human beings that transcends all religions, including Islam.[6]

The opposite of exclusivism is inclusivism. Inclusivism is a modern and mainly western humanistic Christian theological concept which takes many forms. One of these forms is the belief that even though my religion is the only way to salvation, moral women and men of good conscience, even if they be atheists, will attain salvation by being anonymous members of my faith-community.

The well-known German theologian Karl Rahner (1904-1984) coined the term "anonymous Christians" to formulate a theology of Christian inclusivist salvation.[7] He echoed in this the Second Vatican Council declarations *Nostra aetate* and the Dogmatic Constitution on the Church (*lumen gentium*). The Constitution states:

> Those also can attain to everlasting salvation who, through no fault of their own, do not know the gospel of Christ or his Church, yet sincerely seek God and, moved by grace, strive by their deeds to do his will as it is known to them through the dictate of conscience.[8]

Rahner argued for the validity of his theology of universal salvation through the atoning death of Christ on the ground that it is in virtual agreement with the theology of Vatican II. But while Vatican II presupposes faith in God, however erroneous such faith may be, Rahner made everlasting salvation available to all decent men and women of good conscience, even if they are atheists. It must be observed that his theology of salvation ultimately goes against the Christian doctrine of original sin and the need for redemption and atonement through faith in the cross of Christ.

Religious pluralism, as has already been observed, is the recognition of the multiplicity and diversity of religions as a natural or divinely willed phenomenon. Yet if religious pluralism is to serve as a meaningful framework of constructive dialogue among the followers of the various religions, all religions, or at least all theistic religions, must be recognized as legitimate ways to the truth or ultimate reality. It must be further agreed that the followers of every religion have the right to regard their own faith as the true one for them. Since, moreover, the need for everlasting salvation in some form is common to at least all the major religions, no one way should be privileged as the only way to salvation.

It may be argued that acceptance of the equal validity of all the major religions would ultimately lead to religious relativism, or the relativity of the truth. Some have therefore posited a super-religion as a unifying spiritual vision of all religions. This view is, in the final analysis, another form of inclusivism, which reduces all religions to one imaginary ideal faith.[9] That God spoke to every community or nation in its own language, through a long list of prophets and sages, is frequently asserted in the Qur'an and the New Testament.[10] All the major religions hold that the truth is one, and it transcends human understanding. Yet since the goal of all religions is to seek the truth, they must all be ways to that goal, for "...to God do we belong, and to Him we shall return." (2:156).

RELIGIOUS PLURALISM IN ANCIENT IRAN AND THE MEDITERRANEAN BASIN

The period from the eighth to the third century BC can be regarded as the axial age in religious and philosophical creativity in greatly separated areas around the then known world.[11] It witnessed the rise of Chinese philosophy in its Taoist, Confucianist and other forms. In India, during this period of spiritual growth, the great sages of the Upanishads formulated an enduring mystical monistic philosophy which supplanted the somewhat crude Vedic religion. In India too the Buddha "set the wheel of dharma turning" with his moral philosophy of suffering and salvation, and challenged the vast Hindu pantheon with its authoritarian priesthood.

Ancient Israel saw the rise of the prophetic movement with its messianic hopes and ideas of universal salvation. Voices like those of Amos, Mica, Jeremiah and others called for social justice and the worship of YHWH as the sovereign Lord of all nations.

The first man of authority to recognize and promote religious pluralism was Cyrus the great, founder of the Persian empire in the fifth century BC. Cyrus founded an empire that stretched from Iran to Central Asia to Egypt, Iraq, Syria-Palestine, and even into Europe. This great imperial domain was unrivaled until the rise of the Muslim empire following the death of the Prophet Muhammad, and especially after the phenomenal expansion of 711 CE.

Cyrus sought to honor all the deities of his realm. He allowed his foreign subjects to return to their lands, worship their gods and pray for his success and prosperity. He thus gave permission to the Judean exiles to return to Judea and rebuild the Jerusalem Temple of YHWH their God. This earned him the honor of being called YHWH's servant or messiah by the author of Isaiah II.[12]

The next empire builder was Alexander the Great (356-323 BC). Alexander was not only a great conqueror, but also a philosopher. According to classical Islamic hagiography, he was even a prophet.[13]*

Alexander may be regarded as the father of the classical civilizations of Judaism, Christianity and Islam. With Alexander we witness a conscious attempt to impose a single civilization framework on at least the Mediterranean basin, including western Europe, the Middle East and North Africa. This was the Hellenistic civilization, with its rich religious and philosophical heritage, in particular its Platonic and Aristotelian philosophical and scientific worldview.

Within this Hellenistic framework, the Mithraic mystery cult, as well as the inherently dualistic worldview of the religions of ancient Iran, which was expressed in the eternal struggle between good and evil, light and darkness, became a powerful gnostic movement which threatened and deeply influenced early Christianity. The influence of these gnostic philosophies on all three monotheistic religions of the Middle East is undeniable. Less significant in the long run were the mysteries of Isis and Osiris in Egypt, and the Delphic and other Greek mysteries which flourished during this culturally and religiously formative period of western civilization.

It may be argued that the axial age, mentioned above, culminated with Alexander the Great. With Alexander we see the beginning of a

---

*PUBLISHER'S NOTE: The issue of the identity of *dhū al-qarnayn* remains shrouded in mystery. Islamic exegesis has also severely criticized attempts to hypothesize *dhū al-qarnayn*'s equivalence to Alexander. It is clear that Alexander the Great was not a monotheist. According to the *Encyclopedia Britannica*, as well as other sources, towards the end of his life Alexander "seems to have become convinced of the reality of his own divinity and to have required its acceptance by others... a symptom of growing megalomania," *The New Encyclopedia Britannica* (USA: 1989), 15th edn., vol. 13, p. 247.

civilizational synthesis which began with the rise of Christianity and Manichaeism and culminated with Islam. Therefore, the period from Alexander to Muhammad may be viewed as another seminal epoch in the formative history of the civilizations of Judaism, Christianity and Islam.

Jesus and Paul rejected the particularistic Jewish faith to which they both belonged. The new universalistic faith which they founded constituted a sharp contrast with the traditional narrow Jewish view of religion and culture. From the beginning, moreover, Christianity challenged, and soon supplanted, Greek wisdom and Egyptian religiosity.

Christianity did not eliminate Greek philosophy, but absorbed it as the framework of its own theology. As for Hellenized Egyptian and other mystery cults, they survived in Christian hagiography and popular piety. Both Egypt and the East, most likely Iran, are represented in the account of the nativity of Jesus. For instance, the wise men of the East who came seeking the divine child, the new king, are believed to have been Magian or Zoroastrian priests. This account was meant to affirm that the humble child, placed in a lowly manger, was Christ the King.[14]

Religion has always been associated with power and humility. In Christ the King who was laid in a humble manger, the reconciliation was finally achieved between the two warring Egyptian gods Horus and Seth, represented by the ox and the donkey respectively. Through this Hellenistic synthesis, moreover, Christianity rendered the universalistic vision of the ancient Hebrew prophets a message of salvation for all humankind.

It is noteworthy that the first post-Christian religious authority to recognize the plurality and unity of religions was another Iranian, Mani the Babylonian prophet. Mani, who presented yet another vision of the unity of all religions in the third century CE, failed to actualize this vision in a new religious system. He failed because Manichaeism, which was yet another Iranian dualistic faith, denied the unity of the creation under one sovereign, all-powerful and wise God. This unity of creation under a supreme divine being was essentially the message of Zarathustra, the prophet of ancient Zoroastrianism, of which Manichaeism was a later corruption. This message was also propagated by many Greek sages, particularly Plotinus. It may in fact be argued from an Islamic point of view that Plotinus, with his mystical faith in the one divine source of being, was the prophet between Jesus and Muhammad. This is not to say, however, that Mani's explanation of good and evil was quickly forgotten. On the contrary, Manichaeism exerted a deep and lasting influence on the religious thought and piety of Europe and the Middle East.

Mani proclaimed a universal religion of light and salvation. He sought to present himself as the final messenger of God and his religion as a synthesis of Zoroastrianism, Buddhism and Christianity. Yet ironically this great religious genius had a tragic end, and his religion came to be regarded as a great heresy by both Christian and Muslim theologians and heresiographers.[15]

RELIGIOUS PLURALISM IN THE QUR'AN

Among all the scriptures of the theistic religions the Qur'an is unique in that it sets its worldview within the context of divine oneness and human diversity, including the plurality of religions. Furthermore, it regards religious diversity as one of the signs (*āyāt*) of God, second in importance to the "creation of the heavens and earth."[16] The Qur'an does not directly and categorically deny the validity and truth of any religion. Rather it is concerned with individuals and nations and their faith (*imān*), or rejection of faith (*kufr*) in God, witnessing (*shahādah*) to His oneness (*tawḥīd*) and acceptance of humankind's accountability before Him on the Day of Judgment.

The Qur'an presents its view of religious pluralism in a somewhat progressive manner. In a preliminary statement it simply enumerates the religions known to the Prophet's listeners and leaves the question of their truth for God to judge on the Day of Resurrection. It states: "Surely those who have accepted faith [that is the Muslims], those who are Jews, the Sabaeans, the Christians, the Magians and those who have associated other gods with God, verily God will judge among them on the Day of Resurrection. God is witness over all things" (22:17). It should be observed that the verse under consideration first lists the legitimate religions and then mentions those who associate other beings or things with the worship of God alone as people without a legitimate religion.

The Qur'an lays down four basic principles, which are necessary for the truth-claim of any religion. The first is that a true religion must be enshrined in a divinely revealed scripture or sacred law (Shariʿah). Secondly, it must affirm God's absolute Oneness (*tawḥīd*). Thirdly, it must profess active faith in God and the last day. Finally, it should foster righteous living (*iḥsān*). On the basis of these four principles, the Qur'an affirms the truth of the faith of Muslims, Jews, Christians and Sabaeans.[17]

It is to be observed that although a scripture or divinely revealed book is of the utmost importance for the truth of a religion, it is not the sole criterion by which a religious community is to be judged. While the Jews, Christians and Muslims are people of the Book, the Sabaeans may not have had a scripture. Nor is it clear that they were true monotheists, as they are reported to have venerated the stars. They did acknowledge a divine creator, on the basis of which the Qur'an includes them among the people of faith in God. Hence, it may phenomenologically be concluded that the Sabaean faith may spiritually prefigure the truth in the non-prophetic wisdom religions, such as Hinduism, Buddhism and the religions of China and Japan.

It may be further argued that the Qur'an affirms faith in any book that God has or may have revealed.[18] This means that, like the plurality of religions, the plurality of scriptures is open ended. The Zoroastrians, for instance, under Muslim rule collected an impressive canon of sacred books, which they claimed goes back to their ancient prophetic sages.[19]

It is noteworthy that the Prophet himself bestowed on them the status of the people of the Book in his command, "Follow in dealing with them the Sunnah (practice) of the people of the Book."[20] Likewise, the famous young Umayyad general Muḥammad ibn al-Qāsim extended this status to the Hindus, following his conquest of the Indus Valley in 711.

The Qur'an claims to have been revealed as a book confirming all previous scriptures, but particularly the Torah, the Psalms and the

Gospel. Thus the scriptural requirement is understood, and therefore omitted in the following crucial verse for our discussion. The three remaining principles are affirmed, where the Qur'an transcends all religious affiliations:

> Surely those who have faith [that is the Muslims], the Jews, the Christians and the Sabaeans; whoever accepts faith in God and the last day and performs good deeds, those shall have their reward with their Lord; no fear shall come upon them, nor will they grieve. (2:62), and (5:69)

This verse is of decisive importance for several reasons. First, it occurs twice in the Qur'an at the beginning and near the end of the Prophet's career in Madinah, as surah 2 was the first major surah to be revealed in Madinah and surah 5 was revealed before surah 9, which was the last major surah sent down to the Prophet. It must therefore be conclusively argued that this verse could not be abrogated, as many classical and modern jurists and Qur'an commentators have held. This is because abrogation applies only to legislative verses and this is a narrative verse.*

The verse under discussion is important also because it does not limit faith and its rewards to the people of the Book. It has already been observed that the Sabaeans may not have had a sacred scripture.[21] Yet they are included among those who shall have the reward of their faith with God. The identity of the Sabaeans has been under debate. Shahrastānī, in his book *al-Milal wa al-Niḥal* (The Book of Sects and Creeds) presents two sects of the Sabaeans.[22] These are the religious Sabaeans of Iraq and the philosophical Sabaeans of Harran in northern Syria. While the religious Sabaeans, with whom we are here concerned, acknowledged one divine creator, they probably did not have a sacred book and they venerated the stars, as did the Babylonians before them. Yet they are included among the people of faith in God.

---

*PUBLISHER'S NOTE: Abrogation in the Qur'an is a controversial issue. For a detailed and comprehensive understanding of abrogation in the Qur'an, please see: Khan, Israr Ahmad, *Theory of Abrogation: A Critical Evaluation* (Research Management Centre, International Islamic University Malaysia, Kuala Lumpur, 2006.) Also see, Dr. Taha J. Alalwani, *Naḥwa Mawqif Qur'ānī min al-Naskh* [Towards a Qur'anic Position on Abrogation] (Egypt: Maktabah al-Shorouk al-Dawliyyah, 2007), in which he rejects the concept of abrogation entirely.

A close hermeneutical analysis of this verse would reveal two further points. The first is that both the plurality of religions and scriptures are open ended, and closely related. Even though the Qur'an limits the designation "people of the Book" to the Jews and Christians, it speaks of an unspecified number of prophets and messengers who were sent by God as guides and warners to every nation or community. On the basis of this Qur'anic assertion, Muslims, as we have already observed, extended this designation to Zoroastrians and even Hindus. Any other community that could lay credible claim to a sacred scripture would have been included. The second point is that the assertion, "whoever has faith in God and the last day and performs good deeds" provides a universal criterion of divine favor, independent of any religious identity.

According to the principles outlined above, religious affiliation in itself is no guarantee for the attainment of Paradise. The scriptural religions are important frameworks of legal and social identities, but they must be lived within a higher sphere of sincere faith and righteous works. God addresses Muslims and the people of the Book with the warning:

> It is not in accordance with your [Muslims] wishes, nor the wishes of the people of the Book; rather, whoever does evil, he will be recompensed for it, nor will he find for himself any friend or helper besides God. And, anyone who performs righteous deeds – be he male or female – and is a person of faith, those will enter the Garden [of Paradise] and they will not be wronged in the least.[23] (4:123-24)

Thus we see that the criterion for acceptance with God is neither religious identity, nor class or gender but faith and good deeds.

The plurality of religions and scriptures arises ultimately from the great number of prophets and messengers who followed one another, from Adam to Muhammad, in a great universal procession. Relying on the Qur'anic assertion, "...There is no community (Ummah) but that a warner was sent to it" (35:24)[24] later Islamic tradition puts the number of prophets at one hundred and twenty-four thousand. The Qur'an further asserts that God did not send a messenger to a community except in its own language, in order that he may elucidate for them God's commands and prohibitions.[25]

Human history, according to this Qur'anic worldview, is prophetic history. Prophetic history is in reality the history of God's guidance of humankind through the mission of His prophets and messengers. Divine guidance, moreover, is promised to a heedless humanity that must be reminded again and again of its primordial covenant with God.

God tells us in the Qur'an that in primordial time, when humankind were still in the realm of potentiality, called by tradition "the world of atoms" (*ʿālam al-dharrah*), God brought forth from the loins of the children of Adam their progeny and made them witness over themselves. He said, "...Am I not your Lord?" they said, "Yes, indeed, we do bear witness thereto." God then warned humanity, "lest you say on the Day of Resurrection we were heedless of this..." (7:172). The human part of this primordial divine covenant is to affirm in word and deed the sovereign Lordship of the one God. God's part is to guide humankind out of the darkness of heedlessness (*ghaflah*) into the light of faith in Him.

God first renewed this covenant with Adam and his spouse, after they lost the bliss of Paradise through man's first act of heedlessness, first in His saying, "...Their shall come from Me to you guidance; and whoever follows My guidance, no fear shall come upon them nor will they grieve"(2:38).[26] God then renewed this covenant with every prophet until the coming of the last Prophet, Muhammad.

The Qur'an presents religion as such under two distinct, but also interrelated, dimensions. The first is institutionalized religions, such as Islam, Christianity and Judaism. These are the framework of the laws and rituals of worship which give their followers their legal and social identity as Jews, Christians and Muslims. All three traditions should ideally constitute what the Qur'an calls, "*millat abīkum ibrāhīm* (the religion of your father Abraham)," who called all his children Muslims. Institutionalized human religions are the necessary vehicle and framework of the inner dimension which they represent.

The Qur'an calls this inner dimension the *fiṭrah*, or original creation of God of all His human creatures. The Qur'an identifies this divine original creation with the straight (*qayyim*) religion: *"Set [O*

Muhammad] your face straight towards God, a man of pure faith (ḥanīfan), for this is God's original creation (fiṭrah) upon which He created humankind; there is no altering of God's creation...." (30:30).[27]

This divine pure creation is the innate capacity to know God and have faith in Him, with which every human being is born. This means that every child is born pure, and is thus ready to affirm anew the divine primordial covenant of "Am I not your Lord?" This innate capacity to know God is realized through human unaided reason, as was the case with Abraham who took first the luminous star to be his Lord, then when it set, he said, "I love not those that set." He then turned to the moon, and when it set, he exclaimed, "if my Lord guides me not, I shall surely be one of those who had gone astray." He finally took the sun to be his God, but when it set he realized that the sun is not God. Then, in an outburst of adoration, he cried out, "I turn my face towards Him who created the heavens and the earth, a man of pure faith, nor will I be one of the associators (*mushrikīn*)" (6:76-79).[28]

This Qur'anic two-dimensional view of religion in no way implies dichotomy or duality. Rather, institutionalized religion is itself legislated by God as the instrument for the realization of the inner dimension of faith and righteous living. God says in the Qur'an:

> To everyone of you we have appointed a [sacred] law and a course to follow. For, had God so wished, He would have made you all one community. Rather He wished to try you by means of what He had given you; who among you is of the best action. Compete therefore with one another as if in a race in the performance of good deeds. To God shall be your return, and He will inform you concerning the things in which you had differed (5:48).[29]

This verse first stipulates that the exoteric dimension of religion should mirror its inner dimension through the performance of good deeds. Secondly, differences among God's laws which He appointed for different peoples should be respected, and should not lead to conflicts. Finally, the truth concerning these different divine dispensations will be known only on the Day of Judgment when God will inform all faith-communities of all their religious differences. To paraphrase St.

Paul, here we see things through a glass darkly, but then we shall see things as they are.[30] Here we must avoid turning our religious differences into religious conflicts through dialogue in humility and the desire for better understanding. But then God, the absolute Truth (*al-ḥaqq*) will manifest the truth, all the truth.

The Qur'an not only acknowledges religious diversity and plurality, it also lays down the principles that should govern inter-religious relations. It first calls for respect and protection of all places of worship. God says: "...Had God not repelled some people by means of others, synagogues and churches, mosques and monasteries in which God's name is mentioned, would have been demolished...." (22:40)[31] The Prophet himself applied this principle by allowing the delegation of the Christians of Najrān to pray in his mosque. He went even further by calling them and the Muslims to a "just word of common ascent" between the two communities.[32] It took the Muslims fourteen centuries to renew this call, and for some Christians and Jews to listen.

The Qur'an enjoins Muslims to dialogue with Jews and Christians in the fairest manner. It sets forth both the etiquette and theology of dialogue:

> Do not debate with the people of the Book save in the fairest manner, except those among them who do wrong; and say to them 'we accept faith in that which was sent down to us [that is the Qur'an] and that which was sent down to you [that is the Torah and the Gospel]. Our God and your God is one, and to Him we are submitters (Muslims) (29:46).[33]

What then is the ultimate goal of interfaith dialogue from the point of view of the Qur'an? The following few conclusions will, it is hoped, suggest some tentative answers.

CONCLUDING REMARKS

It may first be concluded from the preceding discussion that neither the Qur'an nor the Prophetic tradition demands of Jews and Christians that they give up their religious identity and become Muslims unless they freely choose to do so. The basis of this religious freedom in Islam is the categorical Qur'anic assertion (2:256), "there is no compulsion in religion..." This is a categorical command, not a statement of fact.

Secondly, the Qur'an and Prophetic tradition only enjoined Muslims as well as the followers of other faiths to engage in meaningful dialogue, cooperation and agreement on basic principles. This is what the Qur'an calls "a just word of common ascent," between the Muslims and the people of the Book to worship no one except God and not take one another as lords beside God (3:64).[34] This important call to a unity of faith across the diversity of religions is far more relevant to our time than it was to the time of the Prophet and his people. It goes far beyond the issue of whether Christians actually worship their monks or not. One of the Companions of the Prophet, ʿAdī ibn Ḥātim who was formerly a Christian, said to the Prophet: "But the Jews and the Christians do not worship their Rabbis and their monks." The Prophet said, "Do not they legislate for them and they accept their legislation?" This is tantamount to worshipping them.[35] This is because worship in Islam is obedience and if one obeys anyone other than God it is as though one worships him instead of God.

It is important in this regard to observe that Karaism, a movement within Judaism which arose after Islam, may be regarded as an answer to this call. The Karaite movement continues to this day to call other Jews to return to the law of God as revealed in the Torah, and rejects Rabbinic Judaism. It is with this Rabbinic Judaism that the Qur'an was concerned and with which the Muslim community has been struggling ever since.

Judaism, as it has been observed for nearly 2,000 years, is Rabbinic Judaism. Although Rabbinic Judaism is continuous with biblical religion, the latter has been completely superseded by the former. This is perhaps the reason behind the Qur'anic call for the people of the Torah to judge by what God has revealed in it. For the same reason, the Qur'an calls upon the people of the Gospel to judge by what God has revealed in it (5:44, 47).

To the extent that eastern Christians, more than other peoples, at least at the time of the revelation of the Qur'an, tried to harmonize their faith in God with moral living and humility before Him, they are considered to be the "nearest in amity" to Muslims.[36] This special relation with the Christians does not close the door to dialogue with other religious communities. In fact, the legal designation of *ahl al-Kitāb* (people of the Book) has been quite fluid. It came to include more and more communities as Muslims came to know more and more religious traditions.

To conclude: what then is the challenge that the Qur'an presents to us today? The challenge is this, that we all have faith in God and compete with one another in righteous works. It follows from this challenge that all people of faith respect one another and that they believe in all of God's revelations.

The Qur'an presents the followers of Islam, Christianity and Judaism not only with a great challenge, but with a great promise as well. The promise is this:

> Were the people of the Book to abide by the Torah, the Gospel and that which was sent down to them from their Lord [i.e. the Qur'an], they would be nourished with provisions from above them and from beneath their feet (5:66).[37]

NOTES

1 The present paper has appeared in different forms in the following publications: "Islam and Pluralism," *Encounters* (September, 1997), vol. 3, no.2, pp.103-18; "Islam and the Challenge of Religious Pluralism," *Global Dialogue* (Winter, 2000), vol. 2, no.1, pp.53-64; and "Religious Pluralism and The Challenges of Inclusivism, Exclusivism and Globalism: An Islamic Perspective," *Commitment of Faiths: Identity, Plurality and Gender*, eds. Sumartana et. al (Yogyakarta, Indonesia: Institute of DIAN/Interfidei, 2002).

2 For the role of religion in the rise of human civilizations, see William H. McNeill, *The Rise of the West: A History of the Human Community* (Chicago: University of Chicago Press, 1991).

3 This capacity is called in the Qur'an "*fiṭrat Allah*," God's pure creation. See Qur'an (30:30), to which we shall return later in this discussion.

4 See Mircea Eliade, ed., *Encyclopedia of Religion Volume 2* (New York: Macmillan Publishers, 1987), electronic edition produced by Infobases Inc, Provo, Utah. SV Cyprian. For a modern Protestant defense of Christian exclusivism, see Alvin Plantinga, "Pluralism: A Defense of Religious Exclusivism," *The Philosophical Challenge of Religious Diversity*, eds. K. Meeker and P.Quinn (New York: Oxford University Press, 1999), pp.172-192.

5 See also (3:19), and Mahmoud Ayoub, *The Qur'an and Its Interpreters: The House of 'Imrān* (Albany: State University of New York Press, 1992), vol. 2, pp.56, 66, 240-43 for the views of Qur'an commentators of these verses.

6 For a good study of the term Islam in the Qur'an and exegetical tradition, see Jane Smith, *An Historical and Semantic Study of the Term Islam as seen in a Sequence of Qur'an Commentaries* (Missoula, Montana: Scholars Press for Harvard Theological Review, 1975).

7 Rahner developed his idea into an elaborate theology of salvation through the cross of Christ. See his *Theological Investigations*, 23 vols. (London, Baltimore and New York: 1961-92), particularly vols. 14 and 16, both available in English translations.

8 Dogmatic Constitution on the Church no. 16.

9 See for a penetrating study of the different approaches to religious pluralism, as well as the issue of religious relativism, John Hick, ed., *An Interpretation of Religion; Human Responses to the Transcendent*, 2nd edn. (London and New Haven: Palgrave Macmillan and Yale University Press, 2005).

10 See for examples Qur'an (10:47), (4:41) and (16:36); and the Bible, Acts (2:1-11), I Timothy (2:4) and Hebrews (1:1) ff.

11 This notion was first introduced by Karl Jaspers in his *The Origin and Goal of History* (New Haven: Yale University Press, 1953). For a good discussion of this important period in the development of human civilization and Islam's place in this development, see Marshall Hodgson, *The Venture of Islam: Conscience and History in a World Civilization* (Chicago and London: University of Chicago Press, 1974), vol. 1.

12 See I. Gershevitch, ed., *The Cambridge History of Iran, Volume 2; The Median and Achaemenian Periods* (Cambridge: Cambridge University Press, 1985); and Bible, Isaiah (44:27-28), (45:1-3), (45:12-14); see also II Chronicles (36:21-23); Ezra, (1:1-9), (3:6-8), (5:12-17), (6:2-4).

13 Muslim hagiography identified Alexander with the prophetic figure *dhū al-qarnayn* of (18:83-98).

14 See Bible, Matthew (2:1-12).

15 See for a quick reference on Mani's life and death and his religion, *Encyclopedia of Religion* sv Mani.

16 (30:22). See also (2:213) and (5:48).

17 See Mahmoud Ayoub, *A Muslim View of Christianity: Essays on Dialogue*, ed. Irfan A. Omar (New York: Orbis Books, 2007), pp.17-30. For a more detailed discussion of these four principles from a comparative religion point of view, consult my original lecture, on which this paper is largely based, in the IIIT archives, summer 2008, www.iiit.org.

18 See Fazlur Rahman, *Major Themes of the Qur'an* 2nd edn. (Minneapolis: Bibliothica Islamica, 1994) p.162.

19 Max Muller, ed., *Sacred Books of the East* (Oxford: Oxford University Press, 1897), vol. 47, "Pahlavi Texts, Part 5: Marvels of Zoroastrianism,"

20 Majd al-Dīn Abū al-Saʿādāt al-Mubārak ibn Muḥammad ibn al-Athīr al-Jazarī, *Jāmiʿ al-Uṣūl fī Aḥādīth al-Rasūl*, ed. Abd al-Qadir al-Arnaut, 2nd edn. (Beirut: Dār al-fikr, 1983), vol. 2, p.660, hadith 1161.

21 For a *tafsīr* discussion of the religious identity of the Sabaeans see Mahmoud Ayoub, *The Qur'an and its Interpreters* (Albany: State University of New York Press, 1984), vol. 1, pp.109-110.

22 Muḥammad ibn ʿAbd al-Karīm al-Shahrastānī's *al-Milal wa al-Niḥal* two-volume famous heresiographical work exists in many editions for example Beirut: Mu'assasat al-Kutub al-Thaqāfiyyah, 1994. See the chapter on the Sabaeans in the first volume.

23 This is a cardinal principle of the Qur'an; see for example (2:177), where faith in God, His revelations and prophets and human virtues such as generosity, steadfastness and keeping one's covenants are given as true signs of righteousness.

24 See also (40:78), where the plurality of faiths is clearly asserted.

25 See (14:4); see also (10:47).

26 For the story of Adam's mistake and God's forgiveness, see Ayoub, *The Qur'an and Its Interpreters*, vol. 1, pp.83-93.

27 The Prophet is said to have asserted that every child is born upon this divine *fiṭrah*, and then his parents bring him or her up a Jew, a Christian, or a Magian. See Aḥmad ibn Ḥanbal, *Musnad Ibn Ḥanbal*, ed. Ahmad Muhammad Shakir (Cairo: Dār al-Ḥadīth, ed 1, 1995), vol. 7, p.33, hadith 7182.

28 This human capacity to know God by unaided reason has been recognized by both ancient and classical philosophers and theologians. It is called by Muslim theologians "the way of the friend (*khalīl*) of God," that is Abraham.

29 This is a recurrent theme of the Qur'an.

30 See I Corinthians (13:12).

31 See also (24:36).

32 See (3:61-64), and Ayoub, *The Qur'an and Its Interpreters*, vol. 2, pp.187-208.

33 See also (49:13), which calls upon all the peoples and tribes of humankind to get to know one another through dialogue.

34 It is significant that this call to dialogue follows the only heated debate which the Prophet had with the Christians. This debate is alluded to in the *mubāhalah*, or imprecation verse, (3:61). See Ayoub, *The Qur'an and Its Interpreters*, vol. 2, pp.188-202, 206.

35 Ayoub, *The Qur'an and Its Interpreters*, vol. 2, pp.205-207.

36 The piety and humility of these Christians is touchingly described in the Qur'an. See (5:82-5). See also my paper "Nearest in Amity: Christians in the Qur'an and Contemporary Exegetical Tradition," *Journal of Islam and Christian-Muslim Relations* (July, 1997), vol. 8, no.2, pp.145-64; or in my book *A Muslim View of Christianity*, pp.187-208.

37 This means that they would eat and drink of the bounties of the sky through rain and the rich yield of the earth.

4

Qur'anic Revealed Scripture vs. Judeo-Christian Scripture:

A Muslim Perspective of the Universal & Particular in the Scriptures

KHALED TROUDI

INTRODUCTION

MUSLIMS believe that the Qur'an and the previous Judeo-Christian scriptures represent the very word of God (*kalām Allah*). They claim that these scriptures have been sent throughout human history, before Muhammad, "with universal as well as particular guidance to direct human life in order to achieve the divine goal on earth."[1] The universal guidance is designated to provide a direct discourse that speaks to all human beings, while the particular one has, according to the Islamic tradition, specific spiritual and temporal affairs designated to a specific nation under the leadership of God's prophet.[2] This paper examines why Muslims believe the Qur'an to be the predominant (*muhaymin*) revealed scripture (the "universal") while the Judeo-Christian scriptures represent the "particular." An analysis of various Qur'anic verses will provide the methodology that is used to undertake the different approaches of this study.

The first approach will examine the idea of the unity of all revealed scriptures according to Muslim theology. It will study verses (42:13), (3:95), (2:130-33), and (22:78) to show how Judaism, Christianity, and Islam share the same source of divine revelation, while their original forms can be considered to be one religion, not just part of a religious tradition. These verses help explain how each Abrahamic religion shares a common core of religious and ethical teachings, even though they differ in time and space, especially regarding their doctrines and dogma.

The second approach will study the notion of the true religion in Muslim thought. To further explain this idea, different hermeneutical works on verses (3:19) and (3:85), as upheld by Muslim exegetes since the early days of Islam until the present will be examined. In this case, the validity of Judaism and Christianity according to the Islamic vision will be highlighted, and the theological disputations among the classical and modern Muslim scholars on Qur'anic verses (2:62) and (5:69) will be investigated.

The third approach will study the concept of "Predominant Revealed Scripture" which is mentioned in Qur'anic verses (4:163) and (5:48) and its relationship with the claim which indicates that the Prophet's revelation was a continuation of the inspiration sent previously to earlier prophets of the Abrahamic faith groups. Also, I will examine how such Qur'anic revelation, which is perceived as a "universal" phenomenon, has influenced Muslim visions to classify Judeo-Christian religions as "particular." To further explain this concept, I will analyze how such a Qur'anic verse as (5:48) claims that the "finality" of the prophetic tradition is encoded within the Old and New Testaments. An analysis of verse (6:92) shows that earlier scriptures were actually sent to the people of the Book (*Ahl al-Kitāb*) confirming the concept of "finality." It studies the Qur'anic concept of the end of revelation cycles after universal prophecy had run its course, and demonstrates the universality of Muhammad's prophethood according to verses (5:3) and (33:40). It also highlights the view that although all nations have received prophets with specific scriptural messages that differ in their "details" and/or rituals, they are deeply rooted in the Islamic worldview of the absolute surrender (Islam) of all creation to the will of the creator.

[1]
THE ESSENTIAL UNITY OF ALL REVEALED SCRIPTURES

The idea of the unity of revealed scriptures is deeply rooted in the early days of the history of religions. In Islam, according to Qur'an (42:15), the idea of believing in all revealed books becomes an article of faith. Many Qur'anic passages, such as (43:4), (13:39), and (56:78), indicate that "all scriptures stem from and are parts of a single source, the heavenly archetype called 'the Mother of the Book' (*Umm al-Kitāb*) and also 'The Hidden Book' (*al-Kitāb al-Maknūn*)."[3] Since these scriptures "are universal and identical, it is incumbent on all people to believe in all divine messages."[4] Indeed, the Qur'an itself indicates that, "*The same religion has He established for you as that which He enjoined on Noah – that which We have sent by inspiration to thee – and that which We enjoined on Abraham, Moses, and Jesus*... (42:13).[5]

Thus for Muslims, the Qur'an, especially the narrative passages of the previous prophets, represents the major theological source of the unity of the revealed scriptures in which the prophets are the dominant figures. For this reason, Prophet Muhammad and all Muslims are obligated to be the first believers in the prophethood of Noah, Abraham, Moses, and Jesus and in the truth of the scriptures brought by them, without making any distinction among them. Also, Qur'anic verses (2:136), (2:285), and (3:84) insist that Muslims must not differentiate among the prophets and that each one was given guidance. Jomier states that "the Qur'an speaks very highly of the earlier scriptures that were transmitted by the messengers of God. It is the duty for the Muslim to believe in those scriptures and those messengers of God."[6] However, a critical study of hermeneutical works on the Qur'anic verses reveals that different disputations were provided by Muslim exegetes on this theological issue and its level of understanding in medieval Islam. In fact, most of the exegetes stressed the unity of the three Abrahamic faiths' revealed scriptures to prove the claim that each of them contained a core essentially similar to the others. In addition, exegetes devoted a great deal of time and space to explain that each tradition's prophetic narratives had received the same revelation from one identical source. Through their works, exegetes wanted to demonstrate that this unity of revealed scriptures indicated the fact that the spiritual dimension in which each of those prophets lived was identical. In other words, they sought to demonstrate that each Abrahamic religion shared a common core of religious and ethical teaching, even though the religions differed in time and space, especially with regards to their basic doctrines.

From a Muslim point of view, Qur'anic verses such as (42:13), (3:95), (2:130-33), and (22:78) affirmed Judaism, Christianity, and

Islam to "share a common trunk of divine revelation, and their original forms can be considered to be not just one religious tradition, but one religion."[7] For instance, the Qur'an mentions the Torah (the scripture given by God to the Israelites through Moses), and the Gospel (*Injīl*), given by Jesus to those Jews and others who later became known as Christians. In addition, verses (87:18-19) mention earlier scrolls of Abraham and Moses, which "from the times when the earlier prophets begin to be referred to in the Qur'an, the Prophet is convinced of the identity of his message with theirs."[8] However, Rahman has emphasized that "where the term scrolls has been used for revealed documents; elsewhere it is applied to the heavenly archetype of all revelations."[9]

Historically, most Muslim exegetes have affirmed that throughout the Makkan period, "the word Book is used and applied almost exclusively to the Book of Moses."[10] In interpreting verse (2:213), al-Ṭabarsī and other Muslim commentators have stated that *Kitāb* "refers either to the Torah and the Gospel in which the Qur'an is explained or to them both, meaning that the Qur'an included both the Torah and the Gospel."[11] Others, among them Ibn Kathīr, have opined that it "refers to the preserved Tablet."[12] For instance, according to al-Qurṭubī, "God had promised the people of the Book that he would send down to Muhammad a book."[13] Later, contemporary studies of the scriptures demonstrate that the term *al-Kitāb* (the Book) "is often used in the Qur'an not denoting any specific scripture but as a generic term denoting the totality of revealed scriptures."[14] Semantically, Madigan states, the fundamental pattern of *Kitāb* is symbolically:

> to address the current situation and the prevailing issue. This divine/prophetic address bears the name *Kitāb* not because of its form (which remains oral, fluid, and responsive) but because of its origin and because of its nature as a communication (*n-z-l*, *w-ḥ-y*) of God's knowledge (*'-lm*) and clear statement (*b-y-n*) of God's commends (*ḥ-k-m*).[15]

Muslims however understood these terms according to the sense given by the exegetes, who provided a variety of interpretations. Nevertheless, Muslims regard all of these scriptures as the word of God that came from one revealed source and believe that each of them confirms the truth of its predecessors. McAuliffe states: "Theoretically, at least, there can be no discrepancy in the content of these revelations because they all proceed from the same source."[16] According to (29:46), all Muslims and people of the book believe in the same deity and worship the same God, even though they may differ over how to conceptualize the unique God.

Western scholars, on the other hand, resorted to another methodological analysis to explain the unity of revealed scriptures. By unity is not meant unity in the Qur'anic sense of the term, that is a continuation of original Revelation, but unity in the sense that Islamic references to Judaic and Christian elements were seen as a result of interaction with members of these faiths leading to affinity between them. By focusing on the history and chronological order of the Qur'anic verses, most western scholars limited themselves to studying this phenomenon at its theological level only, during the years of Prophet Muhammad's preaching in Makkah and Madinah. They have claimed that during the early days of the Prophet's preaching (in terms of Qur'anic passages) he makes mention of some earlier prophets, some Arab prophets (e.g., those sent to the tribes of ʿĀd and Thamūd), and biblical figures such as Jesus and other New Testament personalities (i.e. Mary). These figures "do not seem to be referred to in the first Makkan period but appear from the second period onward, while the gospel is mentioned only once in Mecca."[17] Western scholars, then claim that this would indicate that Prophet Muhammad had no connection with earlier scriptures during the first four years of his prophetic career. On the other hand, they also assert that he saw Islam "within the perspective of the earlier Biblical religions."[18]

They furthermore contend that the Qur'anic passages' position toward the older scriptures was rather general, beginning "to become more definite only when Muhammad came into contact with the Jews of Medina."[19] In explaining verses (87:18-19), western scholars indicate that the Qur'an speaks further of the scrolls of Abraham and Moses. They affirm that in the Makkan period, the Qur'an does "not try to distinguish between the Jews and Christians. It does not use those words, though it refers to Moses and Jesus; but speaks of the children of Israel. There is, then, no question as yet of Torah or Gospel, but only of the scripture or the book (*Kitāb*)."[20] For instance, Rahman refers to the general statement of several western scholars, such as Snouck Hurgronje, Theodor Noldeke, and Friedrich Schwally, who claim that at the beginning of his preaching in Makkah:

> the Prophet Muhammad was convinced of bringing to the Arabs the same message which the Christians had received from Jesus and the Jews from Moses, etc., and against the Arab pagans, he confidently appealed to 'the people of knowledge'...whom one has simply to ask in order to obtain a confirmation of the truth of his teaching.[21]

In other words, Prophet Muhammad is regarded as being convinced that he was bringing to the Arabs the same teaching that earlier prophets had brought to their respective communities.

Historically, Western scholars have also maintained that the content and lessons of these Qur'anic passages had been transformed through revelation during the first Makkan period. From a theological standpoint, Rahman refers to this phenomenon to criticize the idea by saying that these Qur'anic passages connected with the narratives of the earlier prophets, which "become numerous, more detailed and are repeated in the Qur'an. There can be little doubt that the Prophet heard these stories during discussions with certain unidentified people, and the Meccans themselves were not slow to point this out."[22] Nevertheless, Western scholars insisted that these passages were revealed to Prophet Muhammad under the impact of his direct religious experience with the Jews and Christians of the Arabian peninsula.

Western scholars further claim that during the Madinan period, because "the Jews and the Christians had refused to accept him [Muhammad] as Prophet; he began appealing to the image of Abraham whom he disassociated from Judaism and Christianity, claiming him exclusively for Islam and linking his community directly with him."[23] Pointing to a passage (3:67) that describes the emergence of Madinah's Muslim community as a separate entity from the Jewish and Christian communities, Western scholars make the case that:

> the people of the book will not recognize him. He must, therefore, seek an authority for himself beyond their control, which at the same time does not contradict his own earlier revelations. He, therefore, seizes upon the ancient prophets whose communities cannot offer him opposition [i.e., whose communities were no longer there: like Abraham, Noah, etc.].[24]

However, the basic problem with these arguments lies in the separation of the chronological study of Prophet Muhammad's career and the Qur'an into two separate periods, the Makkan and the Madinan, a practice that most modern scholars fully endorse. A critical study of the Qur'anic passages, according to Rahman, "reveals rather a gradual development, a definite transition where the late Meccan phase has basic affinities with the early Madinan phase; indeed, one can see the latter in the former."[25] One important development in Madinah, then, is that:

> earlier Revelations, the Torah and the Gospel, are mentioned by name, whereas in Mecca the Gospel is hardly referred to (although, of course, Jesus and other New Testament personalities are certainly there), while the Mosaic Revelation is always called "the Book of Moses," which repeatedly appears as the forerunner of the Qur'ānic Revelation.[26]

In sum, and as this discussion has clearly shown, Islamic theology emphasizes the idea of the essential unity of all revealed scriptures, and this opens the door to examination of an important theological argument with regards to the essential unity of all revealed scriptures that is strongly connected to the notion of the true religion.

[2]
THE NOTION OF THE TRUE RELIGION

The Islamic concept of progressive revelation has led to the idea of the existence of a 'one true religion'. In addition, Muslims claim that the historical legacies within the prophetic traditions are the same, in spite of some specific events that may be explained differently. These concepts have provided specific visions regarding Judeo-Christian scriptures. The most important vision, which becomes the central theme of the Muslim creed, is the notion of the true religion (*al-dīn al-ḥaqq*). Muslims believe that Islam is the *Dīn* of God "which is the commitment to *tawḥīd* and the moral life."[27] However, while Izutsu explains the semantic range of the word *dīn* stating "the word *Dīn* contains among others a remarkable semantic element of obedience (*ṭāʿah*) and (*ʿubūdiyyah*),"[28] he concludes that, "the word *Dīn* has two important meanings distinguishable in the Qur'an: religion and judgment."[29] Other scholars such as Wilfred Smith assume that the word religion (*dīn*) has two different senses: one is religion as a deep personal matter, and the other is religion in a reified sense as something common to a community.[30]

However, Muslim exegetes belonging to different schools of thought have provided extensive hermeneutical works on (3:19) and (3:85), to understand the meaning of the term Islam and *dīn* and show how the Qur'an has conceptualized the notion of true religion in the light of these two verses. For instance, al-Ṭabarī and al-Ṭabarsī have both explained the verse "*Surely the true religion with Allah is Islam*" (3:19) as a second object of Allah's testimony. Accordingly, both have assumed that the previous verse and this verse would then read, "Allah bears witness that there is no God but Allah, and the true religion with Allah is Islam."[31] In this context, al-Ṭabarī and al-Ṭabarsī aim to contend that "Islam as a religion has an eternal and exalted status."[32] Moreover, al-Ṭabarī understood the terms *dīn* and Islam to both have the same meaning, and assumed that *dīn* in this verse "means obedience and humility, which applied to the term Islam."[33] Conversely, Ibn Kathīr claimed the meaning given to the term Islam to be the religion of Islam stating that, "this is a declaration by God that there is no other religion with Him which he would accept from anyone except Islam."[34] Furthermore, Ibn Kathīr explained the meaning of the term Islam as mentioned in these verses as follows: "Islam means following the messengers of God in that with which he sent them at all times until the coming of the Prophet Muhammad, the seal of the messengers."[35] Therefore, Ibn Kathīr specified this meaning of the term Islam by claiming that "God closed all other ways leading to Him except the way through Muhammad. Thus, anyone meeting God after the apostleship of Muhammad, having in this life followed a law

[Sharīʿah] other than Muhammad, it will not be accepted from him."[36] Ibn Kathīr used the general meaning of the term Islam to explain the statement in (3:85), stating, "This is in accordance with God's saying, whosoever desires a faith other that Islam it will not be accepted from him."[37]

Ibn Kathīr supported his ideas by claiming that the Prophet Muhammad had throughout his life "sent messages calling to God all people such as kings, Arabs and non-Arabs, people of the book and unlettered peoples. This he did in obedience to God's command for him to do so."[38] For example, he cites on the authority of Abū Hurayrah that the Prophet said:

> "By Him in whose Hands is my soul, no one of this community, be he Jew or Christian, who hears of me, and he dies without accepting faith in that with which I was sent by God, but that he would be of the people of the fire." The Prophet said, "I am sent to the red and the black," that is, to everyone. He also said, "Every prophet was sent only to his own people, but I was sent to all mankind."[39]

In addition, al-Zamakhsharī who represents the Muʿtazilite school, projects his own doctrinal interpretation of verses (3:19) and (3:85) explaining that theologically the Qur'anic phrase 'Surely the true religion with Allah is Islam' "is further emphasis of the statement of divine Oness in the previous verse. God saying 'there is no God but He,' is the declaration of oneness (*tawḥīd*)."[40] He maintains that, "His saying upholding justice [see 3:18: "...there is no deity save Him, the Upholder of Equity..."] is a proclamation of justice, since he added surely the true faith with God is Islam. He no doubt meant this as a declaration that Islam is the faith of all justice and oneness, which is the true faith with God."[41] He concludes that:

> Any other faith is, therefore, no faith at all with Him. This also means that anyone who holds anthropomorphic views of God, or any views implying anthropomorphism, such as the possibility of the vision (*ru'yā*) of God, or holds *jabr* (divine determinism) which is pure injustice, would not be a follower of God's true faith, which is *islām*.[42]

According to this interpretation, it is quite clear that al-Zamakhsharī's exegesis reflects his Muᶜtazilite view of God and Islam.

Al-Rāzī, literally, defines the term *dīn* according to these verses, "as a divine recompense (*jazā'*) and human obedience because it is the cause of recompense."[43] He interprets the term Islam as having three meanings:

> The first signifies entering into Islam is accepting obedience and submission. The second denotes a person who enters into peace or security (Islam). Third, Ibn al-Anbārī said, a Muslim is one who is sincere in his worship of God. Islam, therefore, means security of faith (*dīn*) and belief (*ᶜaqīdah*) in God.[44]

However, al-Rāzī explained verses (3:19) and (3:85) from a different point of view. Literally, he claimed that the term Islam could not be the synonym of the term *dīn* according to verse (49:14):

> The desert Arabs say, "We believe." Say, "Ye have no faith; but ye (only) say, 'We have submitted our wills to Allah,' For not yet has Faith entered your hearts. But if ye obey Allah and His Messenger, He will not belittle aught of your deeds: for Allah is Oft-Forgiving, Most Merciful."

He understood that the Arab bedouins, "the nomadic people, said: 'we have accepted faith,' and God said, 'you have not accepted faith, rather say, "we have become Muslims,"' which indicates that the term Islam here has a meaning other than *imān*."[45] Even though, al-Rāzī interpreted this verse to show what he felt to be the difference between Islam and *dīn*, he then concludes that verses (3:19) and (3:85) were explained by Muslim exegetes from a legal custom standpoint or *ᶜUrf*, and verse (49:14) from a linguistic principle point of view only.[46]

Al-Qurṭubī, representing the Sunni Ashᶜarite school of thought, summarized the general view of scholastic theologians with regards to the meanings of the terms Islam and *dīn*. He tried to provide different explanations of these terms to indicate the correct definition that could be applied to both from the point of view of the general usage of the Shariᶜah and other theological and linguistic elaborations. Referring to verse 49:14 he defines the term *dīn* and Islam as follows: "The word *dīn* in this verse means obedience and religion (*millah*). And the term Islam is used to mean faith (*imān*) and acts of obedience (*ṭāʿāt*)." Al-Qurṭubī supported his claim by saying that, "In their first implication, the terms *imān* and Islam are different when they are clarified by verse (49:14) and the hadith of the angel Gabriel with the Prophet Muhammad asking about Islam and *imān*."[47] Also, in their second connotation, "the two terms have been used synonymously according to ʿAbd al-Qays's narrative,"[48] and the prophetic hadith that states that "faith consists of seventy-two aspects..."[49] Further, as a third implication, al-Qurṭubī asserts the possibility that "one is implied by the other, as indicated in the verse, where both assent or faith (*imān*) and actions (i.e., Islam) are included."[50]

Mystically interpreting these verses (49:14), Ibn al-ʿArabī considers true faith as follows: "Surely the true faith with God is this divine oneness (*tawḥīd*) which God has determined for Himself. His faith is, therefore, the faith of the surrender of the persons or faces (*wujūh*)."[51] He assumes that "this is in accordance with Abraham's saying, 'I surrender my face to God,' that is, my self and my all."[52] At this level, Ibn al-ʿArabī mystically, interprets verse (49:14) by stating, "I have severed my self from my egotism, and thus achieved annihilation (*fanā'*) in Him. God then commanded His beloved [Muḥammad], peace and blessings be upon him, saying, 'If, therefore, they dispute with you say, I surrendered my person to God, I and those who follow me.'"[53]

Classical Shiite *tafsīrs* also comment on verses (3:19) and (3:85). According to al-Qummī, "the term Islam is submission (*taslīm*) to God and his friends (the imams, *awliyā*). It is also assent or acceptance (*taṣdīq*). God has likewise called *imān taṣdīq*."[54] It is quite clear that al-Qummī differentiates between the meanings of the two terms. He supports his *tafsīr* by reference to a tradition narrated on the authority of the fifth imam, Muḥammad al-Bāqir, who himself clearly advocated the difference between *imān* and Islam, stating, "God has exalted faith over Islam in station."[55] In addition and according to a description of the term Islam provided by ʿAlī, commander of the faithful (*Amīr al-mu'minīn*), it was al-Qummī's belief that "Islam is *taslīm* (submission). *Taslīm* is *yaqīn* (absolute certainty), and *yaqīn* is *taṣdīq*. *Taṣdīq* is *iqrār* (confession). *Iqrār*, that is uttering the *shahādah*, is *idā'* (fulfilling one's duty towards God), and *idā'* is action."[56] He concludes that "the man of faith is he who takes his religion directly from his lord. For the faith, of [the faithful], can be recognized in his actions, while the rejection of faith (*kufr*) by a rejecter of faith can be recognized in his rejection (*inkār*)."[57]

This theological explanation of the term Islam led the modern Shiite Muslim exegete, Muhammad Husain Tabataba'i, to claim that the majority of this surah had been revealed concerning the People of the Book, and to connect reading of this verse (3:19) to the context of the entire Qur'anic passage which includes the verses before and after it. In defining Islam he states that "the true faith with God is one in which there is no contradiction. Nor did God enjoin His servants to follow any other faith except it, or elucidate in the scriptures He sent down to His prophets any other faith except it."[58] He also agreed with al-Qummī's definition of Islam, "which is absolute submission (*taslīm*) to the truth, the truth of belief and the truth of action."[59] Therefore, Tabataba'i stresses Islam to be "one single faith, even though the how and why of it might be diverse in the different dispensations (*sharā'iʿ*) of His prophets."[60] Tabataba'i concludes, "It is clear ... that the true faith, which is with God and in His presence, is one sacred law that differs only in the degrees [of comprehensiveness and perfection] in accordance with the different capacities of the different communities."[61]

The well-known modern Sunni Egyptian commentator Sayyid Qutb claimed that Islam, according to (3:19), was "the totality of faith, belief, and conduct within the context of total submission to the One and only God."[62] Qutb concluded that "true Islam would have no effect on the lives of human beings unless they manifest it [Islam] in a social system in whose pure and bright framework humanity would live."[63]

In interpreting (2:62) and (5:69) much of the exegetical consideration provoked by these verses is designed to construct a theological essence. These passages clearly teach that "the faithful people they are describing will be rewarded by God, and it shows that this is meant in the eschatological sense: they will have nothing to fear at the final judgment."[64] Therefore, these verses seem to provide a "firm basis within Islamic theology for a generous attitude towards at least some people of different faith, affirming that they will share with Muslims in the divine promise."[65] However, it is true that the validity of such universalizing interpretations has been called into question by those who adopt a narrower reading. Accordingly, some scholars claim that the:

> strategy is to identify the groups of the people referred to in these verses as Muslim converts from a Jewish or Christian background or as believers who have kept to uncorrupted versions of Judaism or Christianity – in which case, the religion which wins acceptance from God would be Islam rather that their original faiths.[66]

While arguments between these different views have been conducted on a textual level by appeals to differing parts of the hadith literature, "they also reflect the varying tenor of the relationships Muslims have had with the people of the book, and with other non-Muslims, in various times and contexts."[67] With some sense of restraint, however, Ipgrave states that:

> it has seemed plausible to some commentators to identify in this verse [2:62] a common core of three principles – belief in one true God, acknowledgement of final moral accountability towards Him, and commitment to righteous action in obedience to Him in the present – which an inclusive reading would constitute an authentic divine religion open to all and securing God's favor for all.[68]

However, McAuliffe mentions that "al-Tūsī's analysis of this verse (2:62) begins with the position that finds in these narratives a reference to the Hypocrites, be they Jews, Christians, or Sabians, who finally pay reluctant lip service to belief."[69] She concludes that "this was a critical factor in determining the reception of Muhammad's message."[70] Rida argues that "they would all have seen the truth of this message and accepted it. It was their concern with partisan identification to the exclusion of the truth that blinded them."[71]

As has been demonstrated, most classical Muslim commentators interpreted verses (3:19) and (3:85) literally, understanding the term Islam, in both verses, as referring to "ritualistic or juristic observance and identity."[72] Later on, modern Muslim thinkers and commentators approached the two verses to "argue for the finality and superiority of Islam over all other religions."[73] Therefore, neither classical commentators nor modern thinkers recognized the scriptures of previous religions, including Judaism and Christianity, to have been sent to all humanity underscored by a concept of universal rather than particular discourse. In their *tafsīrs*, a literary approach to the term Islam as synonymous with the term *dīn* has led both classical and modern commentators to assert that the religion of Islam came to abrogate previous religions. In this context, it is clear that the commentators did not distinguish between a universal and a legal Islam to interpret the term Islam. Even Qur'anic scripture itself "does not deny the specificity of various religions,"[74] in many passages it indicates the universal discourse of the previous scriptures.

In addition, Muslim exegetes who have studied verses (2:62) and (5:69), have presented them as showing that Judaism and Christianity were valid only up to a point, with Judaism valid "during the period following God's revelation to Moses until his revelation to Jesus. After this new divine revelation, the Jews [were] under the obligation to follow the Gospel and the laws of Jesus,"[75] and Christianity only valid until the coming of Muhammad. For instance, al-Ṭabarī states that "whoever does not follow Muhammad and renounce his adherence to the tradition of Jesus and the Gospel is damned."[76] In the same vein, Ibn Kathīr claimed that "the Jews acted rightly in their adherence to the Torah and the tradition of Moses, but only until the advent of Jesus. Once Jesus had come, those Jews who did not leave the Mosaic law and adhere to the Gospel and laws of Jesus were liable to eternal damnation"[77] and that "while Christianity was an acceptable belief before the time of Muhammad, those who do not then renounce it in favor of Islam will be damned."[78] This was the commonly held position of the medieval Muslim community's Qur'an commentators and remains in force today. It is a position which modern exegete Rida discusses in his *Tafsīr al-Manār*. Rida writes that "the substance of their [Judaic and Christian] religion has remained recognizable, not distorted to the extent that guidance from its precepts is completely obscured"[79] Concerning the issue of Judaic-Christian legislation, all Muslims exegetes are of the opinion that these have been abrogated or cancelled by the advent of the Qur'an which is regarded as having done away with these earlier legislations. They believe that "Islam allows only Jews and Christians to obey their legislations within their respective communities until both groups embrace Islam and join the community of the last period of history; that is to say, the Islamic dispensation."[80] They claim that Jews and Christians will find in the Qur'an what is essential and best in the Torah and the Gospel. Mahmoud Ayoub claims that:

> the Truth is greater than the expression of any one religious tradition or the understanding of any single individual or community. In order to realize this ideal, Muslims must likewise rethink their own understanding of the true meaning of Islam as the living up to the primordial covenant between God and all human beings and the reaffirmation of this covenant in a variety of expressions in a religiously pluralistic world.[81]

Likewise, Sachedina sees that the "Islamic revelation presents a theology that resonates with the modern pluralistic belief that other faiths are not merely inferior manifestations of religiosity, but variant forms of individual and communal responses to the presence of the transcendent in human life."[82] This means that the universal discourses of the three Abrahamic religions could help establish a new pluralistic discourse, which is seen by many Qur'anic passages especially with regards to the Biblical prophets, to fulfill the divine purpose for humanity.

[3]
THE IDEA OF THE GUARDIAN OR PREDOMINANT (*MUHAYMIN*) REVEALED SCRIPTURE

Deeply rooted in Islamic theology is the idea that all nations have been sent prophets with specific scriptural messages that differ somewhat in their details. This is reflected in the titles "that are customarily given to the great messengers in Islamic texts. Each title designates the special quality of the messenger that distinguishes him from other messengers."[83] According to verse (5:3) of the Qur'an this cycle of

Revelation and prophethood runs its course with the advent of Islam. According to Islamic tradition, "the book with the truth is a summary of God's repeated interference in history, which thereby gains the coherence of a pattern made decisively clear."[84] More precisely, Muslim exegetes have claimed that since the early days of Islam, "revelation continues to figure and the Qur'an upholds itself both as its confirmer and preserver."[85] Qur'anic verse (5:48) and similar verses clearly confirm the idea of a predominant revealed scripture. All Muslims must accept that God sent down the Qur'an in truth as a confirmer of the Books or of all revelations that have come before it and as a protector over them. In addition, the notion of the finality of prophethood is clear in Qur'anic verse (33:40), and similar verses, which mention that all Muslims must believe that Prophet Muhammad is the final prophet sent by God to humanity.

This and verse (14:4), which indicates that every nation has been sent a messenger, led to the idea that the Qur'anic revelation was a universal phenomenon.[86] Thus, Muslims hold that Islam is the religion of all prophets and all righteous people since the beginning of creation. This belief, which has never changed, emphasizes that Islam is to replace all older forms of religion and connects the idea of one true religion with the concept of human nature. For instance, according to the Islamic tradition, this creed represents the identical form of the faith of Adam, Noah, and Abraham and is the core of the message of Moses and Jesus.

However, the Qur'anic message emphasizes that Prophet Muhammad is the only legitimate person who has connected the "new" religion of Islam with the Biblical tradition, especially with the prophets of the *Ahl al-Kitāb*, through which Abraham is a descendant of both Noah and Adam. This creed was confirmed and became the focal point of Muslim religious belief, and is a fact that many Qur'anic verses acknowledge. For example, (42:13) indicates that "God communicates to Muhammad and to all the believers that what is prescribed to them is not something new, but a reproduction of that which previously the earlier prophets revealed to the Israelites."[87] Thus, Muslims believe in the prophetic inspiration, which has guided the great personalities of the Biblical tradition and claim legitimacy as belonging to the religion of Abraham, and consider themselves the ideal continuators and re-newers of it through the message brought by the Prophet Muhammad. Accordingly, Muslims state that all "the Jews, and naturally the Christians, are thus invited to believe the Arab prophet and to consider him as the continuator of their tradition."[88] Therefore, the similarity and the connection of prophethood between these prophets and Prophet Muhammad, as found in the Qur'anic narratives, constitute the fundamental theological element of the Islamic creed and affirm the fundamental continuity between the Biblical revelations and Prophet Muhammad's mission.

In this context and based upon the information provided in the Qur'anic passages, Muslim exegetes connected the idea of predominant revealed scripture with the history of the prophets, and the Jews and Christians. They regarded Judaism and Christianity as true religions that were forms of the one true religion, and which were valid for a certain period of history. According to the Islamic tradition, God sent prophets Moses and Jesus only to the children of Israel, while Prophet Muhammad came with a mission to the whole world. This type of understanding has led Muslim exegetes to state that the missions of Moses and Jesus were limited in time and space. In addition as many Qur'anic verses maintain that "Jews and Christians have not lived up to God's message to them"[89] "many Muslims would like to make this a universal judgment against other religions, claiming that Islam is the only valid religion left on the face of the earth."[90] This issue has been historically debated by classical Muslim exegetes. The majority of them, however, have provided plenty of room to explain it in a theological sense.

CONCLUSION

In sum, it is quite clear that the question of whether a predominant (*Muhaymin*) revealed scripture exists has occupied many pages in *tafsīr* books. However, some western scholars criticize this belief by claiming that "many Muslims prefer to stress the passages that are critical of other religions and ignore or explain away the verses that praise other religions."[91] They claim that "Muslims see other religions in terms of

Islam, which in their eyes is the perfect religion."[92] What they fail to understand is that the majority of Muslim exegetes were in actual fact placing emphasis on Judaism and Christianity whose adherents having been favored with both prophets and a Book (whether the *Injīl* or the Torah) therefore had to be judged by more stringent standards than people of other faiths. In addition, Rida states that the "messenger comes only to confirm what the intellect comprehends, clarifying and elucidating matters of vital significance, such as what the hereafter will be like and the ways of worship not pleasing to God."[93] Rida also wants to clarify the exact limit of human responsibility in relation to God's purpose: the basics are belief in God and the Last Day. Anyone who has been exposed to this message is bound to believe it, whether or not he/she has had the benefit of a prophetic revelation.

Furthermore, while the divine initiative behind revelation and the stages of the revelatory process were important theological issues for the commentators, people's response to revelation was of equal concern. Muslim commentators moreover claim that these (Judeo-Christian) scriptures are different with regards to the scope of the prophetic mission. Most of these missions they contend were limited, largely addressed either to a specific group of people with a few addressed to a wider collective group. This understanding has led Muslims to believe the mission attributed to the Prophet Muhammad to be a universal on, not limited by geographical or ethnological ethnic boundaries.

Reading Qur'anic passages Muslims consider its revelation as a message to all mankind. A Revelation which came to ensure the victory of God's oneness (*tawḥīd*) over paganism and to correct Judeo-Christian misunderstanding of the Bible as well as Christian errors concerning the personality of Jesus. With regards to the existence of a one 'true religion' and the validity of its legislations, Muslim exegetes maintain and always have maintained, that there is a primordial original pure faith, and that Islam is its manifestation to humanity. As such its legislations, although containing different laws and commandments to those of earlier scripture, are fundamentally the same, replacing those no longer suitable for modern times.

REFERENCES

Ayoub, Mahmoud, *The Qur'an and its Interpreters: The House of Imrān* (Albany: State University of New York Press, 1992).

______, "Towards an Islamic Christology: An Image of Jesus in Early Shīʿī Muslim Literature," Part 1, *The Muslim World* (July, 1976), vol. LXVI, no.3, pp.163-188.

Chittick, William C., *Imaginal Worlds: Ibn al-'Arabī and the Problem of Religious Diversity* (Albany: State University of New York Press, 1994).

Chittick, William C., and Sachiko Murata, *The Vision of Islam*, (New York: Aragon House, 1994).

Dirks, Jerald F., *The Abrahamic Faiths: Judaism, Christianity, and Islam: Similarities and Contrasts* (Maryland: Amana Publications, 2004).

Haddad, Yvonne, "The Conceptions of the term *Dīn* in the Qur'ān," *The Muslim World* (April, 1974), vol. 64, pp.114-123.

Ibn Kathīr, Abū al-Fidā' ʿImād al-Dīn Ismāʿīl, *Tafsīr al-Qur'ān al-ʿAẓīm*, 4 vols. (Beirut: Dār al-Fikr, 1970).

Ibn al-ʿArabī, Muḥyi al-Dīn, *Tafsīr al-Qur'ān al-Karīm*, ed. Mustafa Ghalib (Beirut: Dār al-Andalus, 1978).

Ipgrave, Michael, ed., *Scriptures in Dialogue: Christians and Muslims Studying the Bible and the Qur'an Together* (London: Church House Publishing, 2004).

Izutsu, Toshihiko, *God and Man in the Qur'an: Semantics of the Qur'anic Weltanschaung* (North Stratford: Ayer Company Publishers Inc., 1998).

Jomier, Jacques, *The Bible and the Qur'an*, trans. Edward P. Arbez (San Francisco: Ignatius Press, 1964).

Khalidi, Tarif, *Arabic Historical Thought in the Classical Period* (Cambridge, New York and Melbourne: Cambridge University Press, 1994).

Madigan, Daniel, *The Qur'an's Self Image: Writing and Authority in Islam's Scripture* (Princeton University Press, 2001).

McAuliffe, Jane Dammen, "The Prediction and Prefiguration of Muhammad," *Bible and Qur'an: Essays in Scriptural Intertextuality*, ed. John C. Reeves (Atlanta: Society of Biblical Literature, 2003), pp.107-132.

______, *Qur'ānic Christians: An Analysis of Classical and Modern Exegesis* (New York: Cambridge University Press, 1991).

Al-Qummī, Abū al-Ḥasan ʿAlī ibn Ibrāhīm, *Tafsīr al-Qummī*, ed. al-Sayyid Tayyib al-Musawi al-Jaza'iri (Najaf: Maṭbaʿat al-Najaf, 1967).

Al-Qurṭubī, Abū ʿAbd Allāh Muḥammad ibn Aḥmad al-Anṣārī, *Al-Jāmiʿ li Aḥkām al-Qur'ān*. 10 vols. (Cairo: Dār al-Kitāb al-ʿArabī, 1967).

Qutb, Sayyid, *Fī Ẓilāl al-Qur'ān*, 6 vols. (Beirut: Dār Iḥyā' al-Turāth, 1971).

Rahman, Fazlur, "Pre-Foundations of the Muslim Community in Mecca," *Studia Islamica* (1976), no.43, pp.5-24.

Al-Rāzī, Fakhr al-Dīn, *Al-Tafsīr al-Kabīr*, 17 vols. (Beirut: Dār al-Fikr, 1995).

Rida, Rashid, *Tafsīr al-Manār*, 12 vols. (Beirut, 1935).

Sachedina, Abdul-Aziz, "The Nature of Scriptural Reasoning in Islam," *The Journal of Scriptural Reasoning* (April, 2005), vol. 5, no. 1. www.etext.lib.virginia.edu/journals.

______, *The Islamic Roots of Democratic Pluralism* (Oxford: Oxford University Press, 2001).

Smith, Wilfred Cantwell, *The Meaning and End of Religion: A New Approach to the Religious Traditions of Mankind* (New York: Macmillan, 1963).

Al-Ṭabarsī, Abū ʿAlī al-Faḍl ibn al-Ḥasan, *Majmaʿ al-Bayān fī Tafsīr al-Qur'ān*, 10 vols. (Beirut: Dār Maktabat al-Ḥayāt, 1996).

Al-Ṭabarī, Abū Jaʿfar Muḥammad ibn Jarīr, *Jāmiʿ al-Bayān ʿan Ta'wīl Āy al-Qur'ān*, 30 vols. (Cairo: Dār al-Maʿārif, 1969).

Tabataba'i, Sayyid Muhammad Husain, *Al-Mīzān fī Tafsīr al-Qur'ān* (Mu'assasat al-Aʿlamī li al-Maṭbūʿāt, 1974).

Tottoli, Roberto, *Biblical Prophets in the Qur'ān and Muslim Literature* (Richmond, U.K.: Curzon Press, 2002).

Al-Zamakhsharī, Abū al-Qāsim Jār Allāh Maḥmūd ibn ʿUmar, *al-Kashshāf ʿan Ḥaqā'iq al-Tanzīl wa ʿUyūn al-Aqāwīl fī Wujūh al-Tafsīr*, 4 vols. (Cairo: Musṭafā al-Bābī al-Ḥalabī, 1966).

______, *Major Themes of the Qur'an* (Minneapolis: Bibliotheca Islamica Inc., 1989).

NOTES

1 Abdul-Aziz Sachedina, "The Nature of Scriptural Reasoning in Islam," *The Journal of Scriptural Reasoning* (April, 2005), vol. 5, no.1, p.1.

2 Ibid.

3 Fazlur Rahman, "Pre-Foundations of the Muslim Community in Mecca," *Studia Islamica* (1976), no.43, p.10.

4 Fazlur Rahman, *Major Themes of the Qur'an* (Minneapolis: Bibliotheca Islamica Inc., 1989), p163.

5 In this paper I will use the Qur'anic translation of Yusuf Ali: http://www.searchtruth.com/chapter_display.php?chapter=42&translator=2&mac=

6 Jacques Jomier, *The Bible and the Qur'an*, trans. Edward P. Arbez (San Francisco: Ignatius Press, 1964), p.19.

7 Jerald F. Dirks, *The Abrahamic Faiths: Judaism, Christianity, and Islam: Similarities and Contrasts* (Maryland: Amana Publications, 2004), p.27.

8 Rahman, "Pre-Foundations of the Muslim Community in Mecca," p.9.

9 Ibid.

10 Ibid., p.9.

11 Abū ʿAlī al-Faḍl ibn al-Ḥasan al-Ṭabarsī, *Majmaʿ al-Bayān fī Tafsīr al-Qur'ān* (Beirut: Dār Maktabat al-Ḥayāt, 1961), vol. 1, pp.77-78.

12 Abū al-Fidā' ʿImād al-Dīn Ismāʿīl ibn Kathīr, *Tafsīr al-Qur'ān al-ʿAẓīm* (Beirut: Dār al-Fikr, 1970), vol. 1, pp.69-70.

13 Abū ʿAbd Allāh Muḥammad ibn Aḥmad al-Anṣārī al-Qurṭubī, *Al-Jāmiʿ li Aḥkām al-Qur'ān* (Cairo: Dār al-Kitāb al-ʿArabī, 1967), vol. 1, p.158.

14 Rahman, "Pre-Foundations of the Muslim Community in Mecca," p.11.

15 Daniel Madigan, *The Qur'an's Self-Image: Writing and Authority in Islam's Scripture* (Princeton: Princeton University Press, 2001), p.164.

16 Jane Dammen McAuliffe, "The Prediction and Prefiguration of Muhammad," *Bible and Qur'an: Essays in Scriptural Intertextuality*, ed. John C. Reeves (Atlanta: Society of Biblical Literature, 2003), p.108.

17 Rahman, "Pre-Foundations of the Muslim Community in Mecca," p.9.

18 Jomier, *The Bible and the Qur'an*, p.20.

19 Ibid.

20 Ibid.

21 Rahman, "Pre-Foundations of the Muslim Community in Mecca," p.5.

22 Ibid.

23 Ibid.

24 Ibid, p.10.

25 Ibid.

26 Ibid.

27 Yvonne Haddad, "The Conceptions of the term Din in the Qur'ān," *Muslim World* (April, 1974), vol. 64, p.121.

28 Toshihiko Izutsu, *God and Man in the Qur'an: Semantics of the Qur'anic Weltanschuug* (North Stratford: Ayer Company Publishers Inc., 1998), p.220.

29 Ibid.

30 Wilfred Cantwell Smith, *The Meaning and End of Religion: A New Approach to the Religious Traditions of Mankind* (New York: Macmillan, 1963), pp.51-53.

31 Abū Jaʿfar Muḥammad ibn Jarīr al-Ṭabarī, *Jāmiʿal-Bayān ʿan Ta'wīl Āy al-Qur'ān* (Cairo: Dār al-Maʿārif, 1969), vol. 6, pp.267-268. Al-Ṭabarsī, *Majmaʿ al-Bayān*, vol. 3, p.35.

32 Mahmoud Ayoub, *The Qur'an and its Interpreters: The House of 'Imrān* (Albany: State University of New York Press, 1992), vol. 2, p.62.

33 Al-Ṭabarī, *Jāmiʿ al-Bayān*, vol. 6, pp.273-276.

34 Ibn Kathīr, *Tafsīr al-Qur'ān al-ʿAẓīm*, vol. 2, p.22. and see Ayoub, *The Qur'an and its Interpreters: The House of Imrān*, vol. 2, p.62.

35 Ibid.

36 Ibid.

37 Ibid.

38 Ibid., vol. 2, p.23.

39 Ibid.

40 Abū al-Qāsim Jār Allāh Maḥmūd ibn ʿUmar al-Zamakhsharī, *al-Kashshāf ʿan Ḥaqā'iq al-Tanzīl wa ʿUyūn al-Aqāwīl fī Wujūh al-Tafsīr* (Cairo: Muṣṭafā al-Bābī al-Ḥalabī, 1966), vol. 1, pp.344-345. and see Ayoub, *The Qur'an and its Interpreters: The House of 'Imrān*, vol. 2, p.68.

41 Ibid.

42 Ibid.

43 Al-Rāzī Fakhr al-Dīn, *Al-Tafsīr al-Kabīr*, vol. 4, pp.222-223.

44 Ibid.

45 Ibid, p.135.

46 Ibid.

47 Al-Qurṭubī, *Al-Jāmiʿ li Aḥkām al-Qur'ān*, vol. 4, pp.43-44.

48 People from the ʿAbd al-Qays tribe came to the Prophet from the island of Bahrain during the year of the conquest of Makkah. They represented the Arab tribe of *Rabīʿah*. The Prophet enjoined that they have faith in God alone. He then asked them, "do you know what faith is?" They answered, "God and his messenger know best." He said, "it is the witness that there is no God but God and that Muhammad is the apostle of God, observing regular worship, giving the obligatory alms, and observing the fast of Ramadan. It is also that you give in alms the fifth of the booty." The hadith is cited in *Ṣaḥīḥ al-Būkhārī*, Kitāb al-Imān.

49 Al-Qurṭubī, *Al-Jāmi[c] li Aḥkām al-Qur'ān*, vol. 4, pp.43-44.
50 Ibid.
51 Muḥiyy al-Dīn ibn al-[c]Arabī, *Tafsīr al-Qur'ān al-Karīm*, ed. Mustafa Ghalib (Beirut: Dār al-Andalus, 1978), vol. 1, p.174. and see Ayoub, *The Qur'an and its Interpreters: The House of 'Imrān*, vol. 2, p.70.
52 Ibid.
53 Ibid.
54 Abū al-Ḥasan [c]Alī ibn ibrāhīm al-Qummī, *Tafsīr al-Qummī*, ed. Al-Sayyid Tayyib al-Musawi al-Jaza'iri (Najaf: Maṭba[c]at al-Najaf, 1967), vol. 1, pp.99-100. and see Ayoub, *The Qur'an and its Interpreters*: *The House of 'Imrān*, vol. 2, p.70.
55 Ibid.
56 Ibid.
57 Ibid.
58 Sayyid Muhammad Husain Tabataba'i, *Al-Mīzān fī Tafsīr al-Qur'ān* (Mu'assasat al-A[c]lamī li al-Maṭbū[c]āt, 1974), vol. 3, pp.120-121.
59 Ibid.
60 Ibid.
61 Ibid.
62 Sayyid Qutb, *Fī Ẓilāl al-Qur'ān* (Beirut: Dār Iḥyā' al-Turāth, 1971), vol. 1, pp.558-559.
63 Ibid., vol. 1, pp.625-627.
64 Michael Ipgrave, ed., *Scriptures in Dialogue: Christians and Muslims Studying the Bible and the Qur'an Together* (London: Church House Publishing, 2004), p.124.
65 Ibid.
66 Ibid.
67 Ibid.
68 Ibid.
69 Jane Dammen McAuliffe, *Qur'ānic Christians: An Analysis of Classical and Modern Exegesis* (New York: Cambridge University Press, 1991), p115.
70 Ibid.
71 Rashid Rida, *Tafsīr al-Manār*, vol. 1, p.337.
72 Ayoub, *The Qur'an and its Interpreters*, vol. 2, p.241.
73 Ibid.
74 Abdul Aziz Sachedina, *The Islamic Roots of Democratic Pluralism* (Oxford: Oxford University Press, 2001), pp.23-24.
75 McAuliffe, *Qurānic Christians*, p.111.
76 Al-Ṭabarī, *Jāmi[c] al-Bayān*, vol. 1, p.334.
77 Ibn Kathīr, *Tafsīr al-Qur'ān al-[c]Aẓīm*, vol. 1, p.103.
78 Ibid.
79 Rida, *Tafsīr al-Manār*, vol. 1, p.337.

80 Jacques Jomier, *The Bible and the Qur'an*, p20.

81 Mahmoud Ayoub, "Towards an Islamic Christology: An Image of Jesus in Early Shīʿī Muslim Literature," Part 1, *The Muslim World* (July, 1976), vol. LXVI, no.3, pp.163-188.

82 Sachedina, *The Islamic Roots of Democratic Pluralism*, p.14.

83 William C. Chittick and Sachiko Murata, *The Vision of Islam* (New York: Aragon House, 1994), p.166.

84 Tarif Khalidi, *Arabic Historical Thought in the Classical Period* (Cambridge, New York and Melbourne: Cambridge University Press, 1994), p.10.

85 Rahman, "Pre-Foundations of the Muslim Community in Mecca," p.19.

86 William C. Chittick, *Imaginal Worlds: Ibn al-'Arabī and the Problem of Religious Diversity* (Albany: State University of New York Press, 1994), p.124.

87 Roberto Tottoli, *Biblical Prophets in the Qur'ān and Muslim Literature* (Richmond, UK: Curzon Press, 2002), p.9.

88 Ibid.

89 Chittick and Murata, *The Vision of Islam*, p.168.

90 Ibid.

91 Ibid., p.174.

92 Ibid.

93 Rida, *Tafsīr al-Manār*, vol. 1, p.338.

5

Exegesis, Social Science and the Place of the Jews in the Qur'an

MOHAMMED ABU-NIMER

THROUGHOUT Islamic history, religious scholars have been viewed as public intellectuals whose opinions have been valued on all matters. Indeed, in some periods, these scholars excelled in other disciplines, including physics, algebra, chemistry, astronomy, and medicine. Still, views expressed in Qur'anic commentaries received little critical examination, which is a necessary endeavor for contemporary Islamic reform. This paper addresses the views of sixteen exegetes and Qur'an scholars concerning Jews in the Qur'an, and applies both traditional and contemporary approaches to scriptural understanding.

Muḥammad ibn Bahāder ibn ʿAbd Allāh al-Zarkashī (d. 1391) explained that exegesis is needed for three reasons: people differ in their intellectual abilities, so some readers may need assistance to comprehend; parts of the Qur'an are built on certain assumptions that are not apparent to the common person; and some words may carry multiple meanings and can be deciphered only by learned specialists. These factors have become more complex as the usage of the Arabic language and the human condition in general continue to evolve. That the number of highly educated people has reached levels never known before illustrates how change can affect contemporary people's expectations from scholars. Those who specialize in Qur'an studies are no exception.

The process of reform must engage with the established tradition of exegesis and its methods. Al-Zarkashī presented key knowledge requirements for prospective scholars in the field, including classical Arabic diction and phonetics and *asbāb al-nuzūl* (occasions of revelation). He explained that some parts of the Qur'an could be difficult to comprehend because of *ʿumūm al-ṣīghah* (general form) and *khuṣūṣ al-sabab* (particular reason).[1] Some verses may appear general in their wording but may address a specific circumstance.

Jalāl al-Dīn al-Suyūṭī (d. 1505) classified the Qur'anic revelation into two main categories. The first is that which took place after an incident or a question to the Prophet, and the other had no pretext. Al-Suyūṭī added another layer of context that can affect the meaning of Qur'anic verses: the specific place and time of revelation and whether it carried new substance or overlapped with previous revelation.[2] A careful scholar should pay attention to the intricacies of these considerations.

One major approach to exegesis is known as *tafsīr al-Qur'ān bi al-Qur'ān* (interpreting the Qur'an by means of the Qur'an), which is built on the assumption that parts of the Qur'an complement each other. Another approach is called *al-tafsīr bi al-ma'thūr* (exegesis using tradition). Some of these traditions are attributed to the Prophet Muhammad and thus are part of hadith, which comprises his words, deeds, and approvals. Other traditions are only attributed to the Companions of the Prophet or members of his household, while others are narratives that appeared in early writings of *Sīrah* (the biography of the Prophet and the history of the first generation of Muslims). Scholars of hadith developed methodologies to authenticate attributions to the Prophet, but the rest of *ma'thūr* has not been subject to serious scrutiny.

Early scholars of the Qur'an frowned upon *al-tafsīr bi al-ra'y* (exegesis through personal opinion). Muʿtazilite rationalists saw this as an attempt to block ijtihad (independent reasoning). Yet the classical scholars only wanted to protect the status of the scripture as a source of truth telling whose understanding should not be marred by whims or non-scholarly purposes. Despite this theoretical stance, exegetes have often conflated their views on social and political affairs with their attempt to explain the meaning of Qur'anic verses.

The next section briefly reviews the ideas of Seyyed Hossein Nasr and Ismāʿīl al-Fārūqī, who approach the Qur'an as a whole to construct a *tawḥīdī* (monotheistic) worldview. Each generated a unique formula for understanding based on the grand Qur'anic ideas about the relationship between God and his creation. Within this framework, the section constructs the Qur'anic narrative of Jews and Judaism before turning to the critical review of classical exegesis.

THE PLACE OF JEWS IN THE QUR'AN: A HOLISTIC APPROACH

Al-Fārūqī and Nasr offer an understanding of God's relation to man based on the concept of *khilāfah* (vicegerency).[3] God made men and women His deputies on earth, and sent them messengers to teach them how to lead a "God-like" life.[4] Nasr emphasizes the mystical aspects of Islam, while al-Fārūqī focuses on theology, but both postulate that all human beings share a certain *fiṭrah* (nature) that is essentially good but have the capacity to commit wrong.[5] This is why humans are held accountable individually for their own deeds.[6]

Nasr justifies his holistic philosophy by suggesting that the Qur'an "is the source of knowledge, not only metaphysically and religiously, but even in the domain of particular fields of knowledge."[7] Qur'anic wisdom represents "a set of doctrines which expand knowledge of the structure of reality and man's position in it."[8] Al-Fārūqī writes of this same universal message when he expounds on how monotheism can influence the various aspects of human life.[9]

Traditional exegetes typically cited a verse or a *ma'thūr* piece to explain a single verse or a group of verses. The rest of the commentary may have included linguistic explanations and reflections on life events. Viewed from a holistic perspective, this mode of interpretation tends to offer a compartmentalized understanding of the Qur'an. Therefore, the contemporary systematic approaches raise the standard of competence in Islamic studies. Such is the hallmark of the careers of the contemporary exegete Muhammad Asad and religion scholar Mahmoud Ayoub, who do not dismiss tradition.

A holistic view of the scripture requires that an understanding of any part of the Qur'an be congruent with the basic premises of the overall Qur'anic narrative. Al-Fārūqī writes, "Divine unity and unity of truth are inseparable. They are aspects of one and the same reality. This becomes evident when we consider that truthfulness is a quality of the proposition of... *tawḥīd*, namely that God is one."[10] Those who believe the Qur'an is good for all times and places aught to make sure that any conceptions attached to revelation do not contradict its core foundations.

Much of the story of revelation in the Qur'an begins with Abraham, the father of prophets. His story is the most prominent in the Qur'an, save Muhammad's. The Qur'an emphasizes that all prophets preached the core belief in God, which stands as the foundation for the moral principles that all the faiths share. The Qur'an distinguishes between the core message and the expressions of *tawḥīd* in the life of the believers. God willed that there be differences in details, but they are all supposed to lead to the straight path. Louay Safi uses the term "Qur'anic Narrative" to refer to this macro view of the Qur'an.[11]

The Qur'an confronts Jews (and Christians) with its own truth claims. Abraham, Ishmael, Isaac, Jacob, and their descendants were neither Jewish nor Christian.[12] They were all *Muslims* (submitters) to God. The Qur'an essentially tells Jews and Christians that they belong with Muslims to the same family of faith. They are challenged to respond to the unified message of the prophets of God.[13]

The Qur'an recognizes *banū Isrā'īl* (the children of Israel) as a distinct group of people whose existence, struggles, and trials preceded the prophetic career of Moses. They faced oppression with patience and constancy until Moses led their deliverance to the Holy Land, where they enjoyed great wealth and sustenance.[14] They were blessed and favored over all people;[15] they were given a covenant from God through Moses;[16] and were given revelation and wisdom of governance.

Within this framework, the Qur'anic narrative maintains close affinity to Jewish religious history. Bernard Lewis's assertion that the Qur'anic mention of Jews is insignificant is inaccurate.[17] A keyword search of the Qur'an produces 131 verses that mention Musa (Moses).

Other key Jewish figures and terms are featured in many verses.[18] The sum of these occurrences, which do not include other important stories related to the Israelites, e.g., Pharaoh and Exodus, constitute nearly 5 percent of the Qur'an's 6,000 verses.

Most of the prophets mentioned in the Qur'an are Israelite prophets. Indeed much of the history of prophethood is Jewish. The Israelites had internal challenges and disagreements and developed schisms.[19] Among them were literalists who made it hard for themselves to obey God's commands.[20] The Qur'an focuses on the morals of this and other religious experiences rather than the details of what had happened. For example, the Qur'an mentions an unnamed group of Jews identified by having lived after Moses. They asked their unnamed prophet for a leader to fight in the good cause of God, but did not keep their commitment when that leader arose among them.[21] Other Jews were only identified by their actions; e.g., those who violated the fishing ban on the Sabbath[22] these were a small group.

When one considers the totality of the Jewish experience as told in the Qur'an, the Islamic scripture clearly confirms its truths, while showing the diversity of Jews as a people, including those who rejected and even killed prophets,[23] worshiped the calf when Moses was away,[24] and took their rabbis as lords.[25] Others were cursed by David and Jesus for their disbelief.[26]

Christians and Muslims also receive praise and rebuke in the Qur'an. Even the Prophet Muhammad was scolded for ignoring a blind man seeking spiritual understanding. A whole surah (chapter) of the Qur'an was revealed on this occasion.[27] Like the Muslim and Christian experiences, Jewish history offered mirror images of blessing and curse, belief and disbelief, knowledge and ignorance, wisdom and poor judgment, righteousness and wrongdoing.

Some Qur'anic verses describe the entire Jewish experience while others allude to only parts of it. Some of the stories specifically refer to certain Israelite groups. This is illustrated by how the Qur'an engaged the Jews who lived among the Muslims in Madinah. A verse reads that the knowledge of Jewish scholars vindicates the truthfulness of the Qur'an.[28] In another verse, Jews (and the Christians) would like Muslims to follow their ways; the Prophet is instructed not to follow the desires of any people but to remain steadfast on the straight path of God.[29] Jews who were cited as ridiculing God's attributes were cursed.[30] When conflict developed between Jews and Muslims, the Qur'an noted their enmity.[31] Louay Safi explains: "The Qur'an condemned the unscrupulous behavior of several Jewish tribes toward the Prophet and the newly founded Muslim community, in violation of their own religious teachings, while urging the Muslims to respect the religious freedom of the Jews and the religious tradition of Judaism."[32]

The Qur'an therefore informs Muslims about some episodes of Jewish history while highlighting the creedal and moral foundation that the Abrahamic faiths share. In the Qur'anic conception, Jews are just like any others, including Muslims, who have had their own challenges with revelation. All will be held individually accountable to God for their deeds.[33]

Using this understanding of the Qur'anic narrative, the next section focuses on the learning content of the interpretations of verse (5:82) in *tafsīr* sources. The verse reads: "You will find the most hostile among men to the believers the Jews and polytheists; and you will find the most affectionate to the believers those who say we follow Christ; for there are among them monks and scholars and they are not arrogant."[34]

Verse (5:82) is particularly interesting because it makes a clear statement about relations between Muslims, Christians and Jews, and it offers an obvious contrast of amity and enmity within members of the three faiths during the time of revelation. Therefore, it fits the theoretical interest of exploring the relationship between exegesis and important elements of social science. As will be demonstrated below, exegetes make significant observations on human behavior, which raises the question of whether such statements are supported by revelation or require assessment through social science criteria.

EXEGESIS VERSUS STEREOTYPES

Exegetes in the first three centuries refrained from excessive commentary and limited the application of the verse to specific groups of Christians and Jews rather than to all Christians and Jews. Mujāhid (d.

723) was a contemporary of the successors of the Prophet's Companions. He was a student of Ibn ʿAbbās. He is a widely cited source of *ma'thūr*. He did not address the part referring to Jews. Possibly, he thought the verse was a statement of fact, given the growing conflict between Muslims and Jews at the time. Al-Samarqandī (d. 823) and al-Ṣanʿānī (d. 827) wrote that the verse denoted the Jews of Madinah who allied themselves with the pagan Arabs against the Prophet Muhammad. All three works agree that the reference to Christians meant for the kind treatment Muslims received from the Christian King of Abyssinia al-Najāshī.[35]

Several later exegetes concurred with this cautious approach, including al-Thaʿālibī (d. 876), al-Ṭūsī (d. 1067), al-Wāḥidī (d. 1076), and Ibn al-Jawzī (d. 1328). Al-Thaʿālibī cited a hadith warning any Muslim to avoid being alone with Jews out of public sight out of fear for their security. Still, he stressed that neither Jews nor Christians have affection for Muslims. Al-Najāshī and his companions were only an exception. Al-Thaʿālibī saw other Christians as hostile. He did not refer to specific events but mentioned specific actions, including killing Muslims and destroying their property. Perhaps this was in reference to the rising conflict between Muslim and Byzantine forces. In other words, he understood revelation in light of observable facts that appeared not consistent with the statement of (5:82).

A number of these exegetes did not offer Qur'an or *ma'thūr* to support their exposition, including al-Ṭūsī and al-Wāḥidī. It is possible that they were only passing on knowledge they gained from others. At the time, there was not much concern for crediting authors. Qur'an scholarship was generally seen as a way to serve God by sharing His message. This is why it was not considered improper to paraphrase unnamed sources introduced in the passive form *qīla* (it is said). Therefore, exegetes – at least some of them – perceived the most important part of their role was to communicate the message of the Qur'an.

Yet most exegetes drew timeless generalizations about Jewish behavior. Fakhr al-Dīn al-Rāzī al-Shāfiʿī (d. 939) noted that God told of the Christians being more softhearted and thus closer than Jews are to Muslims.[36] Al-Ṣanʿānī (d. 1096) seemed to assume the meaning of a general Jewish enmity, but claimed the verse's reference to Christian affection applies only to forty people from Abyssinia who came to the Prophet to accept Islam, a story that appeared in other sources. He distinguished between those and the disbelieving Christians who are equal to Jews in their hostility to Muslims.[37] In essence, he qualified the message of the verse by offering a generalization about the dominant sentiment among Christians. Al-Ṣanʿānī warned against applying the feeling of amity toward all Christians, but did not substantiate his position. One must assume he counted on his reader's acquiescence due to what was generally known at the time about conflict between Muslims and Christians. When al-Ṣanʿānī died, the Crusades were underway. Whatever the real reason, it could not have stemmed from a method of interpretation because the exegete did not employ the same qualification to his understanding of the other part of the verse.

In contrast, al-Baghawī (d. 1122), who lived in the mid-Crusades period, approached this verse in two ways. First, he agreed with al-Ṣanʿānī's view of the Christians, adding that "they kill Muslims, capture them, destroy their countries and mosques, and burn their Qur'ans."[38] Second, he acknowledged unnamed exegetes suggesting that that verse refers to "all Jews and all Christians because Jews are hardhearted while Christians are softhearted."[39] Al-Baghawī did not offer any support from the Qur'an, hadith, other *ma'thūr*, or behavioral observation for this emphatic characterization.

By then, these social stereotypes of Jews and Christians may have become acceptable in exegetes' circles. Approximately two decades after al-Baghawī, Abū al-Qāsim al-Zamakhsharī al-Khawārizmī (d. 1144) accepted the notion of Christians being "softhearted." He opined that Jews are lumped with the polytheists because they are snobby and will not respond to truth. He cited what he called a "very weak" hadith: "Whenever two Jews are alone with a Muslim they would consider killing him."[40] This narrative presents another dilemma: If Qur'an exposition is about explaining revealed truth, is it proper to support it by a discredited attribution to the Prophet? The irony is that some of the rigidity developed around using *al-tafsīr bi al-ma'thūr* was meant to clear the meaning of the Qur'an from *ra'y* that does not possess truth claim.

By the fourteenth century, Jewish and Christian stereotypes had already been established in exegetical literature. Al-Nasafi (d. 1310) repeated the notion that Jews are hardhearted and Christians are soft-hearted and modest, without reference to supporting evidence from *ma'thūr*.[41] A few decades later, Muḥammad al-Kalbī al-Gharnāṭī (d. 1341) delivered the most equivocal statement of Jew-phobia. He cited their alliance with Makkan polytheists as only an example proving an eternally valid trend. "This remains true until the end of time: every Jew is very hostile to Islam and cunning against its people."[42] Such a notion clearly violates the spirit and text of the Qur'an.

Ibn Kathīr al-Dimashqī (d. 1373) offered a psychological profile of Jews to explain their disbelief: "The disbelief of the Jews is caused by arrogance and the tendency to reject truth. This is why they are cursed until Judgment Day." Like many exegetes, Ibn Kathīr was more careful about generalizations regarding Christians, asserting that verse (5:82) was meant for al-Najāshī and his people.[43] Likewise, al-Bayḍawī (d. 1388) explained Jewish behavior using almost the same words that appeared in earlier exegetical works. He pointed out their snobbish attitude, excessive expression of disbelief, and habit of opposition to prophets. He added to these characterizations charges of whimsical thinking and reliance on imitation. Predictably, he painted Christians with a broad brush as being humble and devoted to knowledge and good works. Interestingly, he concluded by stating that these are praiseworthy attributes "even for non-believers."[44] This idea of goodness that is totally detached from belief is congruent with the Qur'anic concept of *fiṭrah* (human nature), a major theme in contemporary Islamic understanding, as presented above by Nasr and al-Fārūqī.

Al-Suyūṭī (d. 1505) refrained from issuing generalizations, but did not justify the use of a discredited hadith about a Muslim being alone with Jews. One may speculate that he assumed this would not be challenged. He referred to the Christians of Abyssinia who recognized the truthfulness of the Qur'an, but did not suggest that they must have converted to deserve praise. He cited another *ma'thūr* suggesting al-Najāshī, along with Abyssinian monks and scholars, listened to a recitation of the Qur'an.[45]

Abū al-Suʿūd (d. 1544) suggested that this verse only reaffirms what is known about Jews who are "snobbish, extreme disbelievers, and immersed in following whims and desires." He scolded them for their blind following of tradition, lack of inquisitiveness, and propensity to rebel against prophets. Abū al-Suʿūd referred to Christians as *jins* (a distinct category of people). He accepted the generalized notion of Christian affinity to Muslims because, in his words, many Christians are that way. Then he qualified his perception of Jews, stating that although some are guided, most are not. He referred to the alliance between Jews and pagan Arabs but not to the Abyssinian Christians.[46] In other words, he acknowledged that the verse referred to the behavior of Madinah Jews, yet he offered a generalized statement about the religious attitudes of most Jews, never testing it against knowledge of the Jews of his time and/or locale. He paraphrased some other verses of the Qur'an that mentioned wrongdoing of Jews who lived in the past, ignoring the verses praising other Jews.

The same methodological error applies to al-Amadī's characterization of many Christians as believers. Although the statement might actually have been true at the time of revelation and the time of al-Amadī, that knowledge would not be derived from verse (5:82). The verse is not concerned with quantifying the faithful crowd. Even the best quantitative research techniques would have difficulty reaching definitive generalizations about such a difficult topic.

Exegetes who derived meaning from Arabic grammar reached conflicting conclusions. Abū Muḥammad al-Andalusī (d. 1151) wrote that the prefix "*l*" in the word *latajidanna* (verily, you shall find) indicates an absolute affirmation that applies to all times, although he acknowledged that the verse refers to a current state of affairs. Yet, he then excluded Jews with moral character. Like other exegetes, he offered a static profile of all Jews on the basis of Jewish-Muslim relations at the time of the Prophet or on the authority of previously rehashed assumptions regarding the behavior of the great majority among them. Behavioral studies of this nature were not available at the time. Although the verse offers a contrast of Jewish and Christian sentiments vis-à-vis Muslims, al-Andalusī generalized about Jews but remained cautious regarding Christians. He only added the following tweak:

"The Qur'an is not saying Christians feel affection toward Muslims; it only tells that they are *aqrabū* (closer) than the Jews and polytheists to Muslims."[47]

In contrast, Abū ʿAbdullāh al-Qurṭubī (d. 1273) expressed a starkly different understanding of the use of suffix and prefix in Arabic, suggesting that the "*l*" in *latajidanna* denotes an oath for emphasis while the ending with "*nna*" is meant to make a distinction between the present state of affairs and the future. This analysis begs the question of whether al-Andalusī, who lived only a century earlier, missed the meaning of the prefix? Classical Arabic conventions had already been set by then. Al-Qurṭubī did not recall other verses praising Jews and criticizing Christians, but his explanation of the reference to Jews, along with his citation of the story of al-Najāshī to contextualize the reference to Christians, is highly responsive to time and place factors.[48]

Abū al-Faḍl al-Baghdādī al-Ālūsī (d. 1854) used language to stress that Jews are even more hostile than the polytheists because they are mentioned first. This is the only time an exegete made use of the spoken language to indicate emphasis in a written commentary. In Arabic, the word "*wa*" (and) implies equal emphasis.[49] In contrast, Muḥammad al-Shawkānī (d. 1834) used knowledge of grammar and sentence structure to emphasize what is literally apparent in the meaning. His approach is minimalist, assuming that readers would only need an explanation for uncommon words or complex structures.[50]

SCRIPTURE AND THE DYNAMIC NATURE OF HUMAN BEHAVIOR

One cannot infer too much about each exegete by looking at their interpretation of one verse. The focus here is to raise questions and offer answers about the nature of the exegesis field and its possible overlap with behavioral social sciences, given what exegetes actually have done. The review clearly shows substantive disparity not only in the way exegetes understood (5:82) but also in their perception of their own role. Some saw their job as making reading the Qur'an easier; others wanted to amplify the message of the Qur'an; others wanted to read in the Qur'an practical suggestions dealing with the world around them. Some began from their observations in the world and attempted to support them from the Qur'an and other traditions. Asma Afsaruddin demonstrates that Shiite and Sunni scholars used the Qur'an to debate who had the right to succeed the Prophet in political leadership.[51] A holistic approach that seeks to glorify the Qur'an as an eternal source of truth telling would discourage such usage.

Exegesis sources in the first three centuries did not draw generalizations about the character of Jews or Christians from (5:82). In sharp contrast, the twentieth-century work of Seyyid Qutb (d. 1966) reads the Qur'an in light of historical events, including the Crusades, modern western imperialism, and contemporary Israeli colonialism. He accepted the notion that Jews have been Islam's enemies from the start, adding to that clear anti-Jewish rhetoric, accusing Jews of having caused the ills of modern society.[52] Clearly, Qutb infused in his commentary a certain reading of history that he acquired before writing his Qur'an commentary. The shadow of the Arab-Israeli conflict looms large in how he related to Jews. Qutb attributed the mention of Christians in this verse to the people of Najrān, a small Christian group in Arabia that accepted Islam. In this line of thinking, only Christians who convert can be close to Muslims while Jews are always bad and anti-Muslim.

The gist of Qutb's commentary is not completely anomalous. Most of the works reviewed for this paper offer a generalized negative portrayal of Jews. Al-Kalbī even claimed this is simply the nature of Jews and will never change. Al-Baghawī, al-Zamakhsharī, and Ibn Kathīr mentioned the specific context of the conflict with Jewish tribes in Madinah, but still used this as more evidence of the ill-natured quality of Jews as a category of people.

It is worthwhile to contrast this understanding with how these five exegetes dealt with verse (2:47), which reminds the Israelites that God has favored them over all people. All five exegetes express the understanding that the praise applies only to the past, to the time of Moses and other Jewish prophets.[53] In other words, praise is limited to a specific generation of Jews, but the censure pertains to all other Jews (or those since the generation that opposed the Prophet Muhammad). This logic violates the Qur'anic opposition to the notion of collective responsibility. No people should be judged by what their coreligionists did in the past, either individually or collectively.[54]

Jews are described in many *tafsīr* sources as "hardhearted," "snobbish" and "arrogant," while Christians are seen as "softhearted" and "humble." Such descriptions are obviously not general statements about Christian and Jewish ethics; they are presented as collective attributes of members of the two groups. As such, they meet the definition of stereotypes. This finding raises the specific question of whether it is the place of Qur'anic exegesis to profile the behavioral traits of individuals or groups.

People create conventions by which they relate to one another and the world around them. Their shared experiences inform their patterns of thinking and behavior and allow them to form what the Qur'an calls "peoples and tribes." However, nothing in the Qur'an suggests that people are born with cultural characteristics that stay with them and their progeny. Indeed, the Qur'anic narrative supports the notion that people are endowed by their Creator with the ability to make conscious choices with regards to their behavior. This dynamic conception of the human experience renders false any static stereotypes.

The validity of the Qur'an for all times and places does not mean that every statement in it claims to be true everywhere and all the time. As explained above, classical scholars of the Qur'an were usually very particular about noting the context of revelation. The review of (5:82) interpretations shows that many exegetes ignored this important consideration. Many ventured to ascribe eternal behavioral qualities to categories of people based on their religious affiliation. To help future scholars avoid such an error, maybe it would be worthwhile to engage in a classification process that would identify verses whose validity is timeless and those that are bound to time and place.

This will not stop exegetes and others from attempting to relate scripture to personal and public life. There are a number of ways to deal with statements by exegetes implying social learning. The first option is to dismiss them because they lie outside the boundaries of the exegesis specialization. Those with secular scholarly orientation may prefer this response. The risk implied in this choice is clear: excluding oneself from what could be an important discussion. The second option would be to evaluate arguments presented in this sort of discourse based on evidence and logic.

In conclusion, the contemporary holistic understanding of the Qur'an raises several methodological and interpretative challenges to classical exegesis works cited in this study. The main theoretical concern arising from the critique of past works is whether social commentary is a different enterprise than the one concerned with expounding scriptural messages. If it is difficult, impractical, or undesirable to separate the two functions, one still has to ask whether exegetes who are not trained to observe human behavior are qualified to engage in credible expositions of what the Qur'an means to the evolving human condition. In any case, when exegetes delve into such subjects, they automatically cross over to a new interdisciplinary field of knowledge. By doing so, they should welcome critique from a wide range of experts. To deal with the practical implication of this question, one can imagine the possibility of establishing an interdisciplinary field of knowledge that would train scholars in both exegesis and social and behavioral sciences.

REFERENCES

Afsaruddin, Asma, "Sunni-Shi'i Dialectics and the Qur'an," in *Coming to Terms with the Qur'an*, ed. Khalil Muhammad and Andrew Rippin (North Haledon, NJ: Islamic Publications International, 2008).

Al-Amadī, Abū al-Su'ūd, *Irshād al-'Aql al-Salīm ilā Mazāyā al-Qur'ān al-Karīm* (Guiding the Right Mind to the Values of the Noble Qur'an), http://www.aljamea.net/services/viewing/Preview_Books.php, December 2, 2008.

Al-Andalusī, Abū Muḥammad, *Al-Muḥarrir al-Wajīz fī Tafsīr al-Kitāb al-'Azīz* (A Brief Narrative of the Exegesis of the Dignified Book), http://www.aljamea.net/services/viewing/Preview_Books.php, December 2, 2008.

Al-Baghawī, Abū Muḥammad Ḥusayn ibn Mas'ūd, *Tafsīr al-Baghawī*. http://www.aljamea.net/services/viewing/Preview_Books.php, December 2, 2008.

Al-Baghdādī, Abū al-Faḍl, *Rūḥ al-Ma'ānī fī Tafsīr al-Qur'ān al-'Aẓīm wa al-Sab' al-Mathānī* (The Essential Meaning of the Exegesis of the Great Qur'an), http://www.aljamea.net/services/viewing/Preview_Books.php, December 2, 2008.

Al-Bayḍawī, Imām 'Abd Allāh, *Tafsīr al-Bayḍawī*. http://www.aljamea.net/services/viewing/Preview_Books.php, December 2, 2008.

Al-Dimashqī, Ismā'īl Ibn Kathīr, *Tafsīr al-Qur'ān al-'Aẓīm*.

Al-Fārūqī, Ismā'īl, *Al Tawḥīd: Its Implications for Thought and Life* (Herndon: International Institute of Islamic Thought, 1982).

al-Gharnāṭī, Muḥammad al-Kalbī, *Al-Tashīl li 'Ulūm al-Tanzīl*. http://www.aljamea.net/services/viewing/Preview_Books.php, December 2, 2008.

Al-Khawārizmī, Abū al-Qāsim al-Zamakhsharī, *Al-Kashshāf* (The Explorer), http://www.aljamea.net/services/viewing/Preview_Books.php, December 2, 2008.

Lewis, Bernard, *Semites and Anti-Semites* (New York: W.W. Norton & Company, 1986).

Al-Nasafī, Ḥāfiẓ al-Dīn 'Abd Allāh ibn Aḥmad ibn Maḥmūd, *Tafsīr al-Nasafī*. http://www.aljamea.net/services/viewing/Preview_Books.php, December 2, 2008.

Nasr, Seyyed Hossein, *Ideals and Realities of Islam* (Chicago: ABC International Group, 2000).

Al-Qurṭubī, Abū 'Abd Allāh, *Al-Jāmi' li Aḥkām al-Qur'ān* (The Compiler of Qur'an Rules), http://www.aljamea.net/services/viewing/Preview_Books.php, December 2, 2008.

Qutb, Sayyid, *Fī Ẓilāl al-Qur'ān (In the Shade of the Qur'an)* (Beirut: Dār al-Shurūq, 1979).

Al-Rāzī, Fakhr al-Dīn, *Al-Tafsīr al-Kabīr* or *Mafātīḥ al-Ghayb*. http://www.aljamea.net/services/viewing/Preview_Books.php, December 2, 2008.

Safi, Louay, *The Qur'anic Narrative: The Journey of Life as Told in the Qur'an* (Westport: Praeger, 2008).

Al-Samarqandī, Naṣr ibn Muḥammad, *Baḥr al-ʿUlūm* (Sea of Knowledge), http://www.aljamea.net/services/viewing/Preview_Books.php, December 2, 2008.

Al-Ṣanʿānī, *Tafsīr al-Qur'ān* (Qur'an Exegesis), http://www.aljamea.net/services/viewing/Preview_Books.php, December 2, 2008.

Al-Shawkānī, Muḥammad, *Fatḥ al-Qadīr* (Mighty Opening), http://www.aljamea.net/services/viewing/Preview_Books.php, December 2, 2008.

Al-Suyūṭī, Jalāl al-Dīn, *Al-Durr al-Manthūr* (Thrown Pearls), http://www.aljamea.net/services/viewing/Preview_Books.php, December 2, 2008.

______, *Al-Itqān fī ʿUlūm al-Qur'ān*. http://www.aljamea.net/services/viewing/Preview_Books.php, December 2, 2008.

Al-Tābiʿī, Mujāhid ibn Jabr al-Makhzūmī, *Tafsīr Mujāhid* (Exegesis of Mujāhid), http://www.aljamea.net/services/viewing/Preview_Books.php, December 2, 2008.

Al-Zarkashī, Muḥammad ibn Bahāder ibn ʿAbd Allāh, *Al-Burhān fī ʿUlūm al-Qur'ān* (Proof in Qur'an Studies), http://www.aljamea.net/services/viewing/Preview_Books. php, December 6, 2008. http://www.altafsir.com.

NOTES

1 Muḥammad ibn Bahāder ibn ʿAbd Allāh al-Zarkashī, *Al-Burhān fī ʿUlūm al-Qur'ān* (Proof in Qur'an Studies), http://www.aljamea.net/services/viewing/Preview_Books.php, December 6, 2008.

2 Jalāl al-Dīn al-Suyūṭī, *Al-Itqān fī ʿUlūm al-Qur'ān* (Competence in Qur'an Studies), http://www.aljamea.net/services/viewing/Preview_Books.php, December 2, 2008.

3 Seyyed Hossein Nasr, *Ideals and Realities of Islam* (Chicago: ABC International Group, 2000), p.4; Ismāʿīl al- Fārūqī, *Al-Tawḥīd: Its Implications for Thought and Life* (Herndon: International Institute of Islamic Thought, 1982), p.6.

4 Nasr, *Ideals and Realities of Islam*, pp.4-55.

5 Al- Fārūqī, *Al-Tawḥīd*, pp.67-69; Nasr, *Ideals and Realities of Islam*, pp.3, 21.

6 Nasr, Ibid., p.62.

7 Ibid., p.39.

8 Ibid.

9 Al-Fārūqī, *Al-Tawḥīd*, p.6.

10 Ibid., p.43.

11 Louay Safi, *The Qur'anic Narrative: The Journey of Life as Told in the Qur'an* (Westport, CT: Praeger, 2008).

12 See Qur'an (2:140).

13 See Qur'an (2:135-136); (3:84); and (4:163).

14 See Qur'an (7:105); (7:137), (20:80); (26:59); and (44:30).

15 See Qur'an (2:47); and (2:122).

16 See Qur'an (2:40); and (32:23).

17 Bernard Lewis, *Semites and Anti-Semites* (New York: W.W. Norton & Company, 1986), p.127.

18 Israel, 41; *Ahl al-Kitāb* (people of the Book, including Christians), 31; *Hārūn* (Aaron), 20; *Yaʿqūb* (Jacob), 16; *Dāwūd* (David), 16; *Sulaymān* (Solomon), 16; *Isḥāq* (Isaac), 16; *al-Tawrāh* (Torah), 16; and *Yahūd* or *Hūd* (Jews), 10.

19 See Qur'an (10:93).

20 See Qur'an (2:67-71).

21 See Qur'an (2:246).

22 See Qur'an (2:65); and (7:163).

23 See Qur'an (5:70).

24 See Qur'an (2:51); (2:54); (2:92); (4:153); (7:148); and (20:88).

25 See Qur'an (9:31).

26 See Qur'an (5:78).

27 See *Sūrah ʿAbasa* (80).
28 See Qur'an (26:197).
29 See Qur'an (2:120).
30 See Qur'an (5:64).
31 See Qur'an (5:82).
32 Louay Safi, *The Qur'anic Narrative*, p.xiii.
33 See Qur'an (19:93-95).
34 The main sources of information for the cited classical works are http://www.aljamea.net and http://www.altafsir.com. (Al-Jamea is particularly useful; once a certain verse is selected, the contents of exegetical texts are returned as they would appear on a hard copy edition.)
35 Mujāhid ibn Jabr al-Makhzūmī al-Tābiʿī, *Tafsīr Mujāhid* (Exegesis of Mujāhid); Naṣr ibn Muḥammad al-Samarqandī; *Baḥr al-ʿUlūm* (Sea of Knowledge); Al-Ṣanʿānī, *Tafsīr al-Qur'ān* (Qur'an Exegesis), http://www.aljamea.net/services/viewing/Preview_ Books.php, December 1, 2003.
36 Fakhr al-Dīn al-Rāzī al-Shāfiʿī, *Al-Tafsīr al-Kabīr* or *Mafātīḥ al-Ghayb*, http://www.aljamea.net/services/viewing/Preview_Books.php, December 2, 2008.
37 Al-Ṣanʿānī, http://www.aljamea.net/services/viewing/Preview_Books.php, December 1, 2003.
38 Abū Muḥammad Ḥusayn ibn Masʿūd al-Baghawī, *Tafsīr al-Baghawī*, http://www.aljamea.net/services/viewing/Preview_Books.php, December 1, 2003.
39 Ibid.
40 Abū al-Qāsim al-Zamakhsharī al-Khawārizmī, *Al-Kashshāf* (The Explorer), http://www.aljamea.net/services/viewing/Preview_Books.php, December 1, 2003.
41 Ḥāfiẓ al-Dīn ʿAbd Allāh ibn Aḥmad ibn Maḥmūd al-Nasafī, *Tafsīr al-Nasafī*. http://www.aljamea.net/services/viewing/Preview_Books.php, December 1, 2003.
42 al-Gharnāṭī, Muḥammad al-Kalbī, *Al-Tashīl li ʿUlūm al-Tanzīl*, http://www.aljamea.net/services/viewing/Preview_Books.php, December 1, 2003.
43 Ibn Kathīr, *Tafsīr al-Qur'ān al-ʿAẓīm*, http://www.aljamea.net/services/viewing/Preview_Books.php, December 1, 2003.
44 Imām ʿAbd Allāh al-Bayḍawī, *Tafsīr al-Bayḍawī*. http://www.aljamea.net/services/viewing/Preview_Books.php
45 Jalāl al-Dīn al-Suyūṭī, *Al-Durr al-Manthūr* (Thrown Pearls), http://www.aljamea.net/services/viewing/Preview_Books.php, December 1, 2003.
46 Abū al-Suʿūd al-Amadī, *Irshād al-ʿAql al-Salīm ilā Mazāyā al-Qur'ān al-Karīm* (Guiding the Right Mind to the Values of the Noble Qur'an), http://www.aljamea.net/services/viewing/Preview_Books.php, December 1, 2003.
47 Abū Muḥammad al-Andalusī, *Al-Muḥarrir al-Wajīz fī Tafsīr al-Kitāb al-ʿAzīz* (A Brief Narrative of the Exegesis of the Dignified Book), http://www.aljamea.net/services/viewing/Preview_Books.php, December 1, 2003.

48 Abū Abdullāh al-Qurṭubī, *Al-Jāmiʿ li-Aḥkām al-Qur'ān* (The Compiler of Qur'an Rules? A Compendium of the Rulings of the Qur'an), http://www.aljamea.net/services/viewing/Preview_Books.php, December 1, 2003.

49 Abū al-Faḍl al-Baghdādī, *Rūḥ al-Mʿānī fī Tafsīr al-Qur'ān al-ʿAẓīm wa al-Sabʿ al-Mathānī* (The Essential Meaning of the Exegesis of the Great Qur'an), http://www.aljamea.net/services/viewing/Preview_Books.php, December 1, 2003.

50 Muḥammad al-Shawkānī, *Fatḥ al-Qadīr* (Mighty Opening? The Gift [Opening] of the All-powerful), http://www.aljamea.net/services/viewing/Preview_Books.php, December 1, 2003.

51 Asma Afsaruddin, "Sunni-Shiʿi Dialectics and the Qur'an," in *Coming to Terms with the Qur'an*, ed. Khalil Muhammad and Andrew Rippin (North Haledon, NJ: Islamic Publications International, 2008), pp.107-124.

52 Seyyid Qutb, *Fī Ẓilāl al-Qur'ān (In the Shade of the Qur'an)* (Beirut: Dār al-Shurūq, 1979).

53 *Al-jamea.net*, December 11, 2008.

54 See Qur'an (35:18).

6

The Qur'an and Science

IMAD-AD-DEAN AHMAD

IN his work *The Structure of Scientific Revolutions*,[1] Thomas Kuhn discusses the obstacles to the acceptance of revolutionary new scientific ideas that suggest a paradigm shift. Such changes in our entire framework of thinking are not restricted to the hard sciences, but affect every aspect of knowledge and learning. This is especially true when we get so accustomed to old ways of doing things that they actually narrow our perspective.

A famous optical illusion shows a picture of a woman.[2] Observers try to decide if it is a picture of a young woman or an old woman. Different people give different answers. Once one learns to look at the picture in a different way, one's perception of the subject changes. For example, if one perceives an ear just to the left of what appears to be the line of the edge of a headscarf, one may perceive the woman as young. If instead one convinces oneself that this is not an ear, but one of her eyes, one sees an old woman.

The important point is that one cannot see both images at the same time, even once one understands how to see the image. Seeing both simultaneously is impossible. This is what happens with a paradigm shift. We are locked into an old way of perceiving. Unlike with cognition, perceptions are immediate.

Cognition is a gradual process one labors over to understand something. Perception, on the other hand, is instantaneous – we cannot control perception in the way we can control the rational faculty. Yet, when the rational faculty is trapped inside a particular paradigm, we are locked into a narrow range of possible understanding. In other words, to have a new way of understanding Islam and glean new insight from the Qur'an, we must prepare to undergo a paradigm shift.

ANALYZING THE QUR'AN AND SCIENCE

Three general approaches can help us when speaking about the Qur'an and science. In any approach we must adhere to the *tawḥīdī* premise, which requires a rejection of the distinction between the sacred and the secular. In other words, for the Muslim, for the one who believes in *tawḥīd*, there can be no contradiction between the revelations of Allah in the text, the Qur'an, and in the revelation of Allah in the phenomenological world. Nature is as much the book of Allah as is the Qur'an. Therefore, any perceived discrepancy is a reflection of the shortcoming of our understanding.

We can categorize and evaluate the variety of approaches to the question of the relationship of the Qur'an to science. The first is metaphoric, the second literalist, and the third procedural. What does the Qur'an teach us about science? We know without doubt the Qur'an contains many allusions to natural phenomena. Some will say these are metaphors that project some deep-seated spiritual truth. Others will say they are literal and bring some knowledge of the phenomenological world. Without completely discrediting the first two approaches, they have their limitations and can be dangerous. The most important element the Qur'an has to offer is its procedural guidance. One of the most important impacts of Islam on science was its contribution to the development of the methodology of modern science, as we know it today.[3] Understanding why the field of science today differs from the ancient Greek methods is very important for Muslims to grasp. Even those unfamiliar with science itself should understand why modern science developed under Islam.[4]

A central component of science is its procedural structure, which contradicts the fundamentalist Christian view of the relationship of science and religion, where science is treated as a belief system. They will say, "We Christians believe this and we scientists believe that," but what makes science is not the content of their conclusions but how they got to those conclusions. There is a procedure to be followed and the Qur'an encourages that procedure. Furthermore, the Qur'an encourages that procedure in the natural sciences and argues for a similar epistemology in our approach to knowledge in general.

The strictly metaphorical approach to the relationship between the Qur'an and science can overshadow the fact that, with the passage of time, the metaphors in the Qur'an have become more meaningful while the metaphors in, for example, the Bible, become harder to understand as time goes on. They do not become false – because the spiritual truth of an allegory is independent of the truth or falsehood of the physical phenomenon from which it is drawn – but rather that as the paradigm from which it is drawn becomes obsolete, the metaphor becomes antiquated. For example, when one says that someone's reputation has spread to the four corners of the earth, the point of this assertion – that he is famous – may be true, but the phrasing is quaint compared to "his reputation has spread around the globe." When the Bible says that Joshua ordered the sun to stand still, we know what it means, but we have a problem with it in a way that people in Joshua's day did not, because they believed the earth stood still all the time and that the sun rotated the earth once a day; therefore he did not order the earth to stop moving, but for the sun to stand still.

In the case of the Qur'an, many allusions that would have been confusing in the Prophet's time have become meaningful in our own time. Maurice Bucaille (in *The Bible, the Qur'an and Science*) has given an impressive example about the digestion of cows, in that Allah makes a pleasing and nutritious drink from "between" the regions of digestion and the blood.[5] One living in the time of Muhammad would likely not understand this reference, and indeed the scholars of the past offered bizarre interpretations of the meaning. Yet Buccaille, a modern physician, states that the membrane of the intestine allows the nutrients to pass from the partially digested matter into the blood stream, where they pass to the mammary glands and are made into milk. The allusion becomes very easy to understand in light of modern knowledge.

A strictly literal approach, on the other hand, ties the eternal truths of the Qur'an to the changing models of science. Scientific theories constantly change and evolve. Science provides intellectual models for understanding the natural world, and those models are never absolute truth. They are always our best understanding at the moment, and they keep changing. One who takes a verse in the Qur'an and says it presents scientific theory puts oneself in a very dangerous position because when that theory is proven wrong and a new theory comes along, those who tied it to religious doctrine will accuse those who reject the theory (in favor of the new one) of *kufr*. We have seen this in the Christian world. At the time that Christians embraced the Bible they ignored the four corners of the earth statement because they knew the earth to be round. Their own Greek science had taught the earth was round, and they had no problem in accepting the phrase "four corners of the earth" as an antiquated metaphor.

Today, virtually all Christians understand that Joshua in the Bible (Joshua 10: 12-13) could not have ordered the sun to stand still to extend daylight because the cycle of night and day is due to the turning of the earth, but at the time the Bible was adopted by the Christians, Greek science had viewed the sun as moving around the earth. Thus, later when Galileo explained why this was literally untrue, he was accused of heresy. That is a dangerous way to proceed.

The Qur'an is not a scientific textbook. It does not instruct us how Allah created the universe. It instructs us that *He* designed it, and He *urges us to investigate its construction.* Therefore, the Qur'an is pro-science. While not explaining exactly how the world was made, it encourages us to examine God's signs in the heavens and the earth. Particular paradigmatic shifts in the sciences shall demonstrate these points, and we ask how these approaches affect the perception of the relationship of religion and science.

The role Islam played in the development of modern sciences has been explored in great depth elsewhere.[6] There are seven attributes of Islamic civilization that encouraged the development of modern science. Of these seven, six are at least partly from the Qur'an. The seventh relates to the development of hadith science and will be mentioned in passing.[7]

ISLAM AND MODERN SCIENCE

We should first understand the development of modern science and how it differs from Greek science. Westerners often assert that Muslims preserved Greek science. This is a half-truth. Instead, Muslims *transformed* it. Modern science and Islamic science in its later phases differ greatly from Greek science. The Greeks were rationalists. They believed that one could know scientific truths by reason alone. Aristotle said that a scientist is one who grasps that everything is the way it is because it could be no other way. The problem that some Muslim scholars have with scientists getting involved in religion is that they, certain Muslims, confuse modern scientific methods with the Greek method of learning – in which natural law is seen as a narrow, absolutist view of the world.[8] This at the very best makes Allah a slave to nature and at worst removes Him from the picture entirely. If everything is the way it is because it could be no other way, then what is the function of a creator? Indeed, many Greeks believed that things had always been as they are, but the Muslim view was different. The Muslim view is not that everything is the way it is because it could be no other way, but that everything is the way that it is because *Allah willed it to be that way*.

What then are the implications of this assumption? One of the main implications is that *reason is not a sufficient source of knowledge*. There are no self-evident first principles from which you can derive a complete knowledge of reality. Consider, as al-Ghazālī did,[9] the shape of the universe. The philosophers who followed Greek teaching first believed the universe was shaped like an onion. The Earth was at the center of the universe (which they called "the World," the moon in a sphere around it and the other planets in other spheres around it and so on, to the sphere of the fixed stars and divine realm beyond. Al-Ghazālī's critique was significant because he said it might be true, and if so, because Allah willed it that way, not because he had no other choice. There is an infinite number of ways Allah could have constructed the universe, and it was his choice to construct it this way. That is the heart of Islamic critique of what you might think is the natural law theory, and does not deny the existence of natural laws, for such laws are easily demonstrable. Rather, it is a criticism of the monistic epistemology that says reason is a sufficient source of knowledge.

If reason is not a sufficient source of knowledge, what else is needed? Besides reason, which has a role in science under the rubric of "theory," there is also experimentation and observation – precisely what the Qur'an addresses when it commands us to look for Allah's signs in the heavens and on earth. However, beyond these two sources of knowledge, there is a third, which is authority. Authority as a source of knowledge may surprise those used to thinking science and authority are incompatible, but any scientist obtains most of his knowledge not from his own experiments or his own theories but from reading the professional literature. The literature is the authority and is known to be trustworthy because it has been peer-reviewed and because scientists are free to question and challenge it at any time. These three sources of knowledge – reason, experience, and transmission from reliable sources – are in fact the sources of all forms of knowledge.

Waḥī – transmission from particularly reliable sources – is also important. If Allah, the angels, and the prophets are not reliable, then who is? Even these sources are subject to the same sort of questioning. We are all born to different religions. We cannot simply believe whatever has been handed to us as a holy book or the teaching of a professed prophet or priest, or whatever our mothers tell us is true beyond question. These three sources of knowledge have to check one another. When our reason, our experience, and the reliable sources all agree, then we can say that we have knowledge with as much certainty as human beings are capable. Only Allah knows anything with absolute certainty. To the limits of human certainty, we can say that this is our key to knowledge; this is what we know.

Specific elements drove this development from the ancient Greek rationalistic method to the modern method of science just described. The first is *iqra'*, the respect for knowledge. The Qur'an has commanded us to read, meaning to acquire knowledge from exogenous sources. There may be other creatures that are intelligent. Jacques Cousteau once claimed in a radio interview that the killer whale is more intelligent than human beings, yet the whale cannot go to the library or look things up on the Internet. Therefore, the whale's knowledge is forever limited to what it carries in its brain, whereas our knowledge is always open. One does not need to memorize the Hadith to be able to read them and the evaluations of their chains of transmission and soundness of their texts.

A second element is induction. This process is the heart of the scientific method, requiring the rigorous testing of theory by experiment and empirical observation. The role of observation is clearly encouraged in the Qur'an, which says to look for God's signs in the heavens and on earth.

A third element is universality. The Qur'an teaches, and we believe, that all truths come from Allah. Therefore, because Allah sent messengers to every people, all people have access to the truth, and we are not limited to the knowledge of our own history. When the Muslims encountered Greek knowledge, they did not call the Greeks pagans and ignore their books. They translated them all, not for uncritical acceptance, but for critical consideration, to decide what was true and what was false. When we accept the truth and reject what is false, we are better off for having gone through the process.

A fourth very important element is the abolition of the priesthood. Many past scientific civilizations preceded the Islamic one. The ancient Babylonians, for example, possessed fine astronomical sciences, but only among their elites. The idea that the masses should be trusted with this kind of knowledge was unknown. In Islam, the teaching of the prophet is that every Muslim, male or female, has a duty to seek knowledge from the cradle to the grave.[10] Therefore, knowledge is not to be the province of the elites. Indeed, we find that Muslim scholars who made advances in arithmetic, for example, did not just write papers for other scholars, but wrote books on arithmetic for secretaries and scribes,[11] so that people who were providing clerical services to others would be able to do their arithmetic properly.

Furthermore, Islam does not despise material success or advocate asceticism. A materially successful society is one that will conduct research in the hard sciences. For the poor, their main concern is subsistence, and developing low-level technology that will prevent one from starving to death. A materially successful society has people who will dedicate their wealth to setting up *awqāf* to provide not only hospitals, but also to institutions of learning and scientific research. The Muslim society in its heyday had unprecedented wealth that gave birth to the modern university and college.

In an academically free environment, science inevitably moves forward. Conversely, academic freedom is necessary for scientific progress. For Muslims, academic freedom is the corollary of our individual responsibility and duty to Allah. Every Muslim is directly responsible to Allah. Therefore, no one has the right to censor the academic work of another person. When confronted by falsehood one should not censor it, but expose its fallacy: "Nay, We hurl the Truth against falsehood, and it knocks out its brain, and behold, falsehood doth perish!"[12] This approach is a core aspect of the scientific method.

The kind of interference that the Christian church saw with scientific affairs as exemplified by the Galileo episode was the exception, not the rule, in Islam, despite comparisons of Islam to medieval Christian civilization. One excellent scholar contradicted himself when he tried to represent the burning of Ibn Rushd's books as an example of intolerance of science by the orthodoxy of twelfth-century Spain, yet acknowledged that "some strictly scientific ones" were exempt.[13] He missed that Ibn Rushd was persecuted for his philosophical views, not for his scientific views. Abū Yūsuf (the Almohad caliph) should not have burned any of Ibn Rushd's books, but to accuse Islam, or even Muslims, of having a problem with science is erroneous because to the degree that Ibn Rushd's work was purely scientific, it was not censored.

One element behind Islamic science does not derive directly from the Qur'an, and this is the issue of proper citation. Islam played a major role in the development of citation in hadith science. While authority plays a role in science, in modern science authority may be questioned. Therefore, when citing authority, it should be identified clearly and accurately. A scientific paper that cites Einstein as an authority must state where and when he said what was attributed to him, including the name of the book or journal in which he published it, the page number, and so on. If the transmission was claimed to be personal rather than public, the author would need to indicate how the information was obtained – directly, indirectly, and from where/whom. Anyone familiar with hadith science recognizes the *isnād* that is involved in that kind of personal communication. Therefore, hadith science set forth a model that was followed by the other sciences. This kind of care in citation was not part of Greek scholarship, so we should credit Islamic civilization for the contribution of this important part of the scientific method.

The second point involves the limitations of the literalist perspective. Some people try to use the Qur'an as a scientific text, resulting in Muslim pseudo-science. One writer has gone so far as to claim that the miraculous nature of the Qur'an is evident by the fact it has the speed of light to four decimal places.[14, 15] The Qur'an makes allusions, and no doubt the Author of the Qur'an knows more science than anybody ever has. There is also no doubt that He is trying to teach science there. However, one cannot acquire specific scientific knowledge by studying the Qur'an. Instead, one studies nature, acquires scientific knowledge, and looks at the Qur'an and says, "This book is consistent with what I have learned."

The third point is the most complex – the emerging post-modernist paradigm. The West underwent a couple of hundred years of materialism as the dominant philosophy. Although not accepted everywhere, it challenged everything that people believed and was constantly in contention. Its rise was ironic, because the scientists who developed the scientific paradigm behind materialist philosophy were by-and-large believers. Isaac Newton was the most important of them and in the *General Scholium* appended to Newton's magnum opus, the *Principia Mathematica*, he testifies to his belief in God in a way that is reminiscent of the Muslim belief.[16] We know from Newton's religious writings that he rejected the trinity. We also know he believed in God not just as the spirit of the world or just as a Creator of the world who went away (an absent clockmaker as some have described it). Newton believed God is the Creator *and* Sustainer of the world *and* the Lord of the world, whom men worship as Lord, making him a theist, not a deist.[17]

Others looked at Newton's theories and concluded that Newton, Galileo, and others developed a system for understanding the motion of the planets, the mechanics of the universe, and of all physics in a way that did not require God's active intervention. Therefore, they argued, either God created the world and He went away, or maybe the world was always like this and we do not need to assume God's existence at all.

This was the dominant paradigm for centuries until three major discoveries of the twentieth century undermined that paradigm. Taken together, relativity theory, chaos theory, and quantum mechanics destroyed the view of the universe as a three-dimensional billiard table. The next section will analyze the legitimate and illegitimate associations between internal religion and new emerging science.

INTERNAL RELIGION AND EMERGING SCIENCE

Emerging ideas that are somewhat established in the scientific world may not yet have totally seeped into the consciousness of the masses. Just as the idea that the earth circles the sun was quickly established for scientists, common people did not adopt the idea for a couple of hundred more years. Those who may laugh today to think that people believed the sun went around the earth should ask, is it self-evident that the earth goes around the sun? We were raised with that belief so it seems self-evident, but it is not based on our personal experience. Rather, we have learned this from quantum mechanics and relativity.

The Qur'an mentions the *ghayb* and the *shahādah* – the hidden and the manifest – or the unseen and the seen. Problematically, Newton's classical mechanics seemed to make the entire universe a billiard table, with little billiard balls bouncing around. One knowing their positions, motions, and the laws of physics that govern them could predict what they would do next. In this scenario, everything seems determined. If we are made up of matter, as we seem to be, then should not our actions also be determined? It seems as though everything has been determined. Even if these rules were determined by Allah when He set up the universe, they allow no room for further divine intervention, which implies there can be no miracles. The billiard balls can only go a certain way. Allah, even if He wrote the rule on Himself, would seem to have written a rule that prevents miracles.

Furthermore, and very important for religious belief, where is the room for free will? How can one be held responsible for his actions when they have been pre-determined at the time of Creation? Whether one commits adultery, murder, or any kind of sin, is it just the result of many material particles moving in a certain way? Where is the justice in holding me responsible for the choices that seem to be impossible? In other words, where is the room for human will and for God's will? They seem to be absent in this mechanical universe.

The answer to this question of course is that physics and mechanics are not the only components of reality, but in this paradigm, people could not see where the room was for a non-physical action. Physics appeared to occupy all the room for all possible explanations for everything. However, with the discovery of quantum mechanics and chaos theory, everything changed. One item of chaos theory, the Butterfly Effect, is particularly illustrative.[18]

The Butterfly Effect points to the fact that physical systems are extremely sensitive to small changes in the initial conditions. Even if it were true – which it is not – that a given system's future is entirely determined by its present positions and motions, the tiniest conceivable change in that present motion totally changes the future and makes it utterly unrecognizable, no matter how tiny that change is. In other words, a butterfly's decision whether or not to flap its wings somewhere in Kansas right now could change the course of a storm in China six months from now. Miniscule changes like that can have such profound effects.

When combined with quantum mechanics, this hypersensitivity of physical systems to small changes relates to the discussion of religious issues such as human free will and divine intervention. Quantum mechanics seems to undermine the premise that everything is determined from its initial state. On the quantum level of the tiniest subatomic partials, things are not determined. It is helpful to picture an illustrative experiment. First, imagine that we have set up a machine gun randomly firing bullets in the general direction of a wall with two holes in it and behind that wall is another wall. Obviously, the bullets tend to collect directly behind the holes in the near wall.

Now, imagine that you are watching a sea and there are some breakers, or barriers. The outer barrier has two holes in it, and as the waves come in the barrier stops them except for the two holes, and the passing waves, as they come out of those two holes on the other side, interfere with one another. You will see the waves form an "interference pattern," so that as the waves crash against the inner, you would see that the highest waves are not the ones directly behind the two holes but in the middle between them, where the waves constructively interfere with one another. Then, they get smaller and smaller as they go out. If there had only been one hole, then the wave would have been highest after that hole and the other one would be highest after the other one.

Now, what happens when you shine a light in the two holes? You do the same experiment using a thin barrier with two slits in it and a piece of film like the wall on the other side, and you record the light coming through both holes. If both holes are open, the light pattern on the film will be like the wave pattern on the wall, an interference pattern with many peaks and troughs, as if the light is made of waves interacting with one another. However, we understand light comes in the form of little particles called photons. If you close one of the slits, of course the light is brightest behind the slit.

What happens if you take a piece of film and close one slit at one time and the other slit at the other time and let the light accumulate? What if you leave both slits open but shine one photon at a time over a long period of time so the total number of photons is very large? You do it one time, randomly closing one or another of the slits and another time with both slits open. In the first instance, you see the light collected behind the slits but in the second case you see an interference pattern. How does the light going through a slit "know" if the other side is open or closed? Why is it going to have one pattern if they are both open and a different pattern if one of them is closed? This is especially troubling in the light of relativity theory that says that you cannot have instant communication between distant things. How is this information transmitted? This is a serious question and the dominant interpretation of quantum mechanics that derives from this is that you cannot know both the position and the momentum of a particle at the same time. If you do the same experiment with electrons instead of photons, which you would normally think of as particles rather than waves, you get the same result.

In other words, everything in the universe seems to interact with everything else, but how? Quantum mechanics has said that the wave involved here is a wave of probability of the particle's position and momentum, and that the position of a particle or the momentum of a particle do not actually exist until they are observed. There is only a probability that the particles are in a particular place or a probability the particle is at a particular momentum. The only way you can ever hope to know the position or momentum of a particle is to observe or measure it and when you observe it you affect the thing observed i.e. you change it. Therefore, if you ask the question, what is it if I do not observe it? Is the moon there when nobody is looking? We do not know. This is very shocking and hard to believe, and it raises all kinds of questions.

Einstein believed that even if the position or momentum of a particle does not precisely exist at a particular moment, there must be some hidden variable that will determine what it will be at a future moment, and that some day our physics will advance enough to determine what those variables are. Well, some experiments have proven conclusively that Einstein was at least partially wrong. There may be hidden variables but they are not what Einstein would call "local variables." They are not local to the particle. They may be global variables or transcendent variables, but they are beyond the locality of the time and space, which has caused a crisis in the materialistic paradigm.

One scientist, a physicist named David Bohm, tried to resolve this problem.[19] Bohm's very interesting approach boils down to this: Let us accept what is called "the Copenhagen interpretation" of quantum mechanics, that observables do not exist until we observe them. If this is true, we have to assume that reality is divided into two parts, which he calls the explicate and the implicate. The explicate is that which we can observe. The explicate is determined by the implicate, which consists of that which we cannot observe, a whole realm of reality that is forever cut off from our senses. We cannot know it in any way; we only see its effects on the phenomenological world. He calls it explicate and the implicate; we can call it the *shahādah* and *ghayb*.

Notice that this means a couple of things. First, not everything is physics. The *shahādah* is the consequence of the *ghayb*. The *ghayb* may not be physical. Of course, a materialist might say that of course it is material; only physics is hidden from you. Consider the following. A friend walks into the room and another reaches out to embrace him. If it were not a friend, the reaction would be different. What determines whether a person stretches out his arms or not? In the classical mechanical school, many brain atoms that move in certain patterns determine the reaction. Introspectively, one's will drives the decision. The person is happy to see a friend and wants to make a gesture towards him. Where, in physics, is the room for this will? In the emerging paradigm, whether a synapse in one's head fires or not is at the quantum level and therefore is not determined by physics but by will. One can choose whether the synapse fires or not.

In chaos theory, a quantum difference such as whether a synapse fires or not can lead to different chains of events in the macroscopic world, such as whether to embrace someone or to turn away from him. These are questions of human will. There are implications for the divine will when we speak about the entire universe. If a butterfly flapping its wings determines whether a storm goes one way or another in China, this results from Allah's will rather than from a decision made by butterflies. Therefore, how one can believe in the laws of physics and pray for divine intervention at the same time is not problematic. If Allah wants to answer your prayers, He can answer your prayers without contradicting the physical laws He has decreed, because quantum mechanics only tells you how things are going to probably behave in the collective. It says certain things are improbable to a certain degree.

Something only has a fifty-fifty chance of happening; something else has maybe a one in a quintillion chance of happening or one in a googol chance. The odds that all the air in this room will rise to the top half and we will suffocate to death is not zero, but it is so infinitesimally small that we can ignore it, unless Allah wills it to happen, in which case, we cannot ignore it. Therefore, miraculous things like all the air in the room going to one side is not a violation of the laws of physics, but is just something very unusual. Alternatively, as the classical era Muslim scientist might have said, it is not the sunnah of Allah. Allah has a sunnah; He has a usual way of doing things. Quantum mechanics tells you how Allah usually does things, but then in any given instance,

Allah might do something else and it is not a violation of the laws of physics. It is very consistent with the laws of physics.

CONCLUSION

Revelatory and scientific epistemes are not mutually exclusive of alternatives but are instead complementary. The former, the revelatory episteme, gives us access to the hidden or implicate order. In other words, we cannot know it directly by our senses, but Allah can choose to reveal it to us by the methods of revelation that Mahmoud Ayoub has discussed at some length.[20] Such revelations may even come in dreams, since the firing of a synapse in sleep is an obvious interface point between the explicate and implicate. Perhaps we need to be cautious about revelations in dreams, but there may be an infinite variety of means by which Allah may give us knowledge of the hidden so while we do not see the angels helping us as we fight our battles, Allah can tell us that they are there.

The latter approach, the scientific episteme, provides us with an understanding of the manifest of the *shahādah* that Allah does reveal to us through the cognitive process. In the *tawḥīdī* worldview, both are sacred. Rather than view the religious as sacred and the scientific as profane, the work of understanding the manifest, the explicate, the *shahādah*, is as sacred as the work of understanding the word and meaning of the holy text. The book of nature is also a holy text, and understanding it is also an act of worship.

REFERENCES

Ahmad, Imad-ad-Dean, *Signs in the Heavens: A Muslim Astronomer's Perspective on Religion and Science*, 2nd ed. (Beltsville: Amana, 2006).

Al-Bayhaqī, *Shuʿab al-Īmān* and *al-Madkhal*, Ibn ʿAbd al-Barr, *Jāmiʿ Bayān al-ʿIlm*, and al-Khaṭīb, *al-Riḥlah fī Ṭalab al-Ḥadīth*.

Al-Būzjānī, Abu al-Wafā', *Book of the Stations on What Scribes and Secretaries Need of the Science of Calculation*.

Ayoub, Mahmoud, "Qur'an As Revelation," IIIT Summer Institute Proceedings, forthcoming.

Bohm, David, *Wholeness and the Implicate Order* (London: Routledge, 1981).

El-Darymli, Khalid, "Values, Technology and Society: Islam and Science," 2005, http://www.slideshare.net/kkkseld/microsoft-word-the-project-islam-and-science/, citing Sadar, M. Husain, "Science and Islam: Is There a Conflict?" in Sardar, Z., *The Touch of Midas: Islam, Values, and Environment in Islam and the West*. (Manchester: Manchester University Press, 1984).

Encyclopedia Iranica, 2008, http://www.iranica.com/newsite/index. isc?Article=http://www.iranica.com/newsite/articles/unicode/v1f4/v1f4a083.html.

Al-Ghazālī, The Incoherence of the Philosophers, Michael E. Marmura, trans. (Provo, UT: Brigham Young University, 2000).

Gleick, James, *Chaos: Making a New Science* (New York: Viking Penguin, 1987).

Hassab-Elnaby, Mansour, "A New Astronomical Qur'anic Method for the Determination of the Greatest Speed C," http://www.islamicity.com/Science/960703A. SHTML.

Hassab-Elnaby, Mansour, "Review of A New Astronomical Quranic Method for The Determination of the Greatest Speed C," http://www.mat.univie.ac.at/~neum/sciandf/eng/c_in_quran.txt.

Hoodbhoy, Pervez, *Islam and Science: Religious Orthodoxy and the Battle for Rationality* (London: Zed, 1991).

Kuhn, Thomas, *The Structure of Scientific Revolutions*, 3rd ed. (Chicago: University of Chicago Press, 1996).

Punch, 1915, at http://mathworld.wolfram.com/YoungGirl-OldWomanIllusion.html.

NOTES

1 Thomas Kuhn, *The Structure of Scientific Revolutions*, 3rd ed. (Chicago: Univ. of Chicago Press, 1996).

2 This version was originally published in 1915 in *Puck* humor magazine, an American magazine inspired by the British magazine *Punch*. http://mathworld.wolfram.com/YoungGirl-OldWomanIllusion.html.

3 Imad-ad-Dean Ahmad, *Signs in the Heavens: A Muslim Astronomer's Perspective on Religion and Science*, 2nd ed. (Beltsville: Amana, 2006).

4 For a detailed analysis of Islam's contributions to the development of the modern scientific methodology see *Signs in the Heavens* op cit.

5 "And verily in cattle (too) will ye find an instructive Sign. From what is within their bodies, between partially digested matter and blood We produce for your drink milk pure and agreeable to those who drink it" (16:66).

6 See, e.g., Ahmad, *Signs in the Heavens*.

7 I want to emphasize the conclusion from my book, *Signs in the Heavens*.

8 For a more detailed discussion of natural law, see Imad-ad-Dean Ahmad, "On Natural Law and Shariah," a paper delivered August 3, 2009 to the IIIT Summer Institute 2009 on "Contemporary Approaches to Qur'an and Sunna," forthcoming.

9 *Al-Ghazālī, The Incoherence of the Philosophers*, Michael E. Marmura, trans. (Provo, UT: Brigham Young University, 2000), pp.8–9.

10 Narrated from Anas by al-Bayhaqī in *Shuʿab al-Īmān* and *al-Madkhal*, Ibn ʿAbd al-Barr in *Jāmiʿ Bayān al-ʿIlm*, and al-Khaṭīb through three chains at the opening of his *al-Riḥlah fī Ṭalab al-Ḥadīth* (pp.71–76, nos.1–3) "Seek knowledge from the cradle to the grave." "Seeking knowledge is a duty upon every Muslim (male and female)." Quoted by Khalid El-Darymli, "Values, Technology and Society: Islam and Science," 2005, http://www.slideshare.net/kkkseld/microsoft-word-the-project-islam-and-science/, citing M. Husain Sadar, "Science and Islam: Is There a Conflict?" in Z. Sardar, *The Touch of Midas: Islam, Values, and Environment in Islam and the West* (Manchester: Manchester Univ. Press, 1984), p.15.

11 Abū al-Wafā' al-Būzjānī, *Book on the Stations on What Scribes and Secretaries Need in the Science of Calculation*. See "Abu'l-Wafā' al-Būzjānī Mohammad b. Mohammad al-Būzjānī" in *Encyclopedia Iranica*, 2008, http://www.iranica.com/newsite/index.isc?Article= http://www.iranica.com/newsite/articles/unicode/v1f4/v1f4a083.html.

12 Qur'an (21:18).

13 Pervez Hoodbhoy, *Islam and Science: Religious Orthodoxy and the Battle for Rationality* (London: Zed, 1991), pp 114–115.

14 Mansour Hassab-Elnaby, "A New Astronomical Qur'anic Method for the Determination of the Greatest Speed C," http://www.islamicity.com/Science/960703A.SHTML. For a refutation of this argument attributed to Prof. Arnold Neumaier see Dr. Mansour Hassab-Elnaby, "Review of A New Astronomical Quranic Method for The Determination Of The Greatest Speed C," http://www.mat.univie.ac.at/~neum/sciandf/eng/c_in_quran.txt.

15 Ahmad, *Signs*, ch.8.

16 See Ibid, p.122.

17 Ibid.

18 For a lucid and accessible summary of chaos theory see James Gleick, *Chaos: Making a New Science* (New York: Viking Penguin, 1987).

19 See David Bohm, *Wholeness and the Implicate Order* (London: Routledge, 1981).

20 Mahmoud Ayoub, "Qur'an As Revelation," IIIT Summer Institute Proceedings, forthcoming.

7

Translation of Qur'anic Verses with Injunctions: A Theme-based Comparative Review

DAOUD NASSIMI

INTRODUCTION

WHILE the translation of the Qur'an is a challenging task as a whole, the translation of the verses of injunctions in the Qur'an is more challenging. It requires translators to understand and consider many other factors in addition to the knowledge and command of both languages. Since the Qur'an (in its original language) is the perfect word of God, for Muslims, the translation of the Qur'an to any other language is always limited to the understanding of the meanings that the human translators have derived from the Qur'an. Further, the text of the Qur'an has some very unique characteristics that its translation to another language is bound to lose. Therefore, it has been agreed by Islamic scholars and Qur'an translators that any translation of the Qur'an is actually the translation of the meaning of the Qur'an, and not anything like an equivalent to the Qur'an. However, since translation is the only way to help non-Arabic speaking populations to understand the message of the Qur'an and benefit from it, the availability of any faithful translation would be the next best thing and a valuable resource.

In this paper, the translation and commentary of some verses of injunctions are selected from four well known English translations of the Qur'an for a review and comparison. The following four translations have been selected:

1. Abdullah Yusuf Ali, *The Meaning of the Holy Qur'an*, new edition with revised translation, commentary and newly compiled comprehensive index, 10th edition (Beltsville: Amana Publications, first published in 1934, reprinted in 2003).

2. Muhammad Asad, *The Message of The Qur'an*. Translated and explained (Gibraltar: Dār al-Andalus, 1980).

3. Muhammad Taqiyyu al-Din al-Hilali and Muhammad Muhsin Khan, *Interpretation of the Meanings of The Noble Qur'an in the English Language*, 17th revised edition (Riyadh: Darussalam, 1997).

4. Sayyid Abul Aʿlā Mawdūdī, *Towards Understanding The Qur'ān: Abridged Version of Tafhīm al-Qur'ān*. Translated and edited by Zafar Ishaq Ansari (Leicester, UK: The Islamic Foundation, 2006).

In all of these four translations, the translation and commentary of two passages of the Qur'an with injunctions are selected to be studied, compared, and analyzed as samples for this paper. They are analyzed from some or all of the following points of view:

- Clarity of the meaning
- Consideration of the context of the verse, subject, section, and surah
- Consideration of jurisprudence knowledge (fiqh)
- Consideration of the historical background and issues of this age

The passages selected for review in this paper include the injunction of Friday prayers as an act of worship and the injunction of the dress code of women.

To shorten the wording of the frequent references to each translator's name, their names are abbreviated by their initials. The following abbreviation terminology will be used to refer to the four translators:

Yusuf Ali:	YA
Muhammad Asad:	MA

Taqiyyu al-Din Hilali and Muhsin Khan:	H&K
Zafar Ishaq Ansari/Mawdudi:	A/M

SIGNIFICANCE OF INJUNCTIONS (*AḤKĀM*) IN THE QUR'AN

The subject of *aḥkām* is one of the key themes of the Qur'an. *Aḥkām* is plural of *ḥukm*, which can mean a ruling, injunction, command, decree, ordinance, or judgment.[1] The meaning of "injunction" is used in this paper.

The injunctions (*aḥkām*) of the Qur'an are of primary importance in the life of Muslims. They form the primary source of the Shariʿah. The verses that have legal connotations in the Qur'an form the code of conduct for every Muslim from birth to death. They provide the touchstone to distinguish the lawful (*ḥalāl*) from the unlawful (*ḥarām*) and the right from wrong in every sphere of life. This is why the Qur'an is also called "the criterion" (*al-Furqān*). The commands of the Qur'an, unlike any other man-made laws, are not amendable. Therefore, they have remained the same for the last 1,400 years.

There are approximately six hundred or more verses regarding injunctions in the Qur'an. According to one count, about four hundred of these pertain to the acts of worship (*ʿibādāt*) and the remaining is divided as follows: about 70 verses pertain to family law, 80 verses to trade and finance, 13 to oaths, 30 to crimes and sentencing, 10 to constitutional and administrative matters, and 25 to international law.[2]

These counts show the number of verses that deal directly with the laws. There are many other verses in other subjects of the Qur'an; e.g., the stories from which rules have also been derived. The verses related to the acts of worship include purification, ablution (*wuḍū'*), body washing (*ghusl*), symbolic ablution (*tayamum*), prayers (salah), almsgiving (zakah), fasting, pilgrimage (major and minor), oaths and vows, remembrance of Allah (*dhikr*), and invocations (*duʿā'*). The verses related to trade and finance include various types of contracts, donations, loans, authorizations, restrictions, documentation, and guarantees. Family laws include laws related to marriage, divorce, children, and inheritance. Laws related to crimes include murder, adultery, slander, theft, armed robbery, penalties, apostasy, rising against Islamic leadership, etc.

SOME UNIQUE FEATURES OF VERSES OF INJUNCTIONS

The verses related to the injunctions (*aḥkām*) have some unique features that make their translation challenging. The language of the verses of injunctions in the Qur'an often has a unique style. The verses related to many of the commands are very brief and they do not provide much of the rationale for them. This is because a major portion of the Qur'an is dedicated for the areas of beliefs and all kinds of reasoning, evidence, and rationale are provided to convince human beings of the truth of Islamic beliefs. As such, human beings are expected to develop their beliefs based on a rational, voluntary, and independent approach. Once this is achieved, they are asked to submit to God, and then follow His injunctions based on this submission as its rationale even if there is no other explanation provided.

Many of the injunctions of the Qur'an start with a direct address to the believers, such as, "O believers." This could imply that the commands of the Qur'an can be fully understood and appreciated only by the believers of the Qur'an. A true believer is expected to be willing to apply the commands as soon as they hear or learn about them even if they cannot fully comprehend the expected benefits of the commands. This attitude is mentioned in the Qur'an many times. For example:

> The statement (reaction) of the believers, when summoned to Allah and His Messenger, in order that He may judge between (*liyaḥkum* or order) them, is no other than they say, "We hear and we obey": it is such as these that will attain felicity. It is such as obey Allah and His Messenger, and fear Allah and do right, that will win (in the end). (24:51-52)

> It is not fitting for a believer, man or woman, when a matter has been decided by Allah and His Messenger to have any option about their decision: if any one disobeys Allah and His Messenger, he is indeed on a clearly wrong path. (33:36)

The translators of the Qur'an require some additional knowledge to translate the verses of injunctions and comment on them more appropriately. The main areas of this additional knowledge follow.

KNOWLEDGE OF THE TRADITIONS (SUNNAH) OF THE PROPHET MUHAMMAD

The traditions (Sunnah) of the Prophet play an important role in understanding the injunctions of the Qur'an. While the Qur'an is the primary source of law in Islam, the Sunnah is considered as the second source of Islamic law and the explanation of the Qur'an. The Sunnah usually provides necessary and additional information, details, and explanations about the meaning or applications of the teachings of the Qur'an. The Sunnah could affect the application of certain injunctions of the Qur'an in different ways, for example, it could make a rule of the Qur'an that is general, specific, or vice versa. Similarly, hadith could provide many other instructions to help in the implementation of the Qur'an in daily life. These are all based on the facts stated by the Qur'an in many places that the job of the Prophet was, for example, in (3:164) and (62:2), to teach the Qur'an, and in (16:44) to explain the Qur'an to people.

KNOWLEDGE OF JURISPRUDENCE (FIQH)

The *aḥkām* of the Qur'an have been addressed by Muslim scholars under the science of Islamic jurisprudence (fiqh) in a very extensive and comprehensive manner throughout Islamic history. This effort along with the interpretation of the related hadith, have led to the development and establishment of different schools of fiqh. The knowledge of the various interpretations for the legal injunctions of the same verse is often needed by the translator. Further, while the language of some verses is in the command form, it is not meant to be an obligatory act, but rather implies a permissive act. For example, in the injunction of the Friday prayer, as it will be further discussed later, while the statement of spreading out and seeking the provisioning right after the prayer has been worded in a command form, it is not meant to be a command, but a permission or option to seek the provisioning right after the prayer. Therefore, such details cannot be understood and reflected on unless the translator has some knowledge of fiqh.

KNOWLEDGE OF ISSUES OF TODAY'S WORLD RELATED TO THE QUR'AN

There are certain subjects in Islamic law that have become the concern of many people, especially in the English-speaking world, such as jihad (striving/struggling), rights of women, and so forth. There are some verses in the Qur'an on these subjects that have often been quoted to claim some issues with the Qur'anic teachings. The translators of the Qur'an need to have a proper knowledge of such issues so they can carefully render the related verses in the light of those issues without making any compromise in the accuracy of the meaning of the verses. Such care can be attained, for example, by providing the necessary context of those verses in the commentary.

With this background in mind, a comparative review of two samples of injunctions verses are presented in the following sections. The two samples selected include the injunction of Friday prayers as an act of worship and the injunction of the dress code of women.

INJUNCTION OF FRIDAY PRAYERS

In this section, the translations and commentary of the verses of the Qur'an related to the injunction of the Friday prayers will be reviewed. This subject is covered in verses (9-11) of *Sūrah al-Jumuʿah* (surah no. 62) which means "Friday" and is named after this day.

The Friday prayer is one of the most important acts of worship in Islam. It is also one of the most important gatherings for Muslims. Especially in the countries where Muslims live as a minority, the Friday prayer is one of the few opportunities for them to be together and be reminded of their religion.[3] Every week, in tens of thousands of mosques throughout the world, millions of Muslims from all walks of life sit patiently, listen to the Friday sermon (*khuṭbah*), and observe the obligatory prayers in obedience to Allah's direct command in verse (62:9) of the Qur'an. The weekly Friday prayer and *khuṭbah* are powerful institutions established to build communities. They provide an opportunity for spiritual nourishment, learning, and group bonding.[4]

The Friday prayers and *khuṭbah* have detailed descriptions in the books of jurisprudence (fiqh).[5] The various aspects of this subject have been explained according to the teachings of the Prophet and his practice as well as the understandings of the various schools of fiqh.[6]

1.1. The Qur'anic Text

Verses (62:9-11)

يَٰٓأَيُّهَا ٱلَّذِينَ ءَامَنُوٓا۟ إِذَا نُودِىَ لِلصَّلَوٰةِ مِن يَوْمِ ٱلْجُمُعَةِ فَٱسْعَوْا۟ إِلَىٰ
ذِكْرِ ٱللَّهِ وَذَرُوا۟ ٱلْبَيْعَ ۚ ذَٰلِكُمْ خَيْرٌ لَّكُمْ إِن كُنتُمْ تَعْلَمُونَ ﴿٩﴾ فَإِذَا
قُضِيَتِ ٱلصَّلَوٰةُ فَٱنتَشِرُوا۟ فِى ٱلْأَرْضِ وَٱبْتَغُوا۟ مِن فَضْلِ ٱللَّهِ وَٱذْكُرُوا۟
ٱللَّهَ كَثِيرًا لَّعَلَّكُمْ تُفْلِحُونَ ﴿١٠﴾ وَإِذَا رَأَوْا۟ تِجَٰرَةً أَوْ لَهْوًا ٱنفَضُّوٓا۟
إِلَيْهَا وَتَرَكُوكَ قَآئِمًا ۚ قُلْ مَا عِندَ ٱللَّهِ خَيْرٌ مِّنَ ٱللَّهْوِ وَمِنَ ٱلتِّجَٰرَةِ ۚ وَٱللَّهُ
خَيْرُ ٱلرَّٰزِقِينَ ﴿١١﴾

1.2. Text of Translations and Commentary

YA:

(62:9) O ye who believe! When the call is proclaimed to prayer on Friday (*5461) [the Day of Assembly], hasten earnestly to the Remembrance of Allah, and leave off business [and traffic]: (*5462) That is best for you if ye but knew! (*5463)

(62:10) And when the Prayer is finished, then may ye disperse through the land, and seek of the Bounty of Allah. And celebrate the Praises of Allah often [and without stint]: that ye may prosper. (*5464)

(62:11) But when they see some bargain or some amusement, they disperse headlong to it, and leave thee standing. Say: "The [blessing] from the presence of Allah is better than any amusement or bargain! And Allah is the best to provide [for all needs]." (*5465)

***5461:** Friday is primarily the Day of Assembly, the weekly meeting of the congregation, when Muslims show their unity by sharing in common public worship, preceded by a *khuṭbah*, in which the Imam (leader) reviews the week's spiritual life of the community and offers advice and exhortation on holy living.

Notice the gradations of social contact for Muslims if they follow the wise ordinances of their faith. (1) Each individual remembers Allah for himself or herself five or more times everyday in the home or place of business, or local mosque, or open air, as the case may be. (2) On Friday in every week there is a local meeting in the central mosque of each local centre – it may be a village, or town, or ward of a big city. (3) At the two *ʿĪds* every year, there is a large local area meeting in one center. (4) Once at least in a lifetime, where possible, a Muslim shares in the vast international assemblage of the world, in the center of Islam, at the Makkan Pilgrimage, a happy combination of decentralization and centralization, of individual liberty and collective meeting, and contact at various stages or grades. The mechanical part of this ordinance is easy to carry out. Are we carrying out the more difficult part – the spirit of unity, brotherhood, mutual consultation, and collective understanding and action?

***5462:** The idea behind the Muslim weekly "Day of Assembly" is different from that behind the Jewish Sabbath (Saturday) or the Christian Sunday. The Jewish Sabbath is primarily a commemoration of God's ending His work and resting on the seventh day (Genesis 2:2; Exodus 20:11), we are taught that Allah needs no rest, nor does He feel fatigue (2:255). The Jewish command forbids work on that day but says nothing about worship or prayer (Exodus 20:10); our ordinance lays chief stress on the remembrance of Allah. Jewish formalism went so far as to kill the spirit of the Sabbath, and call forth the protest of Jesus: "the Sabbath was made for man, and not man for the Sabbath" (Mark 2:27). But the Christian Church, although it changed the day from Saturday to Sunday, has inherited the Jewish spirit: witness the Scottish Sabbath; except insofar as it has been secularized. Our teaching says: 'When the time for *Jumuʿah* Prayer comes, close your business and answer the summons loyally and earnestly, meet earnestly, pray, consult and learn by social contact: when the meeting is over, scatter and go about your business.'

***5463:** The immediate and temporal worldly gain may be the ultimate and spiritual loss, and *vice versa*.

***5464:** Prosperity is not to be measured by wealth or worldly gains. There is a higher prosperity – the health of the mind and the spirit.

***5465:** Do not be distracted by the craze for amusement or gain. If you lead a righteous and sober life, Allah will provide for you in all senses, better than any provision you can possibly think of.

MA:

(62:9) O YOU who have attained to faith! When the call to prayer is sounded on the day of congregation, (*10) hasten to the remembrance of God, and leave all worldly commerce: this is for your own good, if you but knew it.

(62:10) And when the prayer is ended, disperse freely on earth (*11) and seek to obtain [something] of God's bounty; but remember God often, so that you might attain to a happy state!

(62:11) Yet [it does happen that] when people (*12) become aware of [an occasion for] worldly gain (*13) or a passing delight, they rush headlong towards it, and leave thee standing [and preaching]. (*14) Say: "That which is with God is far better than all passing delight and all gain! And God is the best of providers!"

***10:** i.e., on Friday, when the congregational prayer at noon is obligatory. Nevertheless, as the sequence shows, Friday is not a day of compulsory rest in Islamic law.

***11:** i.e., "you may devote yourselves to worldly pursuits."

***12:** Lit., "they."

***13:** Lit., "trade" or "a bargain."

*14: Se., "O Prophet" – thus alluding to a historical incident, when most of the congregation, on hearing that a long-expected trade caravan had come from Syria, rushed out of the mosque in the midst of the Prophet's Friday sermon. In a wider timeless sense, the above verse contains an allusion to an all-too-human weakness against which even true believers are not always immune: namely, the tendency to overlook religious obligations for the sake of a transitory, worldly advantage.

H&K:

(62:9) O you who believe [Muslims]! When the call is proclaimed for the salah [prayer] on the day of Friday [*Jumuᶜah* prayer], come to the remembrance of Allah [*Jumuᶜah* religious talk (*khuṭbah*) and salah (prayer)] and leave off business [and every other thing], that is better for you if you did but know!

(62:10) Then when the [*Jumuᶜah*] salah [prayer] is finished, you may disperse through the land, and seek the Bounty of Allah [by working, etc.], and remember Allah much, that you may be successful.

(62:11) And when they see some merchandise or some amusement [beating of Tambur (drum), etc.] they disperse headlong to it, and leave you [Muhammad] standing [while delivering *Jumuᶜah's* religious talk (*khuṭbah*)]. Say "That which Allah has is better than any amusement or merchandise! And Allah is the Best of providers."

A/M:

(62:9) Believers, when the call for Prayer is made on Friday, hasten to the remembrance of Allah and give up all trading. (*7) That is better for you, if you only knew.

(62:10) But when the Prayer is ended, disperse in the land and seek Allah's Bounty, (*8) and remember Allah much so that you may prosper. (*9)

(62:11) Yet no sooner than they saw some trading or amusement, they flocked to it and left you standing by yourself. (*10) Tell them: "That which is with Allah is far better than amusement and trading. (*11) Allah is the best provider of sustenance. (*12)

***7:** The word "remembrance" here signifies the Friday sermon. This is because the first thing to which the Prophet paid attention after the *adhān* (call to prayer) was not prayer itself but the Friday sermon that always preceded the Friday prayer. Furthermore, the words "hasten to the remembrance of Allah" mean that one should proceed to the Friday sermon with a sense of urgency and importance, and not that one should literally run to it. The directive "to give up all trading" means that after the call to Friday prayer has been made, one should not only give up trading but also concern oneself solely with the Friday service and shun every other occupation. It is also pertinent to mention that Muslim jurists are agreed that every kind of business transaction after the call to Friday prayer is forbidden. It is also pertinent to note that according to a hadith, children, women, slaves, sick people, and travelers are exempt from the obligation to perform Friday prayer.

***8:** This does not mean that everybody is obligated to disperse in the land and engage in seeking their livelihood following the Friday prayer. Instead, people may disperse in the land and proceed with their economic activities. One should bear in mind the context in which these words occur. The words "disperse in the land and seek Allah's Bounty" follow the directive to stop all business activities after the call to the Friday prayer is made. Therefore, when the prayer is over, it is natural that believers be told that they may proceed with whatever economic activities they wish.

This is similar to what was said in the Qur'an on another occasion. People were ordered not to engage in hunting when they were in the state of *iḥrām*. But once they had completed the obligatory requirements of pilgrimage, "...then hunt" (5:2). This does not mean it was obligatory for such people to hunt; rather, what is meant is that the restrictions on hunting were now terminated and so they might hunt if they so wanted.

Those who argue on the basis of this verse that there is no holiday on Friday in Islam, however, put forward a flawed argument. For if the

Muslims have to have a weekly holiday it should obviously be on Friday in the same manner that the Jews have it on Saturday and the Christians on Sunday.

***9:** We have translated this verse as follows: "...so that you may prosper." If we take the Arabic word *la'alla* used in the verse literally, we would have translated it as "...perhaps you will prosper." Our present translation, however, is appropriate because here the word *la'alla* is not used to indicate any doubt. To comprehend the true purport of *la'alla* (literally, "perhaps") it should be borne in mind that the statement here is analogous to a royal declaration and is couched in terms befitting royalty. The statement is like a boss saying to his subordinates: "Carry out this duty well, and perhaps you will be promoted." The tenor of the address subtly implies a promise in expectation of which subordinates will perform their tasks with full devotion.

***10:** This refers to an incident that took place in the early Madinah period of the Prophet's life. A trading caravan had arrived in Madinah from Syria exactly at the time of Friday Prayer and its arrival was announced by the beating of drums. The Prophet was then delivering his Friday sermon. The sound of the drums made people impatient with the result that all but twelve persons left the mosque and headed for the caravan.

***11:** These words indicate a kind of lapse on the part of the Companions. Had the underlying cause of this lapse been their weakness of faith or their willful preference for worldly benefits over the Hereafter, God's reproach would have been couched in much sterner terms. But what caused the incident was the fact that the Muslims had not yet received any extensive training to live according to Islamic principles. In view of this, the rules pertaining to the Friday prayer were enunciated much in the manner a teacher would do. This was followed by expressing disapproval of the Companions' actions after which it was declared that the reward they would receive by listening to the Friday Sermon and offering the Friday prayer would be far greater than anything they could gain from engaging in business and recreation.

12: God is a much better Provider of sustenance than all those who are ostensibly a means to provide sustenance to God's creatures.

1.3. Comparative Review

Verses 62:9-11 of the Qur'an describe the injunctions related to the Friday prayers. The quoted translations and commentaries of these verses in the above present the understanding of the meaning of these verses by the four translators in the light of the related hadith and fiqh knowledge. The key terms, phrases, and points that could affect the understanding of the related injunctions of these verses are the following items:

- To whom this injunction is obligatory
- The clear meanings of *Idhā nūdiya*
- *Fasʿaw*
- *Dhikrillāh*
- *Al-bayʿ*
- *Fantashirū fī al-arḍi wabtaghū*
- The historical context of verse 11.

These items need to become clear either in the translation text by selecting appropriate terms to communicate the intent or using parenthesis, or in the commentary of these verses. The following provides a comparison of the four translations from these points of view:

1. Although the address is to all the believers, there are certain people who are exempted from the obligation of this injunction, such as women, travelers, the sick, etc.[7] A/M is the only one who has explained this point in the last part of comment *7.

2. *Idhā nūdiya*: In the translation of this term, the important point to be clarified is that it is meant to say that "when it is the time for the Friday prayer." Thus, even if a person cannot hear the call for the prayer, the command applies to him. MA is the only one who has tried to clarify this point in his comment *10.

3. *Fas*ᶜ*aw*: In the translation of this term, it is important to clarify that the intent is to give it a sense of urgency and importance, and not physical running. A/M has nicely explained this point. H&K have translated it as "come to" which is meant to avoid the literal running, but does not communicate its intended urgency. YA has translated it as "hasten earnestly" which could make the point indirectly. MA has left it with its literal translation as "hasten to."

4. *Dhikrillāh*: In the translation of this term, it is important to clarify that the intent of "remembrance of Allah" is "the *khuṭbah* and the prayer of Friday."[8] H&K have clarified this point inside a parenthesis within the translated text. A/M has explained it in the beginning of his comment *7. YA and MA have left it to its literal translation without clarifying it.

5. *Al-bay*ᶜ: The intent is "any kind of financial and worldly occupations." YA has explained it but not more than the literal translation. MA has clarified it in his translation as "all worldly commerce." A/M has explained it very clearly in his comment *7. H&K have clarified it by adding "and every other thing" within a parenthesis in the translation.

6. *Fantashirū fī al-arḍi wabtaghū*: In the translation of this phrase, the intent is not an order to make it obligatory, but an instruction to make it permissible. YA has clarified it in his translation by using the word "may." MA has used the word "freely" in his translation and has explained it in his comment *11. H&K have done it in their translation by using the word "may." A/M has translated it literally, but he has explained it very clearly in his comment *8.

7. While verse 11 has a lesson for Muslims of all times, its historical context should be clarified. YA has translated it nicely to cover the lesson, but does not mention its historical context. MA has covered both aspects very clearly. H&K do not mention its historical context. A/M has clearly translated it as a past event and has elaborated on its historical context in his comments *10 and *11 along with clarifica-

tion of the fact that the Prophet's Companions did not have enough training/instructions at that time.

It can be noted from the work of the four translators that YA and A/M have provided detailed and useful commentary for these verses. YA provides a good introduction about the Friday prayer and a useful comparison to the Judeo-Christian weekly religious days. A/M has explained the verses with useful fiqh details. MA has minimal commentary, but enough to clarify some of the major points. H&K do not offer any commentary on these verses except some parenthetical words within the translated text in order to clarify the meaning.

2. *Injunction of Women's Dress Code (Ḥijāb)*

In this section, the various translations of verses (24:31) and (33:59), which provide a description of the dress code of Muslim women, will be reviewed. This injunction is referred to as *aḥkām al-ḥijāb*. Although *ḥijāb* applies to both males and females, it is often referred to the dress code of women.

These two verses are chosen because the topic of *ḥijāb* is often debated, especially in western societies, as an issue of Muslim women's rights. Many people consider *ḥijāb* as a sign of oppression of Muslim women. On the other hand, those who observe *ḥijāb* consider it not only an Islamic duty, but also feel that it liberates them from the constraints of some uncongenial aspects of western modernity.

For Muslims, *ḥijāb* is prescribed by Allah, the Creator of all human beings. It is a prescription for modest dressing that applies to both males and females. It is a part of the overall rules of behavior and appearance to be observed when men and women interact with one another in a social milieu. *ḥijāb* is the proper Islamic dress code that is primarily intended to safeguard the modesty, dignity, and honor of men and women. *ḥijāb* thus forms part of a holistic program of Islamic ethics and morals governing male and female interaction.

The word *ḥijāb* comes from the Arabic word *Ḥajaba*, meaning to hide from view, to conceal, to screen, to veil, and to cover.[9] Therefore, *ḥijāb* means a covering or a curtain. The Qur'an has used the term *ḥijāb* in its common meaning, i.e. curtain, whether real or proverbial. However, because a curtain covers and conceals, it is commonly used as a verb for a woman covering herself to avoid being seen by unauthorized males. Therefore, in the common usage, the term *ḥijāb* refers to the dress code and modest covering of a Muslim woman.

As a book of guidance for all aspects of human life, the Qur'an provides some essential and useful guidelines about the dress code of men and women. While the dress of human beings is often considered as a means of protection and adornment of the body only, notably overlooking and ignoring its purpose of providing modesty, God calls the attention of mankind to its full and great aspect in the following words: "O children of Adam! We have indeed sent down to you clothing to cover your nakedness, as well as to be an adornment and protection. But the raiment of *taqwā* – that is the best. This is of the signs of Allah that they may be mindful" (7:26).

This verse makes clear that the first objective of human dress is to provide modesty and decency. To help achieve this objective, Islam provides specific guidelines for the believers to follow in their clothing. A major portion of these guidelines is provided in verses (33:59) and (24:31), which are being reviewed here.

The context of verse (33:59) is that immediately before this verse, there is condemnation of the behavior of the hypocrites and troublemakers who had been abusing Muslim women by their practice of sexual harassment, false rumors, and undue accusations. They were warned of severe punishment in the Hereafter for their depraved behavior. Then, in verse (33:59), Muslim women were told that, in order to avoid harassment, they should give a clear signal by their Islamic attire of their being chaste and God-fearing Muslim women. Immediately after this verse, the perpetrators of harassment are warned of dire consequences at the hands of the Prophet and his Companions. In other words, the culprits were condemned and warned both of the punishment in this world and in the Hereafter to ensure that they did not dare to harass Muslim women; at the same time, Muslim women were commanded to take their own precautions.[10]

Verse (24:31) is preceded by a verse that commands Muslim males first to lower their gaze and to be mindful of their chastity. Both

Muslim men and women have been commanded to lower their gazes and protect their private parts. This is a general command applicable to whenever and wherever men and women come across each other. Lowering the gaze does not mean that Muslims should always keep their heads down and not look up. Actually, the words used are "they should lower some of their looks," indicating that only certain types of looks are being talked about, meaning that they should not look intently at someone of the opposite sex with a lustful eye.

While lowering of one's gaze and protection of one's private parts have to be observed by both men and women as explained in verse (24:30), verse (24:31) requires women to cover their *zīnah*. The *zīnah* of women is defined as natural physical beauty (except certain parts that have to be revealed) and their ornaments.[11] As explained in the middle part of verse (24:31), *zīnah* has to be covered from everyone except certain relatives and people: her fathers, including grandfathers, fathers of the husband, her own or her husband's sons, her brothers, and her nephews (sons of sisters and brothers), her female friends or relatives, those feeble dependent males who do not have any sexual inclinations, and children who do not have exposure to sexual matters.

The next part of verse (24:31) calls on women to walk without stamping their feet lest they attract people's attention because of the sounds produced by such walking. Verse (24:31) ends with an invitation to all of the believers to turn to God for true success.

Both for men and women, there exists a minimum area/part of the body that must be covered, this is called the *ʿawrah*. The *ʿawrah* must be covered with loosely fitting clothing that does not show details of the physical figure and through which neither skin nor its tone is visible. The *ʿawrah* of a person's body must be protected from anyone's sight or touch, male or female, except from spouses. It should be kept covered even if no one is around, and is also the minimum that must be covered for a person's prayer (salah) to be valid, even if the person is praying alone at home. The *ʿawrah* for males consists of the part of the body from the height of the navel to the knees. A woman's *ʿawrah* consists of her whole body except the face, hands, and feet. General scholarly opinion is that the minimum part of the body that has to be exposed to perform the daily chores and functions of life is not included in the

ʿ*awrah*. That is why even if some portions of the forearm close to the wrist or of the calves close to the ankles are exposed during performing tasks, it is considered acceptable.[12]

The following review will provide a more detailed understanding of the requirements and issues of *ḥijāb*.

1.3.1. The Qur'anic Text

Verse (33:59)

يَٰٓأَيُّهَا ٱلنَّبِيُّ قُل لِّأَزْوَٰجِكَ وَبَنَاتِكَ وَنِسَآءِ ٱلْمُؤْمِنِينَ يُدْنِينَ عَلَيْهِنَّ مِن جَلَٰبِيبِهِنَّ
ذَٰلِكَ أَدْنَىٰٓ أَن يُعْرَفْنَ فَلَا يُؤْذَيْنَ ۗ وَكَانَ ٱللَّهُ غَفُورًا رَّحِيمًا ﴿٥٩﴾

Verse (24:31)

وَقُل لِّلْمُؤْمِنَٰتِ يَغْضُضْنَ مِنْ أَبْصَٰرِهِنَّ
وَيَحْفَظْنَ فُرُوجَهُنَّ وَلَا يُبْدِينَ زِينَتَهُنَّ إِلَّا مَا ظَهَرَ مِنْهَا ۖ وَلْيَضْرِبْنَ
بِخُمُرِهِنَّ عَلَىٰ جُيُوبِهِنَّ ۖ وَلَا يُبْدِينَ زِينَتَهُنَّ إِلَّا لِبُعُولَتِهِنَّ أَوْ ءَابَآئِهِنَّ
أَوْ ءَابَآءِ بُعُولَتِهِنَّ أَوْ أَبْنَآئِهِنَّ أَوْ أَبْنَآءِ بُعُولَتِهِنَّ أَوْ إِخْوَٰنِهِنَّ أَوْ بَنِىٓ
إِخْوَٰنِهِنَّ أَوْ بَنِىٓ أَخَوَٰتِهِنَّ أَوْ نِسَآئِهِنَّ أَوْ مَا مَلَكَتْ أَيْمَٰنُهُنَّ أَوِ
ٱلتَّٰبِعِينَ غَيْرِ أُو۟لِى ٱلْإِرْبَةِ مِنَ ٱلرِّجَالِ أَوِ ٱلطِّفْلِ ٱلَّذِينَ لَمْ يَظْهَرُوا۟
عَلَىٰ عَوْرَٰتِ ٱلنِّسَآءِ ۖ وَلَا يَضْرِبْنَ بِأَرْجُلِهِنَّ لِيُعْلَمَ مَا يُخْفِينَ مِن
زِينَتِهِنَّ ۚ وَتُوبُوٓا۟ إِلَى ٱللَّهِ جَمِيعًا أَيُّهَ ٱلْمُؤْمِنُونَ لَعَلَّكُمْ تُفْلِحُونَ ﴿٣١﴾

1.4. Text of Translations and Commentary

YA:

(33:59) O Prophet! Tell thy wives and daughters, and the believing women, (*3764) that they should cast their outer garments over (*3765) their persons [when abroad]: that is most convenient, that they should be known (*3766) (as such) and not molested. And Allah is Oft-Forgiving, (*3767) Most Merciful.

***3764:** This is for all Muslim women, those of the Prophet's household, as well as the others...they were asked to cover themselves with outer garments when walking around.

***3765:** *Jilbāb*, plural *jalābīb*: an outer garment: a long gown covering the whole body, or a cloak covering the neck and bosom.

***3766:** The object was not to restrict the liberty of women but to protect them from harm and molestation. In the East and the West, a distinctive public dress of some sort or another has always been a badge of honor or distinction, both among men and women. This can be traced back to the earliest civilizations. Assyrian Law in its palmiest days (7th century B.C.), enjoined the veiling of married women and forbade the veiling of slaves and women of ill fame.

***3767:** That is, if a Muslim woman sincerely tries to observe this rule, but owing to human weakness falls short of the ideal, then "Allah is Oft-Forgiving, Most Merciful."

(24:31). And say to the believing women that they should lower their gaze and guard (*2984) their modesty; that they should not display their beauty and ornaments (*2985) except what [must ordinarily] appear thereof; that they should draw their veils over their bosoms and not display their beauty except to their husbands, their fathers, their husband's fathers, their sons, their husbands' sons, their brothers or their brothers' sons, or their sisters' sons, or their women, or the slaves whom their right hands possess, or male servants free of physical needs, or small children who have no sense of the shame of sex; and that they should not strike their feet in order to draw attention to their hidden ornaments. (*2986) And O ye Believers! turn ye all together towards Allah, that ye may attain Bliss. (*2987)

***2984:** The need for modesty is the same in both men and women. However, due to the differentiation of the sexes in nature, temperaments, and social life, a greater amount of privacy is required for women than for men, especially in the matter of dress and the uncovering of the bosom.

***2985:** *Zīnah* means both natural beauty and artificial ornaments. Both are implied here, but chiefly the former. The woman is asked not to make a display of her figure or appear in undress except to the following classes of people: 1. her husband, 2. her near relatives who would be living in the same house, and with whom a certain amount of *negligee* is permissible; 3. her women, *i.e.*, her maidservants who would be constantly in attendance on her: some commentators include all believing women; it is not good form in a Muslim household for women to meet other women, except when they are properly dressed; 4. slaves, male and female as they would be in constant attendance (but with the abolition of slavery this no longer applies); 5. old or infirm men-servants; and 6. infants or small children before they get a sense of sex. [*Cf.* also 33:59.]

***2986:** It is one of the tricks of showy or unchaste women to tinkle their ankle ornaments, to draw attention to themselves.

***2987:** While all these details of the purity and good form of domestic life are being brought to our attention, we are clearly reminded that the chief object we should hold in view is our spiritual welfare. All our life on this earth is a probation, and we must make our individual, domestic, and social life all contribute to our holiness, so that we can obtain the real success and bliss that is the aim of our spiritual endeavor.

MA:

(33:59) O Prophet! Tell thy wives and thy daughters, as well as all [other] believing women, that they should draw over themselves some of their outer garments [when in public]: this will be more conducive to their being recognized [as decent women] and not annoyed. (*74) But [withal,] God is indeed much-forgiving, a dispenser of grace! (*75)

***74:** *Cf.* the first two sentences of (24:31) and the corresponding notes.

***75:** The specific, time-bound formulation of the above verse (evident in the reference to the wives and daughters of the Prophet), as well as the deliberate vagueness of the recommendation that women "should draw upon themselves some of their outer garments (*min jalābībihinna*)" when in public, makes it clear that this verse was not meant to be an injunction (*ḥukm*) in the general, timeless sense of this term but, rather, as a moral guideline to be observed against the ever-changing background of time and social environment. This finding is reinforced by the concluding reference to God's forgiveness and grace.

(24:31) And tell the believing women to lower their gaze and to be mindful of their chastity, and not to display their charms [in public] beyond what may [decently] be apparent thereof; (*37) hence, let them draw their head-coverings over their bosoms. (*38) And let them not display [more of] their charms to any but their husbands, or their fathers, or their husbands' fathers, or their sons, or their husbands' sons, or their brothers, or their brothers' sons, or their sisters' sons, or their women folk, or those whom they rightfully possess, or such male attendants as are beyond all sexual desire, (*39) or children that are as yet unaware of women's nakedness; and let them not swing their legs [in walking] so as to draw attention to their hidden charms (*40) And [always], O you believers – all of you – turn unto God in repentance, so that you might attain to a happy state! (*41)

***37:** This interpolation of the word "decently" reflects the interpretation of the phrase *illā mā ẓahara minhā* by several of the earliest Islamic scholars, and particularly by al-Qiffāl (quoted by al-Rāzī), as "that which a human being may openly show in accordance with prevailing custom (*al-ʿādah al-jāriyah*)." Although the traditional exponents of

Islamic Law have for centuries been inclined to restrict the definition of "what may [decently] be apparent" to a woman's face, hands and feet – and sometimes even less than that – we may safely assume that the meaning of *illā mā ẓahara minhā* is much wider, and that the deliberate vagueness of this phrase is meant to allow for all the time-bound changes that are necessary for man's moral and social growth. The pivotal clause in the above injunction is the demand, addressed in identical terms to men as well as to women, to "lower their gaze and be mindful of their chastity": and this determines the extent of what, at any given time, may legitimately – i.e., in consonance with the Qur'anic principles of social morality – be considered "decent" or "indecent" in a person's outward appearance.

***38:** The noun *khimār* (of which *khumur* is the plural) denotes the head-covering customarily used by Arabian women before and after the advent of Islam. According to most of the classical commentators, it was worn in pre-Islamic times more or less as an ornament and was let down loosely over the wearer's back; and since, in accordance with the fashion prevalent at the time, the upper part of a woman's tunic had a wide opening in the front, her breasts were left bare. Hence, the injunction to cover the bosom by means of a *khimār*, (a term so familiar to the contemporaries of the Prophet) does not necessarily relate to the use of a *khimār* as such but is, rather, meant to make it clear that a woman's breasts are not included in the concept of "what may decently be apparent" of her body and should not, therefore, be displayed.

***39:** i.e., very old men. The preceding phrase "those whom they rightfully possess" (lit., "whom their right hands possess") denotes slaves; but see also second note on verse 58.

***40:** Lit., "so that those of their charms which they keep hidden may become known." The phrase *yaḍribna bi-arjulihinna* is idiomatically similar to the phrase *ḍaraba bi-yadayhi fī mishyatihi*, "he swung his arms in walking" (quoted in this context in *Tāj al-ᶜArūs*), and alludes to a deliberately provocative gait.

***41:** The implication of this general call to repentance is that "since man has been created weak" (4:28), no one is ever free of faults and temptations – so much so that even the Prophet used to say, "Verily, I turn unto Him in repentance a hundred times every day" (Ibn Ḥanbal, Bukhārī and Bayhaqī, all of them on the authority of ʿAbd Allāh ibn ʿUmar).

H&K:

(33:59) O Prophet! Tell your wives and your daughters and the women of the believers to draw their cloaks [veils] all over their bodies [i.e. screen themselves completely except the eyes or one eye to see the way]. That will be better, that they should be known [as free respectable women] so as not to be annoyed. And Allah is Ever Oft-Forgiving, Most Merciful. (* 1)

***1**: See the footnote of (24:31).

(24:31) And tell the believing women to lower their gaze [from looking at forbidden things], and protect their private parts [from illegal sexual acts, etc.] and not to show off their adornment except only that which is apparent [like palms of hands or one eye or both eyes for necessity to see the way, or outer dress like veil, gloves, head-cover, apron, etc.], and to draw their veils all over *Juyūbihinna* [i.e. their bodies, faces, necks and bosoms] and not to reveal their adornment except to their husbands, their fathers, their husband's fathers, their sons, their husband's sons, their brothers or their brother's sons, or their sister's sons, or their [Muslim] women [i.e. their sisters in Islam], or the [female] slaves whom their right hands possess, or old male servants who lack vigor, or small children who have no sense of the shame of sex. And let them not stamp their feet so as to reveal what they hide of their adornment. And all of you beg Allah to forgive you all, O believers, that you may be successful (* 1).

***1**: About "And to draw their veils all over *Juyūbihinna* (i.e. their bodies, faces, necks and bosoms) and not to reveal their adornment..." Narrated ʿĀishah: "May Allah bestow His mercy on the early immigrant women. When Allah revealed: "And to draw their veils all over

Juyūbihinna [i.e. their bodies, faces, necks and bosoms]" – they tore their *Muroots* [a woolen dress, or a waist-binding cloth or an apron] and covered their heads and faces with those torn *Muroots*." (*Ṣahīh Bukhārī*, hadith no.4758). Narrated Ṣafiyyah bint Shaybah: "ʿĀishah used to say: when the verse "And to draw their veils all over *Juyūbihinna* [i.e. their bodies, faces, necks and bosoms]" was revealed, [the ladies] cut their waist sheets at the edges and covered their heads and faces with those cut pieces of cloth." (*Ṣaḥiḥ Bukhārī*, hadith no.4759).

A/M:

(33:59) O Prophet, enjoin your wives and your daughters and the wives of believers, to draw a part of their outer coverings around them. (*20) It is likelier that they will be recognized and not molested. (*21) Allah is Most Forgiving, Most Merciful.

***20:** That is, they should wear their over-garment (*chaadar*) and veil. In other words, they should not move about with their faces uncovered.

***21:** " ...It is likelier that they will thus be recognized..." that is, when people see them dressed in garments exuding simplicity and modesty they will be recognized as honorable and chaste women. They will appear distinct from women of loose character who are ever on the hunt for lewd encounters. These women are unlike those whom immoral men would seek out to gratify their desires. As for the words "and will not be molested," they mean that since those women will be perceived as decent ladies they will not be subjected to teasing and harassment to which men of vile character have recourse when they encounter women not particularly known for their uprightness and firmness of character.

(24:31) And enjoin believing women to cast down their looks and guard their private parts and (*20) not reveal their adornment except that which is revealed of itself, and to draw their veils over their bosoms, and not to reveal their adornment save to their husbands, or their fathers, or the fathers of their husbands, (*21) or of their own sons, or the sons of their husbands, (*22) or their brothers, (*23) or the sons of their brothers, or the sons of their sisters, (*24) or the women with whom they associate, (*25) or those that are in their bondage, or the male attendants in their service free of sexual interest, (*26) or boys that are yet unaware of illicit matters pertaining to women. Nor should they stamp their feet on the ground in such manner that their hidden ornament becomes revealed.

***20:** It should be noted that the demands that the Divine Law makes on women, (as mentioned in this verse), are not just what is expected of men, i.e. avoiding to look at what is improper to look at and guarding one's private parts. It also demands of women more than what it requires men to do. This clearly shows that women are not equated with men as far as this matter is concerned.

***21:** The word *abā'* used in this verse covers one's father, both maternal and paternal grandfathers and great-grandfathers. A woman may, therefore, appear before these elders of either her own family or of her husband's family in the same manner as she may appear before both her father and father-in-law.

***22:** The word *abnā'ihinna* ("their sons") covers, apart from their own sons, their grandsons and great-grandsons, i.e. those born both of one's sons and daughters. Furthermore, no distinction is made between one's own sons and one's stepsons. A woman may appear freely before the children of her stepsons as she may appear before her own children and grandchildren.

***23:** "Brothers" here covers both real and stepbrothers.

***24:** This refers to a woman's nieces and nephews, whether they are born of her brother or sister, and whether those brothers and sisters are real or are stepbrothers and stepsisters.

***25:** This by itself shows that a Muslim woman should not display her attractions before immoral and immodest women.

***26:** That is, as they are in a state of subservience there is no room to suspect that they would dare harbor evil designs regarding the women of the household.

1.5. Comparative Review

The review of these two verses is carried out based on how some of the key words and phrases that affect the understanding of the teachings of the verses and its legal aspects are rendered and commented upon. The key words and phrases in these two verses are:

- *Zīnah*
- *Khimār*
- *Jilbāb*
- *Yudnīna ᶜalayhinna min jalābībihinna*
- *Illā mā ẓahara minhā*
- *Wal yaḍribna bi khumurihinna ᶜalā juyūbihinna*

1. ***Zīnah***: This includes natural or bodily beauty and acquired adornments such as rings, bracelets, and clothes.[13] It includes female decorations, ornaments, clothing, hairstyle, etc.[14] It includes the natural physical beauty of a woman as well as all beautification aids and adornments used to increase her attractiveness such as hairstyle, make-up, and jewelery.[15] YA has translated it as "beauty and ornaments" that covers both aspects. MA has translated it as "charms" which means attractive features. It is an alternative idiomatic usage. H&K and A/M have translated it as "adornment" that may not cover the natural beauty.

2. ***Khimār*** (of which *khumur* is the plural): *Khimār* means anything that covers the head of something.[16] It is what covers the head of the woman.[17] *Khimār* means a head cover.[18] *Khimār* is a cloth to be worn or wrapped that must be big enough to cover hair, neck and bosom, and must not be transparent so that it can truly cover up or hide *zīnah*. To hide the *zīnah*, they must wear *khimār* in such a way that it covers their chests as well as adornments.[19] MA translated *Khimār* as "head covering," but the rest have translated it as "veil." Thus, they do not differ much. However, MA and H&K have made some comments related to the usage of *khimār* that will be addressed later.

3. ***Jalābīb***: This is the plural of *jilbāb*. *Jilbāb* means a big sheet that covers the head and the whole body.[20] It is a cloak or a big sheet of

cloth that is wrapped around the body as an outer garment.[21] It is a sheet that covers the head and the entire body and clothing of a lady.[22] YA and MA rendered it as "outer garments," but YA has further explained it in his comment *3765 as "an outer garment: a long gown covering the whole body, or a cloak covering the neck and bosom." H&K have rendered it as "cloaks (veil)" and A/M has rendered it as "outer coverings." Basically, they all have covered the essence of the meaning and there is not much of a difference between their translations of this term.

4. ***Yudnīna ʿalayhinna min jalābībihinna***: The translators have rendered this phrase as follows:

YA: "They should cast their outer garment over their persons [when abroad]."

MA: "They should draw over themselves some of their outer garments [in public]*75."

H&K: "To draw their cloaks [veils] all over their bodies [i.e. screen themselves completely except the eyes or one eye to see the way]."

A/M: "To draw a part of their outer coverings around them."

In the translation, they all use similar wording except that MA and A/M have translated the word *min* in its discriminatory (*tabʿīd*) meaning as "some of" and "a part of," respectively. However, more significant differences appear in the commentary of MA and A/M, and what is added inside the parenthesis by H&K. MA explains this phrase in his comment *75 that this is a time-bound formula and it is not meant to be an injunction, but only a moral guideline. His reasoning for this argument is that there is a deliberate vagueness in this phrase and there is a reference to God's forgiveness at the end of the verse.

However, this conclusion and reasoning is very weak for many reasons, such as: (i) The wording of the verse is a clear order on the Prophet to convey. (ii) The orders (injunctions) of the Qur'an are for all times unless there is an evidence for its time limitation from the Qur'an or the Sunnah. (iii) The claimed vagueness is not confirmed by any of the famous commentators of the Qur'an. (iv) Allah's forgiveness at the end of the verse is often mentioned at the end of orders to show Allah's mercy and pardon for any disobedience that takes place due to one's inability or forgetfulness, etc. Therefore, MA's commentary for this phrase is problematic and his reasons are not based on any solid position.

H&K have added a statement to the translation of this phrase inside parenthesis reading: (i.e. screen themselves completely except the eyes or one eye to see the way). The main intent of adding this statement is to imply that the face should also be covered. A/M has also mentioned covering of the face in his comment *20 to this phrase. This issue will be discussed in the review of the next phrase.

5. ***Illā mā ẓahara minhā***: The translators have rendered this phrase as follows:

YA: "except what [must ordinarily] appear thereof."
MA: "beyond what may [decently] be apparent thereof."
H&K: "except only that which is apparent [like palms of hands or one eye or both eyes for necessity to see the way, or outer dress like veil, gloves, head-cover, apron, etc.]"
A/M: "except that which is revealed of itself."

The meaning of this phrase, which offers an exception to the rule of not revealing the beauty and ornaments of women, has been discussed and debated extensively by commentators of the Qur'an. The majority understand it as "the face and hands of women and that part of the ornaments that cannot be hidden," but some do not agree with the exception of the face and hands. Among these four translators, as apparent, differences are indicated in what is added inside the parenthesis.

YA has clarified it as that which is beyond one's ability, leaving it there without further explanation. MA has added the word "decently" in parenthesis and explains it in his comment *37. He argues that this exception of "what not to reveal" depends on the prevailing custom and time-bound changes of society. However, this argument seems weak from many points of view. The Qur'an's injunctions are for all times and places unless there is an evidence for its limitation. Even in the case of difference with regards to the exception of revealing the face and hands, this is not due to customs, but to the technical differences in the approaches of some scholars. For example, those who insist that a woman's face should not be revealed, and that women should cover the face wherever they live, including Europe and the U.S.

H&K have added a description inside parenthesis and have provided commentary *1 to indicate the necessity of covering the face and the hands of women as part of their *ḥijāb*. Further, they have even added extra words in the translation of the hadith in the commentary to prove that the face should be covered. The wording of both *aḥādīth* of Bukhārī, which have been referred to in comment *1, ends with "*fakhtamarna bihā*," which simply means "they covered with it." But H&K have added the words "heads and faces" which are not in the original Arabic text at all.

The issue of whether a woman's face and hands are exempted from the requirements of their *ḥijāb* has been extensively discussed among some scholars for centuries. Shaykh Ahmad Kutty summarizes the issue as follows:

> The majority of Imams – including those of the four Schools as well as others – share the interpretation of Ibn ʿAbbās that hands and face are exempted per the interpretation of the phrase "except what is apparent," and thus hold the opinion that a woman is not obliged to cover her face and hands. However, a group of scholars, the majority of whom belong to the Hanbalite Juristic School, teaches that a woman must cover her face and hands as well. In support of their position, they invoke a tradition attributed to the Prophet, stating, "Woman is all *ʿawrah*," and hence as such, needs to cover up completely. They also reason by saying that the most attractive parts of a woman's body capable of enticing men are her face and hands.[23]

Kutty further explains the validity of Ibn ʿAbbās' position as follows:

> The aforementioned position of the majority on this issue seems to be more consistent with the general understanding and evidences of the Qur'an and Sunnah than of those who advocate covering the face and hands as well. There are several proofs that point to this conclusion:

> Firstly, the verse quoted above from the Qur'an, seems to presume that the women it addresses are not wholly covered (i.e. face and hands), since otherwise, there is no sense in ordering both genders to lower their gazes. Secondly, it is a general consensus among scholars that a woman is not required to cover her face and hands while performing salah; if these were deemed to be *ᶜawrah*, it would certainly have been necessary to cover them. Thirdly, a woman is required to bare her face while she is in a state of *Iḥrām* (during hajj and *ᶜumrah*), which again, confirms what we said earlier. Moreover, the evidences in the sources – the Qur'an and the Sunnah – are overwhelming in showing that the *ḥijāb* as prescribed by Islam was not meant to segregate women or shut them out of the social involvement and participation in the affairs of the Muslim community since the participation of Muslim women – at all levels of Islamic life – is fully documented beyond a shadow of doubt in the sources of Shariᶜah. Such active participation as described in the sources is conceivable only if we assume that women were not wholly covered from head to toe. In light of the above, we conclude: a Muslim woman is required to cover all her body except her face and hands, according to the majority of scholars belonging to all schools. Covering the head, however, is not at all a disputed issue among them – they all agree that this is a necessary part of *ḥijāb*.[24]

Al-Albani[25] and Abu Shuqqah[26] have written outstanding books on Muslim women's *ḥijāb*, both proving with extensive references that the covering of the face and hands by women is not required by Islam. Similarly, ad-Darsh addressed this topic as *ḥijāb* or *niqāb* in his book dealing with the *ḥijāb*.[27] Meanwhile, some scholars have argued this position defending the covering of the face and hands, such as al-Barazi.[28]

6. ***Wal yaḍribna bi khumurihinna ᶜalā juyūbihinna***: This phrase has been translated in the following ways:

YA: "they should draw their veils over their bosoms."
MA: "let them draw their head-coverings over their bosoms."
H&K: "to draw their veils all over *Juyūbihinna* [i.e. their bodies, faces, necks, and bosoms]."
A/M: "to draw their veils over their bosoms."

The translations of all four are not much different from each other except H&K who provide a parenthetical description. In this description, the words "bodies" and "faces" are added which do not necessarily correspond to the meaning of the word *Juyūbihinna* in the verse. *Juyūb* is the plural of *jayb* and means "bosoms, breasts, cavity, and opening."[29]

MA makes some remarks in the last part of his comment *38 that need to be addressed. He argues that "the injunction to cover the bosom by means of a *khimār* does not necessarily relate to the use of a *khimār* as such," but is only meant to clarify that a woman's breasts should be covered. This argument can be interpreted in two ways. If it is meant to confirm the necessity of covering the bosom, it is fine. However, if MA has tried to state that the intent is to cover only the breasts, then the meaning of both the words *jayb* and *khimār*, as explained earlier cannot support it.

In reviewing the translations of the verses containing women's dress code injunction, it is apparent that of the four translators, YA has provided much of the necessary details in his commentary to explain and clarify the subject. While the other three translators have tried to expound, each one of them has made some statements that need to be clarified and addressed.

The theme-based approach applied in this paper to assess various translations of the Qur'an allows, as demonstrated, for meaningful differences among translators to be highlighted, as well as identifying the need for certain qualifications among translators to augment their expertise.

REFERENCES

Abu Shuqqah, Abdul Halim, *Taḥrīr al-Mar'ah fī ʿAṣr Risālah* (Kuwait: Dār al-Qalam, 1990), vol. 4.

Ad-Darsh, Syed Mutawalli, *Muslim Women's Dress: Ḥijāb or Niqāb* (Kuala Lumpur: Islamic Book Trust, 1997).

Al-Albani, Muhammad Nasr al-Din, *Ḥijāb al-Mar'ah al-Muslimah fī al-Kitāb wa al-Sunnah* (Beirut: Al-Maktab al-Islāmī, 1969).

Ali, Muhammad Mohar, *A Word for Word Meaning of the Qur'ân*, (Oxford: Jam'iat Ihyaa' Minhaaj al-Sunnah, 2003), vol. 2.

Alkhairo, Wael, *Speaking for Change: A Guide to Making Effective Friday Sermons* (Maryland: Amana Publications, 1998).

Baalbaki, Munir, *Al-Mawrid Arabic-English Dictionary* (Beirut: Dār al-ʿIlm li al-Malāyīn, 1998).

Badawi, Jamal, *The Muslim Woman's Dress* (Indiana: MSA, 1980).

Al-Barazi, Muhammad Fuad, *Ḥijāb al-Muslimah* (Riyādh: Maktab Aḍwā' al-Salaf, 1995).

Doi, Abdur Rahman I., *Women in Shari 'ah* (London: Ta-Ha Publishers, 1989).

Al-Fayrūzābādī, Muḥammad ibn Yaʿqūb, *Al-Qāmūs al-Muḥīṭ* (Beirut: Dār Iḥyā' al-Turāth al-ʿArabī, 2003).

Hamid, Ayub A., *Unveiling the Commands: The Truth about Hijaab, Jilbaab and Khimaar* (Ontario: Bayān Communications and Publications, 2004).

Ibn al-ʿArabī, *Aḥkām al-Qur'ān*, (Beirut: Dār al-Maʿrifah, 1982), vol. 4.

Ibn Manẓūr, Jamāl al-Dīn Muḥammad ibn Mukarram, *Lisān al-ʿArab* (Beirut: Dār Ṣādir li al-Ṭibāʿah wa al-Nashr, 1955).

Al-Jaṣṣāṣ, Abū Bakr, *Aḥkām al-Qur'ān* (Beirut: Dār Iḥyā' al-Turāth al-ʿArabī, 1985), vol. 5.

Nyazee, Imran Ahsan Khan, *Islamic Jurisprudence* (Islamabad: The International Institute of Islamic Thought, 2000).

Sabiq, As-Sayyid, *Fiqh us-Sunnah* (Illinois: American Trust Publications, 1996).

Kutty, Ahmad. http://www.islamonline.net/servlet/Satellite%3Fcid %3D1123996016280%26pagename%3DIslamOnline-English-AAbout_Islam%252FAskAboutIslamE%252FPrintAskAboutIslamE. Accessed on October 20, 2007.

Tahmaz, Abdul Hamid, *Al-Fiqh al-Ḥanafī* (Damascus: Dār al-Qalam, 1998).

Zarabozo, Jamal Aldin, *The Friday Prayer* (Aurora, Co.: Islamic Assembly of North America, 1994).

NOTES

1 Munir Baalbaki, *Al-Mawrid Arabic-English Dictionary* (Beirut: Dār al-ʿIlm Li al-Malāyīn, 1998), p.483.
2 Imran Ahsan Khan Nyazee, *Islamic Jurisprudence* (Islamabad: The International Institute of Islamic Thought, 2000), p.161.
3 Jamal Aldin Zarabozo, *The Friday Prayer* (Aurora, Co.: Islamic Assembly of North America, 1994), p.1.
4 Wael Alkhairo, *Speaking for Change: A Guide to Making Effective Friday Sermons* (Maryland: Amana Publications, 1998), p.1.
5 For example: As-Sayyid Sabiq, *Fiqh us-Sunnah* (Illinois: American Trust Publications, 1996).
6 For example: Abdul Hamid Tahmaz, *Al-Fiqh al-Ḥanafī* (Damascus: Dār al-Qalam, 1998).
7 Abū Bakr al-Jaṣṣāṣ, *Aḥkām al-Qur'ān* (Beirut: Dār Iḥyā' al-Turāth al-ʿArabī, 1985), vol. 5, p.340.
8 Ibn al-ʿArabī, *Aḥkām al-Qur'ān* (Beirut: Dār al-Maʿrifah, 1982), vol. 4, p.1805.
9 Baalbakī, *Al-Mawrid*, p.454.
10 Al-Jaṣṣāṣ, *Aḥkām al-Qur'ān*, vol. 5, p.245.
11 Jamal Badawi, *The Muslim Woman's Dress* (Indiana: MSA, 1980), p.5.
12 Ayub A. Hamid, *Unveiling the Commands: The Truth about Hijaab, Jilbaab and Khimaar* (Ontario: Bayan Communications and Publications, 2004), p.10.
13 Badawi, *The Muslim Woman's Dress*, p.6.
14 Abdur Rahman I. Doi, *Women in Shari'ah* (London: Ta-Ha Publishers, 1989), p.25.
15 Hamid, *Unveiling the Commands*, p.26.
16 Muḥammad ibn Yaʿqūb al-Fayrūzābādī, *Al-Qāmūs al-Muḥīṭ* (Beirut: Dār Iḥyā' al-Turāth al-ʿArabī, 2003).
17 Muhammad Fuad al-Barazi, *Ḥijāb al-Muslimah* (Riyādh: Maktabat Aḍwā' al-Salaf, 1995), p.36.
18 Muhammad Nasr al-Din al-Albani, *Ḥijāb al-Mar'at al-Muslimah fī al-Kitāb wa al-Sunnah* (Beirut: Al-Maktab al-Islāmī, 1969).
19 Hamid, *Unveiling the Commands*, p.26.
20 Jamāl al-Dīn Muḥammad ibn Mukarram ibn Manẓūr, , *Lisān al-ʿArab* (Beirut: Dār Ṣādir li al-Ṭibāʿah wa al-Nashr, 1955), p.139.
21 Hamid, *Unveiling the Commands*, p.18.
22 Al-Barazi, *Ḥijāb al-Muslimah*, p.33.

23 Shaykh Ahmad Kutty. http://www.islamonline.net/servlet/Satellite%3Fcid%3D1123996016280%26pagename%3DIslamOnline-English-AAbout_Islam%252FAskAboutIslamE%252FPrintAskAboutIslamE, accessed on October 20, 2007.

24 Ibid.

25 Al-Albani, *Ḥijāb al-Mar'ah al-Muslimah.*

26 Abdul Halim Abu Shuqqah, *Taḥrīr al-Mar'ah fī ʿAṣr Risālah* (Kuwait: Dār al-Qalam, 1990), vol. 4.

27 Syed Mutawalli ad-Darsh, *Muslim Women's Dress: Ḥijāb or Niqāb* (Kuala Lumpur: Islamic Book Trust, 1997).

28 Al-Barazi, *Ḥijāb al-Muslimah*, pp.143-238.

29 Muhammad Mohar Ali, *A Word for Word Meaning of the Qur'ân* (Oxford: Jam'iat Ihyaa' Minhaaj al-Sunnah, 2003), vol. 2, p.1116.

PART III

8

Finding a Principled Approach to Matn Analysis

SAMI CATOVIC

"THE Sunnah was the iron framework of the House of Islam; and if you remove the framework from a building, can you be surprised if it breaks down like a house of cards"? Here, the twentieth century scholar Muhammad Asad clearly articulated the role Sunnah plays in the construction of the "house of Islam." Attempts have been made historically, as well as in contemporary times, to dissociate the Sunnah of the Prophet Muhammad from the Message he brought, the Qur'an.[1] This approach is academically unsound, as well as having no real import for the masses.

The Qur'an clearly establishes the authority of the Prophet in numerous cases, such as, "Surely you have in the Messenger of Allah the pattern of excellence for anyone whose hope is in Allah and the Last Day and who remembers Allah much" (33:21). The *uswah*, or pattern, is only available to us through the Sunnah of the Prophet, which is primarily found in the hadith. The believer is instructed throughout the Qur'an to not only obey God, but also His messenger.[2]

The majority of scholars have held to the principle that obeying God (the Qur'an) cannot be separated from obedience to the Prophet.[3] In other words, the authority of the Qur'an and the Prophet are equal in conveying teachings and establishing a pattern of behavior. The Qur'an and hadith, however, are not necessarily equal in authority. The authenticity of the Qur'an, for Muslims, is not questioned, and those hadith that attain to the authenticity of the Qur'an in establishing a normative practice of the Prophet are on an equal footing with the Qur'an. However, hadith that do not rise to a sufficient level of authenticity would not necessarily be considered on equal footing with the Qur'an; rather they would provide auxiliary material for legislation.

The example of the Prophet is transmitted to us primarily through reports.[4] The stages of transmission begin with the Companions, who lived with the Prophet and observed his example. They transmitted what they heard or saw during the life of the Prophet to those who were not present. After the Prophet's death, they became the vehicle by which those who followed could learn about the Prophet. This was done primarily through the oral tradition, but evidence also shows that from the time of the Prophet, his hadith were in fact written down, contrary to what has been asserted by some orientalists that the traditions were actually written down much later.[5]

There is also early evidence for the actual compilation of hadith. For example, the Umayyad caliph ʿUmar ibn ʿAbd al-ʿAzīz (d. 101 AH/720 CE) called for the compilation of hadith during his time. Among other commands to collect hadith, he wrote in a letter to his governor in Madinah, Abū Bakr ibn Ḥazm, instructing him to, "Accept nothing other than the hadith of the Prophet."[6]

Sunnah as practice differs from written or oral validation, or the hadith literature. Practice depends on established practice and is not necessarily validated from written or oral documentation. The documenting of the Sunnah was maintained through oral and written tradition. Writing, however, was to aid memory, not necessarily for establishing the validity of a tradition.[7]

However, at the end of the second century we see the first comprehensive collections of narrations in book form. The most famous was the *Muwaṭṭā'* of Imam Mālik. Thereafter, the *musnad* collections began, with the chain of narrators being listed in the hadith. By this time, the traditions of the Prophet were narrated and recorded with their chains. Thereafter, compilation of the *jāmiʿ* collections was established. Here, not only the chain was important but also an evaluation of the narrators in the chain to determine the probable authenticity of a particular narration. In the centuries that followed, it was generally agreed upon that there were six canonical collections of hadith. These were Bukhārī (d. 256 AH/870 CE), Muslim (d. 261 AH/875 CE), Abū Dāwūd (d. 275 AH/888 CE), al-Tirmidhī (d. 279 AH/892 CE), Ibn Mājah (d. 283 AH/887 CE) and al-Nasā'ī (d. 303 AH/915 CE).[8]

SCIENCE OF HADITH CRITICISM

The early development of hadith criticism primarily focused on the structure of the chain and the evaluation of the narrators of the tradition. Specialists in the field developed a highly complex system by which to judge the narrators in the chain of transmission to determine the level of their trustworthiness in conveying a particular hadith. This science, the *al-ᶜadl wa al-tarjīḥ* (impugnment and validation) contributed to the classification of alleged hadith from authentic to fabricated. The highest level of authenticity were those hadiths that reached the status of *mutawātir*.

The general principle behind the reliability of the hadiths which reached the status of *mutawātir* was that they were transmitted in the first three generations on such a large scale, with multiple chains of narration, that the chance of fabrication was inconceivable. Scholars differed as to how many chains were necessary to rise to this status.[9] If a hadith was not at the level of *mutawātir* it fell into the category of *āḥād*. *Āḥād* traditions were those hadith that did not reach the status of *mutawātir*,[10] and therefore, could be one chain of transmission or several.

According to most scholars of hadith, the *āḥād* traditions were further divided into two sub-categories: the *maqbūl* (accepted) and the *mardūd* (rejected).[11] The *maqbūl* in turn were broken down into *ṣaḥīḥ* (sound) and *ḥasan* (fair). Whether a hadith was *ḥasan* or *ṣaḥīḥ* depended largely in part on the integrity of the chain and the evaluation of the narrators in the chain. In other words, the level of trustworthiness of the narrators in the chain and the overall integrity of the chain, along with the scholars' methodology of evaluation, resulted in the appropriate categorization of the hadith.

Along with this determination was the principle that both the chain and the *matn*, the chain and content of the hadith, also had to be sound. It has been argued that although the *matn* also had to have been sound, the hadith scholars did not develop or focus their attention on developing a system by which the *matn* could be analyzed. For example, Khaled Abou El Fadl, citing Ibn Khaldūn, observed:

> When it comes to reports, if one relies only on the [method] of transmission without evaluating [these reports] in light of the principles of human conduct, the fundamentals of politics, the nature of civilization, and the conditions for social associations, and without comparing ancient sources to contemporary sources and the present to the past, he could fall into errors and mistakes and could deviate from the path of truth. Historians, [Qur'anic] interpreters and leading transmitters have often fallen into error by accepting [the authenticity of certain] reports and incidents. This is because they relied only on the transmission, whether of value or worthless. They did not [carefully] inspect [these reports] in light of [fundamental] principles of [historical analysis] or compare the reports to each other or examine them according to the standards of wisdom or investigate the nature of beings. Furthermore, they did not decide on the authenticity of these reports according to the standards of reason and discernment. Consequently, they were led astray from the truth and became lost in the wilderness of error and delusion.[12]

While Ibn Khaldūn outlined some of the challenges faced in evaluating a tradition, the numerous criteria he proposed are mostly untenable. Further, it would be incorrect to hold that no analysis of the *matn* was undertaken by hadith scholars. Any hesitancy by the scholars to work out and develop a comprehensive detailed approach to *matn* stemmed possibly from their fear of being conclusion-driven or subjective in their understanding of the hadith. In other words, the science of hadith criticism focusing on the narrators and the integrity of the chain of transmission lent itself to a more objective evaluation of a particular hadith. The principles of evaluating the chain were established, those principles were applied to a particular narration, and the resulting tradition was graded accordingly – whether the scholar was inclined to agree to the content (i.e., the *matn*) of the resulting tradition was irrelevant.

However, scholars did emphasize the importance of the text also being sound and not just the chain. As Ibn Abī Ḥātim al-Rāzī state:

> The goodness of a dinar is known when it is measured against another. Thus if it differs in redness and purity, it will be known that it is counterfeit. A diamond is evaluated by measuring it against another one. If it

> differs in brilliance and hardness, it will be known to be glass. The authenticity of hadith is known by its coming from reliable narrators and the statement itself must be worthy of being a statement of Prophethood.[13]

Principles by which the scholars of hadith evaluated the *matn* of a hadith included the following: fanciful statements the Prophet could not have made; statements that were against reason and history; statements that contradict the Qur'an or *mutawātir* traditions; statements that promised disproportionate reward for minor good deeds and vice versa; statements that violate the rules of Arabic grammar; and traditions that were unbefitting to the prophetic office.[14]

In addition to identifying suspect hadith based on the *matn*, various methods were developed when an apparent conflict between hadith occurred. This was the science of *mukhtalif al-ḥadīth* (conflict in hadith) and *mushkil al-ḥadīth* (difficulty in hadith).[15] This science attempted to reconcile apparently conflicting hadith, via the various tools of textual analysis including *ta'wīl* (interpretation to reconcile conflicting hadith), *takhṣīṣ* (a method by which one is reconciled with the other through particularization of the general), and *al-jamʿ wa al-tawfīq* (reconciling through providing background information to particularize the hadith to a specific set of circumstances). The scholar needed not only a strong background in hadith but also in the sciences of fiqh and *uṣūl al-fiqh*.

When a conflict could not be resolved, scholars such as al-Suyūṭī proposed the following methodology. If the chronology of the conflicting hadith could be determined then *naskh* (abrogation) would take place, by which the later hadith would have abrogated the earlier hadith. If it were not possible to determine the chronology, then the rules of preference – *al-tarjīḥ* – would be invoked. Al-Suyūṭī outlined a series of factors by which preference could be guided, which include the following:

- Conditions of narrators – ages, knowledge, number, etc – stronger narration should take preference.
- Clarity of language used in narration.
- Whether the narration is verbatim verses conceptual.
- Preference to time – *madanī* take preference to *makkī*.

- Wording of hadith – specific takes preference to general, literal to metaphoric, one that expounds cause to one that does not, explicit over implicit, verbal to the actual, longer to the shorter, etc.
- Prohibition takes preference over permissibility, imposition of penalty, over one that does not.
- Preference to hadith that complies with the Qur'an and other *aḥādīth*.[16]

When not possible to determine a preference, the hadith would be suspended (*al-tawaqquf*), whereby the conflict remained unresolved but no action was to be taken based on the hadith. The order, therefore, of the methodology for the evaluation of apparently conflicting authenticated hadith (as this occurs only in dealing with *maqbūl* traditions) is reconciliation, abrogation, preference, then suspension.

An example of reconciliation occurs in the following analysis. In the *Sunan* of Ibn Mājah is a reported hadith that states, "O My Lord! Help me live as a pauper, let me die as a pauper, and resurrect me among the paupers."[17] This hadith appears to conflict with several hadith and verses from the Qur'an dealing with poverty, such as the tradition narrated by ʿĀ'ishah that "the Prophet prayed to God against the evil of poverty (*fitnat al-faqr*)." In *Ṣaḥīḥ Muslim* it is also narrated that he said, "God loves His Servant who is affluent, pious, and modest." Further there is a tradition that states, "O Lord, I seek Thy refuge from disbelief and poverty."[18]

In *Sūrah al-Ḍūḥā* in the Qur'an, God says about the Prophet, "and He found you poor and made you affluent" (93:8). There are several ways to deal with the initial hadith of Ibn Mājah that apparently conflicts with the other traditions and the implications in the Qur'anic text. However, following al-Suyūṭī's categorization, one would begin with an attempt at reconciliation. This was done, for example, by Shaykh Qaradawi, where he argued that the initial hadith was to be understood metaphorically. Poverty in this tradition is meant to convey modesty and humility. Thus the traditions were reconciled with one another and the validity of the first tradition is maintained.[19]

Other traditions provided greater challenges for reconciliation and required other tools of analysis. For example, in the hadith narrated in

Abū Dāwūd we find the following: "Umm Salamah said: I was with the Messenger of God when Maymūnah was also present, at which time Ibn Maktūm turned up, and this was after we were ordered to practice veiling. So the Prophet told us to 'hide from him.' We said, 'O Messenger of God! Is he not blind? He can neither see nor recognize us!' Then the Prophet said: 'Are you blind too then? Can you not see him?'"[20] This tradition demonstrates that the Prophet forbade women from looking at men, whether they could see them or not. Yet we find in the *sīrah* and hadith literature numerous traditions of women looking at men, without condemnation of the Prophet.

Further, there is a specific hadith involving the blind companion Ibn Maktūm, where the Prophet told Fāṭima bint Qays "to observe your waiting period in the house of Ibn Umm Maktūm, for he is a blind man, you may be changing your clothes but he would not be able to see you."[21] The initial hadith is difficult to uphold and reconcile with other traditions that are in direct conflict with it. Therefore, the approach taken by some scholars classical and contemporary has been to reject the initial hadith in preference for the other evidence, which permits women to look upon men.[22]

Another example of irreconcilable conflict is an alleged hadith found in Abū Dāwūd regarding female infanticide, which states, "both the perpetrator of infanticide and its victim are in Hell." This is clearly in conflict with the Qur'anic verse "and when the female child buried alive is questioned: for what crime was she killed?" (81:8-9). There is no way to uphold the validity of the alleged hadith in light of the Qur'anic verse, and therefore the hadith is rejected.

PRINCIPLED APPROACH TO *MATN* ANALYSIS

The *matn* criticisms outlined above focus more on the tools that can be used to look at apparently conflicting statements or practices attributed to the Prophet. However, another complementary approach is based on the establishment of certain principles by which a tradition is evaluated. This approach has been invoked in the times of the Companions and the succeeding generations, although it may not have been specifically articulated as such. Qāḍī Abū Yūsuf referred to this approach in his warning during the period of proliferation of numerous forged traditions. He said, "Hadith multiplies so much so that some hadiths which are traced back through chains of transmission are not well-known to legal experts, nor do they conform to the Qur'an and the Sunnah. Beware of solitary hadiths and keep close to the collective spirit of hadith...therefore make the Qur'an and the well-known Sunnah your guide and follow it."[23]

Judging a tradition based on a principle was something that the Companions themselves had invoked at times. For example, the famous tradition of the woman who had starved her cat is found in both Bukhārī and Muslim. The cat was kept in captivity until it died of hunger and thus the woman was sent to Hell. According to one tradition, God said to her, "You did not feed the cat nor watered her while you tied her, nor did you send her out so that she could feed herself from the cast of the earth." However, in another tradition, we find ʿĀ'ishah confronting Abū Hurayrah regarding this tradition. She told him: "Are you the one who reported the hadith that 'a woman was tortured concerning a cat that she had kept in captivity and refused to feed or water the cat?'" To this he said, "I heard it from the Prophet." Then she said, "Did you know who that woman was? The woman who did so was a disbeliever. For a believer is much too honored by God Most High to let him be tortured for the sake of a cat. When you speak concerning the Prophet, you must be careful as to what you are saying."[24]

This debate between ʿĀ'ishah and Abū Hurayrah is significant because ʿĀ'ishah did not merely tell Abū Hurayrah that he made a mistake in relating the tradition. She also said that the tradition itself, as narrated by Abū Hurayrah violated a certain principle which she then articulated, "A believer is much too honored...to be tortured for the sake of a cat." She challenged the *matn* of the hadith by demonstrating how it conflicted with the principle she put forth.

In another tradition narrated by Bukhārī regarding the Night Journey (*al-isrā' wa al-miʿrāj*), ʿĀ'ishah again analyzed the narration of the event as articulated by some of the Companions based on it violating a Qur'anic verse. The relevant portion of the tradition is as follows:

> Narrated Masrūq: I said to ʿĀ'ishah, "O Mother! Did Prophet Muhammad see his Lord?" ʿĀ'ishah said, "What you have said makes my hair stand on end! Know that if somebody tells you one of the following three things, he is a liar: Whoever tells you that Muhammad saw his Lord, is a liar." Then ʿĀ'ishah recited the Verse: "No vision can grasp Him, but His grasp is over all vision. He is the Most Courteous well-acquainted with all things" (6:103). "It is not fitting for a human being that Allah should speak to him except by inspiration or from behind a veil..." (42:51).[25]

ʿĀ'ishah's strong language (using the term "liars") addressed to those who claimed that the Prophet saw his Lord on the night journey is based on her understanding of the verse: "No vision can grasp Him" and that He does not speak "except by inspiration or from behind a veil." For ʿĀ'ishah, what was articulated by some in describing what happened clearly contradicted the Qur'an and thus had to be rejected based on the Qur'anic principle. The validity, arguments, or evidence that may contradict ʿĀ'ishah's conclusion may be debated and in fact was. The point however is that she judged a tradition based on certain principles that she derived and articulated.

The use of a principled approach is commonly found in the area of theology. Many theologians adopted a certain methodology in dealing with verses from the Qur'an as well as hadith that speak about God. Positive knowledge about God had to be based on the Qur'an and hadith that reached the status of *mutawātir*. Who God is and the implications and understanding of *tawḥīd* had to be based on evidence that was free from all doubt and possible speculation or error. Thus, the requirement of Qur'anic texts and *mutawātir* hadith to establish positive knowledge. *Āḥād* traditions were to be understood within the context of the principles derived from the Qur'an and *mutawātir* traditions.

For example, ʿAbd al-Raḥmān ibn al-Jawzī in *Dafʿ Shubah al-Tashbīh bi-Akaff al-Tanzīh* established his first principles by which he evaluated verses and traditions that speak about God. The Qur'anic verse (amongst others that convey a similar meaning) "There is nothing like Him" was the guiding principle by which he looked at the various traditions narrated concerning God. In light of this clear unequivocal verse, all traditions that seem to indicate a place, space, or form for the Creator are dismissed as inauthentic due to the chain, and if the chain is sound, they are interpreted metaphorically where possible. Ibn al-Jawzī stated, "Any text [of the Qur'an and Sunnah] is only held according to its literal meaning when it is possible and feasible. If something would redirect or negate this being done, it is understood and held according to its figurative understanding."[26] In other words, literal meaning is only appropriate when it does not violate the principle that "God is not like His creation." If a tradition indicates similarity then it is either a forged hadith or one that must be interpreted in a way that does not violate the guiding principle.

For example, we find in Bukhārī and Muslim traditions references to God "laughing." For Ibn al-Jawzī, laughing is something that is done by humans and therefore it cannot be understood as referring to God. He explained those traditions by what occurs when one laughs, and then interpreted accordingly. He says: "Laughter that seizes people is merely a reference to when someone manifests the teeth that are concealed by the mouth. But this is impossible with respect to God, Glorified and Exalted is He. It is [therefore] necessary to construe it to mean, 'God manifested His generosity and graciousness.'"[27] The analysis thus breaks down into the following:

- The literal meaning of the text states that God laughs
- Laughing is something that is done by creatures
- God cannot be similar to creatures
- The tradition is either incorrect or must be interpreted metaphorically in order not to violate the initial principle – God cannot be similar to creatures

What is important to note from this line of argument is that God is not understood by gathering all traditions relating to Him and His alleged attributes and thus constructing an image of the Creator. Rather, an initial principle is established, as set forth by God Himself in the Qur'an, and then the traditions are understood within the context of that principle. Ibn al-Jawzī goes to great length in his text to show how others have begun with a principle that God is like us (although they deny this by word) and then find in various traditions and verses those that confirm this pre-conceived notion.

MATN ANALYSIS AND THE AUTHORIAL ENTERPRISE

Khaled Abou El Fadl develops a theory of hadith criticism based on what he calls the authorial enterprise.[28] For Fadl, one cannot divorce the role of the narrators in contributing to the narration of the hadith. In other words, what we have narrated to us may contain what the Prophet had said, but we heard it through people who contributed to the text of the hadith, either intentionally or not. One may have narrated a tradition in a certain way based on their own circumstances and biases, which colored their understanding and selection of narration. There was a reason why one person remembered a certain tradition, but not others. The reporters may have remembered the specific saying accurately, but failed to see the relevance in the context in which it was given, and therefore may or may not have narrated the context in which it was given. However, according to Fadl, the context itself may be critical to understanding the import of the tradition.

Further, these traditions were integrated into existing legal structures by which some may have placed more value in the tradition as compared to others. For Fadl it is unrealistic to think that one can merely state that the Prophet declared something, unless one also looks to the authorial enterprise in the chain of transmission. The Prophetic voice may be found to be stronger or less strong when the authorial enterprise is considered.

For an example of his evaluation of the authorial enterprise, Fadl looks to the tradition found in Bukhārī: "No people will succeed who entrust their affairs to a woman." According to Fadl, the majority of these reports go back to the Companion Nufayᶜ ibn al-Ḥārith, known as Abū Bakrah al-Thaqafī (d. 52 AH/672 CE). Although hadith scholars have found him trustworthy, Fadl finds his life, opinions, and hadith narrated by him as reflecting a person who is politically a pacifist and as one who sought to uphold the traditional role of men in society. For example, Abū Bakrah did not seek to get involved in the disputes between ᶜĀ'ishah and ᶜAlī, and ᶜAlī and Muᶜāwiyah. The circumstances surrounding the tradition are that the Prophet apparently said it upon hearing that a woman had assumed power in Persia.

Fadl speculates that it was possible Abū Bakrah's subjectivities caused him to mishear what the Prophet had said. It may have been that he said, "A people who are led by this woman will not succeed." But Abū Bakrah's bias caused him to have heard it as a general statement, rather than referring specifically to what was occurring in Persia.[29] For Fadl the authorial enterprise does not end with an analysis of the narrator but also to whom he narrated to and why it was popular and easily accepted. For example, was it easily accepted because this was a patriarchal society? Fadl argues that these issues raise serious doubts about the competency of the tradition, irrespective of Bukhārī's acceptance of it as authentic.

Fadl's investigation of Abū Bakrah as a narrator is rather extensive but it does contain a significant amount of speculation. Further, this approach toward critiquing a hadith makes one subject to being accused of being result-driven and subjective, rather than objectively evaluating the evidence presented. One's own biases and prejudices are also brought to the analysis of the text. One equipped with a modern education, influenced by modern (predominantly western) ideas of patriarchy could result in an analysis that is skewed in favor of one's current opinions and ideas. Such an approach could result in the allegation that one sought to investigate a hadith one was troubled by in order to undermine its alleged authenticity. The scholars of hadith of old have established their own grades of what they consider appropriate guidelines in evaluating whether someone is trustworthy or not. It is from those initial premises that they decided whether a tradition was accepted or not. This minimized the amount of bias and prejudice that the scholar brought to his analysis.

Further, not only the evaluation of those within the chain of narration and their alleged biases, but the Companions themselves become subject to criticism. This line of reasoning put forward by Fadl calls into question the accepted principle, as articulated by Ibn Ḥajar, that, "The *Ahl al-Sunnah* are unanimous that all [the Companions] are *ʿudūl*, i.e. truthful." The *ʿAdālah* is that there has been no intentional deviation from the truth. This does not mean that they were infallible (as some may understand it) but rather that they did not intentionally deviate from the truth. Fadl's critique lends to questioning this foundational principle in the transmission of hadith, for it can delve into potential motives of the Companions, which would undermine their accepted status as truthful.

However, Fadl provides a useful principle or tool that can be used in evaluating a particular hadith. This principle is that a higher standard should be employed for traditions that have a strong social impact, transcending a specific legal obligation. For example, the tradition that is reported in various forms contains the statement, "It is not lawful for anyone to prostrate to anyone. If I would have ordered any person to prostrate to another, I would have commanded wives to prostrate to their husbands because of the enormity of the rights of husbands over their wives." After citing the various versions of this tradition (at times conflicting) Fadl observes these reports reach beyond other traditions that specify narrow legal obligation; these reports explicate a fundamental principle that is supposed to impact all marriages and all gender relations. While the physical act of prostration to the husband is not permitted, the moral substance of prostration does apply through such traditions.[30]

For Fadl, this tradition and similar ones establish a widespread moral and social structure and therefore require a high level of scrutiny. According to Fadl, "In considering each report, we need to think about the effect or impact of applying this report in a normative fashion, and the greater the impact, the stricter the scrutiny. The greater the impact the heavier the burden of proof that a report will be required to meet."[31]

The principle of the impact of a report on social norms in shaping a society can be somewhat objectively applied. In other words, any report that has a strong and broad social impact should cause one to pause before acting upon it. It should not be accepted merely because it is found in one of the six canonical collections. Nor should it be rejected off-hand as not meeting our sensibilities (as that would cause us to fall into the subjective), but should cause one to investigate the matter further and see if it meets a higher standard.

This approach is fairly normal in traditions that relate to *tawḥīd*. When a conscientious person comes across an authentic tradition that seems to conflict with an established principle of *tawḥīd*, one pauses before accepting it outright (or rejecting it). A conscientious individual will suspend his judgment until he or she investigates the tradition further. A principled approach is also found in the area of *Sīrah* literature as articulated by Shaykh Muhammad al-Ghazali. He "accepted the narrations whose wordings conform to the fixed principles and laws even if their chains of narrators were not sound and...[he] rejected those *aḥādīth* which are described as authentic because they do not conform to the fixed principles and laws according to... [his] understanding of Allah's religion and the methodology of the *daʿwah*."[32]

In contemporary times people have free access to nearly all the hadith collections by merely surfing the web. The traditions collected in the canonical collections are deemed by most Muslims to be authentic, especially those found in Bukhārī and Muslim. Any attempt to undermine or raise doubts as to the science of hadith criticism in the chains of transmission will prove unsuccessful, first because the compilers put forth the best human effort in determining authenticity, and second, because undermining that system will potentially undermine the whole corpus of hadith. However, if scholars establish some basic overriding principles, not necessarily to automatically reject or accept a particular tradition, but to provide a framework that would cause one to pause when they come across a particular tradition and inquire further, it may control the quick judgment people reach merely by finding a particular hadith in an authentic collection.

REFERENCES

Abū Yūsuf, *al-Radd ʿalā Siyar al-Awzāʿī*, ed. Abu al-Wafa al-Afghani (Cairo: Maktabat Dār al-Hidāyah, 1357 AH).

Azami, Muhammad Mustafa, *Studies in Hadith Methodology and Literature* (Indianapolis: American Trust Publications, 1992).

Azami, Muhammad Mustafa, *Studies in Early Ḥadīth Literature* (Beirut: al-Maktab al-Islāmī, 1968)

Brown, Daniel, *Rethinking Tradition in Modern Islamic Thought* (Cambridge: Cambridge University Press, 2003).

Doi, Abdur Rahman I., *Hadith: An Introduction* (Chicago: Kazi Publications, 1980).

El Fadl, Khaled Abou, *Speaking in God's Name: Islamic Law, Authority and Women* (Oxford: Oneworld Publications, 2001).

Al-Ghazali, Muhammad, *Understanding The Life of Prophet Muhammad* (Riyadh: International Islamic Publishing House, 1997).

Al-Jawzī, ʿAbd al-Raḥmān ibn, *The Attributes of God Dafʿ Shubah al-Tashbih Bi-Akaff al-Tanzih*, Abdullah bin Hamid Ali, trans. (Bristol: Amal Press Ltd., 2006).

Kamali, Muhammad Hashim, *A Textbook of Ḥadīth Studies* (Leicester: Islamic Foundation, 2005).

Al-Ṣalāḥ, Al-Shahrazūrī ibn, *An Introduction to the Science of the Ḥadīth* (Reading: Garnet Publishing, 2006).

Siddiqi, Muhammad Zubayr, *Ḥadīth Literature: Its Origin, Development and Special Features* (Cambridge: Islamic Texts Society, 1996).

NOTES

1 See, e.g., Daniel Brown, *Rethinking Tradition in Modern Islamic Thought* (Cambridge: Cambridge University Press, 2003).

2 See, for example, Qur'an (4:59) and (3:164).

3 See Brown, *Rethinking Tradition*, pp.10-12.

4 This was not the only means, as the practices of the Companions and subsequent generations also reflected the practices of the Prophet.

5 Muhammad Zubayr Siddiqi, *Ḥadīth Literature: Its Origin, Development and Special Features* (Cambridge: Islamic Texts Society, 1996), p.6.

6 Muhammad Hashim Kamali, *A Textbook of Ḥadīth Studies* (Leicester: Islamic Foundation, 2005), p.28.

7 Muhammad Mustafa Azami, *Studies in Early Ḥadīth Literature* (Beirut: al-Maktab al-Islāmī, 1968), p.20,25.

8 As of the 5th century AH this was not generally agreed upon, as is evidenced by Shahrazūrī, who lists five canonical collections, not including Ibn Mājah. See Ibn al-Ṣalāḥ al-Shahrazūrī, *An Introduction to the Science of the Ḥadīth* (Reading: Garnet Publishing, 2006), p.22.

9 See Kamali, *A Textbook of Ḥadīth Studies*, pp.169-170.

10 *Āḥād* is sometimes mistakenly translated as "solitary" or "single transmission" giving the impression that there is only one chain of transmission.

11 Muhammad Mustafa Azami, *Studies in Hadith Methodology and Literature* (American Trust Publications, Indianapolis 1992), p.61.

12 Ibn Khaldūn referred more generally to the transmission of history and not necessarily just the transmission of hadith. See Khaled Abou El Fadl, *Speaking in God's Name: Islamic Law, Authority and Women* (Oxford: Oneworld Publications, 2001), p.110.

13 See al-Azami, *Studies in Hadith Methodology and Literature* (Indianapolis: American Trust Publications, 1992), p.57.

14 See Siddiqi, *Hadith Literature*, p.114; and Abdur Rahman I. Doi, *Hadith: An Introduction* (Chicago: Kazi Publications, 1980), p.32.

15 See Kamali, *A Textbook of Ḥadīth Studies*, pp.109-122.

16 Ibid., p.110.

17 Ibid., p.113.

18 Ibid.

19 Ibid.

20 Ibid., p.114.

21 Ibid.

22 Of course this would be conditional upon the look not invoking unlawful desire.

23 Abū Yūsuf, *al-Radd ʿalā Siyar al-Awzāʿī*, ed. Abu al-Wafa al-Afghani (Cairo: Maktabat Dār al-Hidāyah, 1357 AH).

24 See Kamali, *A Textbook of Ḥadīth Studies*, pp.115-116.

25 *Ṣaḥīḥ al-Bukhārī*, 60:378.

26 ʿAbd al-Raḥmān ibn al-Jawzī, *The Attributes of God: Dafʿ Shubah al-Tashbīh bi-Akaff Al-Tanzīh*, Abdullah bin Hamid Ali, trans. (Bristol: Amal Press Ltd., 2006), p.43.

27 Ibid., p.82.

28 See El Fadl, *Speaking in God's Name*, Chapter Four: "The Text and Authority."

29 See El Fadl, *Speaking in God's Name*, p.113.

30 See El Fadl, *Speaking in God's Name*, pp.212-213.

31 Ibid. p.88.

32 Muhammad al-Ghazali, *Understanding The Life of Prophet Muhammad* (Riyadh: International Islamic Publishing House, 1997), p.15.

9

Post-Divorce Financial Support from the Islamic Perspective (Mutᶜat al-Ṭalāq)

MOHAMAD ADAM EL SHEIKH

INTRODUCTION

THE subject of this paper is post-divorce financial support and its affinity to *Mutᶜat al-Ṭalāq*, as we know it in Islamic jurisprudence. The target audience is Muslim jurists who should fully appreciate the fairness and justice of Islamic Shariᶜah law in all matters, including the care of women in general and divorced Muslim women in particular. As such, Muslim jurists should strongly uphold the right of divorcee women, as illustrated in the Qur'an and applied by the Prophet, and work jointly to develop an effective approach for reviving Qur'anic and prophetic injunctions pertaining to post-divorce financial support, both for the protection of contemporary divorced Muslim women in general, and those in the western hemisphere in particular.

Predominant scholastic understanding and prevailing judicial applications in the Muslim world today indicate that women are not entitled to any post-divorce financial support (*mutᶜat al-ṭalāq*), property settlement, or indeed any wealth of their household accumulated during the course of their marital life. The pretext being that the shelter, food and clothing provided by husbands during marriage fully exhausts any share ex-wives can expect to receive post-marriage. This understanding considers women as being only entitled to three months of spousal support during the religiously prescribed waiting period known as *ᶜiddat al-ṭalāq*.

As a former judge of Shariᶜah courts in Sudan, as a former resident imam of one of the largest Islamic centers in the U.S., as an Islamic adjudicator and arbitrator for the Muslim community for more than twenty years in North America, I have encountered and been involved in numerous cases of this nature. In addition, I have witnessed the injustices imposed against divorced women and their suffering due to the neglect of Islamic rules of post-divorce financial support (*mutʿat al-ṭalāq*). This un-Islamic and inhumane treatment of divorced Muslim women affected me deeply motivating a desire to study the issue for myself in the interests of women and to examine the correct Islamic position with regards to compensation.

Although the Qur'an addresses the subject in several verses, and the Sunnah confirms its application during the lifetime of the Prophet, as well as his Companions, and the Successors, nevertheless the issue has become one of the most marginalized and neglected elements of Islamic transactional jurisprudence.

Mutʿah is an Arabic term which linguistically means enjoyment and happiness as opposed to gloominess, depression, and grief. Idiomatically, it refers to the post-divorce financial support, or post-divorce payment, made by a divorcer to a divorcee, in an attempt to uplift the divorcee's sense of self-esteem (many women unfortunately feel a sense of social humiliation associated with the term "divorced woman") and tone down the negative impacts of the divorce.

Although this definition reflects the psychological component of the aftermath of divorce, it does not inclusively cover the fact that *mutʿat al-ṭalāq* is first the right of the divorcee from the accumulated wealth of the household whereof she was part and a full partner in ownership. In accordance with Islamic Shariʿah, *mutʿat al-ṭalāq* is one of the three fixed rights due to women beside their owed shares of inheritance. Altogether these rights are thus: dowry on the occasion of marriage; maintenance provided throughout the course of the marriage; *mutʿat al-ṭalāq* after occurrence of the irrevocable divorce;[1] and their allocated shares of inheritance upon the death of the husband.

POST-DIVORCE SUPPORT (*MUTʿAT AL-ṬALĀQ*) IN THE QUR'AN

Mutʿat al-Ṭalāq is profoundly rooted in the divine Scripture as clearly illustrated in the following Qur'anic verses:

> There is no blame on you if you divorce women before consummation or the fixation of their dowry; but bestow on them provision [*matiʿuhunna*], the wealthy according to his means and the poor according to his means; such [*matāʿan*] of a reasonable amount is due from those who wish to do the right thing. (2:236)

> And for divorced women is a suitable [*matāʿun]*. This is a duty on the righteous. (2:241)

> O, Prophet, say to your wives: "if you desire the life of this world and its glitter, then come! I will make a provision for you and set you free in a handsome manner" [i.e. divorce you all]. (33:28)

> O you who believe! When you marry believing women and then divorce them before you have touched them, no prescribed waiting period should be imposed on them, but grant them the *mutʿah* and set them free in a handsome manner. (33:49)

QUR'ANIC COMMENTARIES ON *MUTʿAT AL-ṬALĀQ*

It is remarkable that most existing commentaries of the Qur'an are largely identical, not only in terms of meaning and concepts employed, but also on many occasions the words used.

Tafsīr al-Ṭabarī

It is worth noting that one of the oldest Qur'anic commentators, Imam al-Ṭabarī, in his commentary on the foregoing Qur'anic verses, strongly advocated the rights of women with regards to the *mutʿah*. He sturdily defended his belief that payment of *mutʿat al-ṭalāq* to a divorced woman was an obligation on the husband by virtue of these Qur'anic verses. After detailing the different opinion of jurists on the matter, he states, "I believe what represents the truth among all of the above jurists' arguments is the argument of those who say that post-divorce *mutʿah* is mandatory for all divorced women, because Allah has said: 'For all divorced women *mutʿah* is a duty on the *muttaqīn*.'"[2]

Al-Ṭabarī was an authoritative, not a passive jurist, meaning that unlike many other jurists who simply reiterated / repeated what had been reported by others he remained independent expressing his viewpoints intellectually, honestly, rationally, and even sometimes aggressively, refuting the faulty arguments of his opponents. He was quoted in his *tafsīr* as saying:

> It is my conviction that post-divorce *Mutᶜah* is an obligatory payment on the husband who divorced his wife, and he is liable to pay her *mutᶜat al-ṭalāq* just like he is liable to pay her due dowry, and he will never be exonerated from such obligation until he pays her or her proxies or heirs, and that *mutᶜat al-ṭalāq* is like other debts that are due to her, and the husband is subject to incarceration and his property can be sold for not paying his divorced wife her post-divorce due *mutᶜah*.[3]

Tafsīr al-Qurṭubī

Muḥammad ibn Aḥmad al-Anṣārī al-Qurṭubī's[4] commentary of the Qur'an is among the most famous of his works. Imam al-Qurṭubī's commentary on the Qur'anic verses in question is among the more instructive, and like al-Ṭabarī, he demonstrates his independent opinion with regards to post-divorce *mutᶜah*. Although a Mālikī (one of the four schools of Islamic jurisprudence) scholar like other North West African jurists, (he was from Cordoba), his independent conscience enabled him to depart from the prevailing fetters of the Mālikī School with regards to women's post-divorce right to *mutᶜah* such that where Imam Mālik considered post-divorce *mutᶜah* to be not mandatory but rather just recommended, al-Qurṭubī nevertheless did not endorse Imam Mālik's or indeed any other Mālikī jurists view on this matter audaciously declaring his dissatisfaction with the position.

Hence, although Mālik, Judge Shurayḥ, and other jurists considered it as a non-binding Islamic rule, regarding it as recommended only, al-Qurṭubī quoted ᶜAbd Allāh ibn ᶜUmar, ᶜAlī ibn Abī Ṭālib, Saᶜīd ibn Jubayr, and other prominent scholars of the Successors who held that the rule of *mutᶜat al-ṭalāq* had come in the form of a command and therefore was a binding rule (*wājib*). Al-Qurṭubī continued to state that the supporters' argument was based on the wording of the Qur'anic verse as an imperative and binding command from Allah, while the second party did not deny that the wording was in command form, but based its understanding of its implementation in terms of to whom it was addressed, claiming that the verse addressed the *muḥsinīn* and the *muttaqīn* only, so it was binding only upon the *muḥsinīn* (righteous people) and the *muttaqīn* (pious people of means). Further, they stated that if *mutᶜat al-ṭalāq* had been a binding Islamic rule, it would have been imposed on all people, not only on the righteous and pious.

After having discussed these conflicting opinions, al-Qurṭubī strongly endorsed the first party's viewpoint, mentioning the second party's argument to be indefensible, because the contextual indication and understanding thereof demonstrated that the command of *mutᶜat al-ṭalāq* referred to divorcees, and the preposition letter (*lām*) in the word (*li al-muṭallaqāt*) was a possessive letter and an indicative element that gives divorced women an undeniable right to their post-divorce financial shares.

Furthermore, al-Qurṭubī pointed out that *muḥsinīn* and *muttaqīn* in fact emphasize and further assure the right of divorced women to post-divorce *mutᶜah*, because to be a *muḥsin* and a *muttaqī* is a duty on all Muslims. He then refuted the opinion of jurists who believed that *mutᶜah* was prescribed for women whose marriage had not been consummated and whose *mahr* had not been fixed, jurists such as i.e. Ibn ᶜAbbās, Ibn ᶜUmar, Jābir ibn Zayd, al-Ḥasan, ᶜAṭā' ibn Rabāḥ, Isḥāq, Imam al-Shāfiᶜī, Imam Aḥmad, etc.[5]

Tafsīr Ibn Kathīr

Abū al-Fidā' Ismāᶜīl Ibn Kathīr,[6] in addition to what he shares with other commentators, added some considerable points in his famous *tafsīr*. First, he defined *mutᶜat al-ṭalāq* by saying that *mutᶜah* was something paid by the husband to his divorced wife, according to the husband's means, so as to compensate the divorced wife for what she lost due to the divorce. He then quoted ᶜAbd Allāh ibn ᶜAbbās who determined the amount of *mutᶜat al-ṭalāq*, saying, "...If the husband is wealthy, he should compensate his divorced wife by providing her with a servant or the like, but if he is of limited resources then he should provide her with four pieces of clothing." He defines the clothing by quoting al-Shābī, one of the successor jurists, who determined the amount of *mutᶜat al-ṭalāq* to be "a vest, a head scarf, a blanket, and a dress."

Tafsīr Fakhr al-Rāzī

Imam Fakhr al-Dīn al-Rāzī[7] one of the most prominent jurists of his time was in favor of the opinion of jurists who believed that *mutᶜat al-ṭalāq* was not an optional matter but fittingly mandatory. According to his understanding, both Imam Abū Ḥanīfah and Imam al-Shāfiᶜī supported the opinion of *mutᶜat al-ṭalāq* being obligatory on the husband. His comments on verse (2:236) divide divorced women into three categories:

- Women divorced before the fixation of a dowry and before the consummation of marriage. For these *mutᶜah* is mandatory by husbands upon divorce.
- Women divorced after the fixation of a dowry but before the consummation of marriage. For these no *mutᶜah* is due but they are entitled to 50 percent of the fixed dowry.
- Women divorced after the fixation of a dowry and after the consummation of marriage. For these *mutᶜat al-ṭalāq* is mandatory.

Imam al-Rāzī quoted ᶜAbd Allāh ibn ᶜUmar as saying that *mutᶜat al-ṭalāq* was prescribed for all divorced women. Al-Rāzī did not hesitate to support his argument by the same points made by al-Qurṭubī, mentioned earlier, then added that the preposition letter *ᶜalā* in Arabic indicates that the matter in question is neither optional nor recommendable, but rather is obligatory.[8]

Tafsīr al-Zamakhsharī

Al-Zamakhsharī[9] is also among the most famous jurists and scholars of Islam. In his well-accepted *tafsīr* known as *al-Kashshāf*, he comments on the foregoing Qur'anic verses quoting the opinion of Saᶜīd ibn Jubayr, Abū al-ᶜĀliyah, and al-Zuhrī, jurists who believed *mutᶜah* to be mandatory compensation due to all divorced women. Al-Zamakhsharī does not endorse their opinion. Rather, like other commentators, he supported Mālik, who believed post-divorce support to be mandatory only for women divorced before the consummation of marriage, and only recommendable for other divorcees.[10]

Tafsīr al-Manār

Tafsīr al-Manār by Shaykh Rashid Rida,[11] a relatively modern twentieth century scholar, conversely discusses and impressively defends the enforcement of post-divorce support. Rida supported scholars who endorsed the eligibility and the right of divorced women to post-divorce support as a mandatory duty upon the divorcing husband.[12]

THE ROLE OF TRANSLATION OF THE QUR'AN

There is no doubt that translators of the Qur'an have done a great service to humanity in their attempt to understand and then render the meaning of the Qur'an from its original Arabic into other languages.

However, translation alone cannot convey the exact meaning of certain Qur'anic terms. Therefore, speakers of Qur'anic Arabic, translators of Qur'an, as well as end users of the translation should join hands in helping one other to understand the exact intended meaning of certain Qur'anic terms and terminologies. This should occur preferably before the final stage of the translation production process and of course before publication, in order to avoid some vital mistakes in terminology, particularly when the meaning of a specific word determines the rights of a human being, in which case the accuracy of the translation becomes crucially imperative.

For instance, most Qur'anic translators have translated the term *mutʿah* as a gift. Some translators have taken this erroneous translation from earlier translators apparently, out of respect and good faith.

We know that there exist Five Rules of Islamic Law: *ḥalāl* (lawful or permitted); *ḥarām* (unlawful or not permitted); *mandūb* (Sunnah); *makrūh* (disapproved but lawful); and *mubāḥ* (permissible). According to Islamic law, "gift" does not fit into the first or third category. Rather, it is classified under the last category, *mubāḥ*. However, Muslim jurists have determined that a gift is not a mandatory transaction, but rather a social non-binding transaction, unless and until it is fully acquired by the recipient, when it would be governed by another form of rules. Moreover, in accordance with Islamic Shariʿah law, a gift has its own jurisprudential rules which differ completely from that of post-divorce financial support.[13]

POST-DIVORCE FINANCIAL SUPPORT FROM THE PERSPECTIVE OF THE SUNNAH

In accordance with the Prophetic Sunnah, the Prophet was married to a woman known as ʿUmrah, daughter of Yazīd, son of John, from the tribe of Kilāb, but due to an uncertain reason the marriage was not consummated. Upon divorcing her, the Prophet paid her what was due according to her post-divorce right and sent her back to her family. In this Prophetic practice, we learn that despite the short time she spent in the Prophet house, when he pronounced an irrevocable divorce upon her, he granted her post-divorce *mutʿah.*[14] In another Prophetic narrative, a man from the al-Anṣār married a woman from the tribe of Ḥanīf, but divorced her before the consummation of the marriage. The Prophet commanded him to pay her post-divorce financial support (*mutʿah*).[15] Many of the Prophet's Companions, including ʿUthmān Ibn ʿAffān, ʿAbd al-Raḥmān ibn ʿAwf, judge Shurayḥ, and Ḥasan ibn ʿAlī ibn Abī Ṭālib gave *mutʿah* to their divorced wives.[16]

POST-DIVORCE FINANCIAL SUPPORT FROM THE PERSPECTIVE OF MUSLIM JURISTS

Muslim jurists hold two different opinions on post-divorce financial support. Some jurists regard it as mandatory (*wājib*), in the first category of Islamic rulings; and some as *mundūb* (recommendable), in the second category of rulings. However, in terms of practicality, Muslim jurists do not hold post-divorce support as obligatory. Even those who believe it to be a mandatory command from Allah do not advocate it, much less apply it. The principle is almost totally ignored, and buried under the prevailing rubble of custom.

Ninety percent or more of our revered jurisprudential resources were either compiled or can be traced back to the second century after the hijrah – more than twelve hundred years ago – during the time of Imam Abū Ḥanīfah,[17] Imam Mālik, and Imam al-Shāfiʿī.[18] Until now in some Muslim countries and in remote isolated villages, it has been customary for divorced women, along with their children, to be returned back to their family home, where they are accommodated and financially supported by the extended family. However in today's society many women have to fend for themselves and earn an income to support themselves and their children. In circumstances such as these compensation for divorce becomes even more important because the safety net of extended family systems is fast eroding.

Imam Abū Ḥanīfah[19]

The Ḥanafī Jurisprudential School is the oldest Sunni school of fiqh. The prevailing opinions of its jurists endorse post-divorce support as mandatory (*wājib*) in two cases. The first is in the case of *al-mufāwadah*,[20] referring to a woman married without fixation of a dowry and divorced before consummation of the marriage. In this case post-divorce financial support is mandatory, because it is a substitute of her right to 50 percent of the dower (*mahr*). The Qur'an states that there is no blame if a man divorces a woman before consummation or fixation of the dower, but mentions bestowing on her a suitable gift, the wealthy according to his means and the poor according to his means (2:236).

The second is in the case of a divorced woman whose *mahr* was fixed but who was divorced before consummation of the marriage:

> O you who believe! When you marry believing women and then divorce them before you have touched them, no prescribed waiting period (*ᶜiddah*) should be imposed on them, but grant them the *mutᶜah* [post-divorce support] and set them free in a handsome manner. (33:49)

The Ḥanafī position is not precisely clear with regard to divorcee women in other situations. According to the majority of Ḥanafī jurists, post-divorce support is just recommendable.[21] This position drives many Muslim jurists, judges, and common people to treat post-divorce support as an optional matter.

Imam Mālik Ibn Anas

Imam Mālik[22] and the majority of his disciples state that post-divorce support is not mandatory at all but is instead recommendable for all divorced women except those with fixed dowries and who were divorced before the consummation of the marriage. Women with a fixed dowry are not entitled to *mutʿat al-ṭalāq*.[23]

The argument provided by the Mālikī school to justify the dispensability of post-divorce support is based on the words *muḥsinīn* and *muttaqīn*, which say *mutʿah* is mandatory only for these two categories of people. The best repudiation of the Mālikī school position is that of Imam al-Qurṭubī, a Mālikī jurist, who as discussed earlier truly represented the Mālikī school in his reply meaning that his opinion represents the best juristic opinion in the Mālikī school.

Imam al-Shāfiʿī

Al-Shāfiʿī's recent and most publicly publicized opinion holds that any divorced woman who is not the direct reason for the divorce is entitled to post-divorce support.[24] Although al-Shāfiʿī's opinion on this matter has been reputed as the most balanced among the Islamic jurisprudential schools, he did not offer a blank check to all divorcee women. He found that divorcee women fall into two categories (listed below) with those eligible for post-divorce financial support falling under category A, as opposed to B.

Category A:

- A woman divorced without any fault on her part
- A woman whose divorce occurs before fixing of the *mahr* and before the consummation of marriage
- A woman divorced via a competent court due to the husband's impotence
- A woman divorced due to her husband's bad attitude or his physical and mental cruelty
- A woman divorced due to a husband's desertion
- A woman divorced due to her husband's failure to secure necessary maintenance for her
- A woman divorced due to *ʿillāh* (that is chronic sickness) or *ẓihār* (an ancient Arab custom, where the husband foreswears any marital relations with his wife, declaring her to be "like the back of his mother)" undertaken against her by her husband.

Category B:

- A divorced woman whose dowry has been fixed but whose marriage has not been consummated.
- A woman who demands a *khulʿa* divorce (divorce sought by the wife through a Muslim judge).
- A woman whose marriage has been revoked by a competent court due to her being accused by the husband of having an extramarital affair (*mulāʿanah,* an Islamic legal term meaning the mutual act of swearing an oath is carried out before a judge when a husband accuses his wife of adultery and cannot prove it with four witnesses. see Yusuf Ali commentary on 24:6-7).
- A woman whose divorce was based on a defect attributed to her.
- A woman who chooses to divorce her husband over maintaining her marriage with him.[25]

Furthermore, like all other human life paradigms, mutual benefit is the central point of human interactions, which is true even in the relations between parents and their children as suggested in the Qur'an: "...You know not whether your parents or your children are nearest to you in benefit...." (4:11). As such, marriage in Islam is based on benefit reciprocity. Spouses should know that a useless person in the family and in the community can be tolerated only for a limited period before people start to feel that his very existence has turned burdensome.

It is natural that a husband desires to have children and enjoy a physical and personal life, but if due to chronic illness or the like, his wife cannot bear him children or falls short physically, husbands should not divorce their wives for this reason. Divorcing a wife due to what is out of her control is a gross betrayal of the matrimonial bond. In the best interests of children and the extended family, husbands should remain married. At the same time, women with chronic health disorders such as these should not deprive their husbands of taking another wife. Not doing so would otherwise furnish a ground for losing their post-divorce financial support.

Ibn Ḥajar al-ʿAsqalānī states that a Qur'anic verse[26] was revealed to address such type of family disputes: "If a wife fears cruelty or desertion on her husband's part, there is no blame on them if they arrange an amicable settlement between themselves, and such settlement is best, even though men's' souls are swayed by greed, but if you do good and practice self-restraint, Allah is well-acquainted with all that you do."[27]

Husbands and wives who are undergoing this kind of trial should apply the wisdom of Sawdah bint Zamʿah, the wife of the Prophet. When she grew old and lost her strength and beauty, in recognition of the norm that Allah has created in the nature of men, she handed over her spousal rights to ʿĀi'shah, the youngest wife of the Prophet.

Aḥmad Ibn Ḥanbal[28]

The Ḥanbalī jurisprudential position towards post-divorce support is almost the same as those of the Ḥanafī and Shafiʿī schools.[29] ʿAbd al-Raḥmān al-ʿĀṣimī al-Najdī al-Ḥanbalī highlighted the consensus between the three major Islamic jurisprudential schools as he pointed out the similarities among them.[30] In his famous *Majmūʿ Fatāwā*, Shaykh al-Islām Imam Ibn Taymiyyah states that ʿAbd Allāh ibn ʿUmar, Imam al-Shāfiʿī, and Imam Aḥmad ibn Ḥanbal all considered post-divorce support (*mutʿah*) to be mandatory for every divorced woman, except those divorced after the fixation of the dowry but before consummation of the marriage. For such divorcees with a fixed dower, no post-divorce support was required.

In contrast, Imam Ibn Taymiyyah makes an excellent point, this being that as Islamic Shariʿah considers a marriage contract the reason for the prerogative of acquiring a bridal dowry *mahr al-nikāḥ*, likewise divorce is the reason for the prerogative of acquiring post-divorce support, *mutʿat al-ṭalāq*. He states that married women whose dower had not been fixed were entitled to a *mahr* similar to that of her peers based on the marriage contract, and such prerogative was to be delivered even after the death of the husband. He then quotes the case of *Barwaʿ bint Wāshiq*, whose husband died before her dower had been fixed, and the Prophet awarded her the *mahr* of her peers.[31] After discussing the opponents' arguments against post-divorce support (*mutʿah*), he reports the other opinion of Imam Aḥmad ibn Ḥanbal stating that the accurate opinion reported from Imam Aḥmad is what was previously quoted, which described post-divorce support as mandatory for each divorced woman.[32]

During Ibn Taymiyyah's time, the need for imposing post-divorce support was less pressing than in our present time. In his time, social consolidation and extended family accommodations were in full operation. Today, in many cases, divorced women have no such places of refuge and no financial means to support themselves or their children.

ASSESSMENT OF POST-DIVORCE FINANCIAL SUPPORT

Regrettably, our predecessor jurists left us with a very limited legacy on the subject of assessment for post-divorce financial support, and almost nothing on property settlement. Most assessments were reported from either the Companions of the Prophet, such as ʿAbd Allāh ibn ʿAbbās and al-Ḥasan ibn ʿAlī or there is the incident of the Prophet himself when he divorced one of his wives before consummation of the marriage, gave her *mutʿah* and asked Abū Usayd to take her to her family:

> Al-Bukhari reported in his Sahih that Sahl bin Sa`d and Abu Usayd said that Allah's Messenger married Umaymah bint Sharahil. When she was brought to the Prophet he extended his hand to her, but she did not like that. The Prophet then ordered Abu Usayd to provide provisions for her along with a gift of two garments.[33]

ʿAbd Allāh ibn ʿAbbās was reported to have assessed post-divorce financial support for a woman who had been married to a wealthy man, stating that she was entitled to a servant man or woman, and that a woman who was married to a man of limited income was entitled to three or four pieces of clothing.

Wahbah al-Zuhayli, a prominent contemporary Muslim jurist, reported all the opinions of highly regarded Muslim jurists on the matter of post-divorce financial support, in his famous book *al-Fiqh al-Islāmī wa Adillatuhu*. According to al-Zuhayli, post-divorce financial support is based on the financial and social status of the couple, as in the prevailing jurist opinion (fatwa) on this matter that purports if the couple is from a wealthy and high background, the divorcee's compensation should be in accordance with this, and if the couple is of limited income, then the divorcee shall be entitled accordingly, and if the couple are from different social backgrounds, the divorcee shall be granted the average between the two.

In his conclusion, al-Zuhayli seems to support the opinion of Imam Abū Ḥanīfah, Imam Mālik, and Imām Shāfiʿī with regard to the assessment of post-divorce financial support. He states that the assessment of the financial support should depend on the discretion of the trial judge. He also hints that there should be no ceiling for post-divorce financial support (amount of *mutʿah*) because the Qur'an does not put a limit on it.[34]

The strongest evidence with regards to the assessment of post-divorce financial support is the hadith of ʿAbd Allāh ibn ʿAbbās, which determines that the highest type of post-divorce support is to give the divorcee a servant, the second to provide her with sustenance, and the lowest to clothe her.[35]

The assessment of post-divorce financial support made during the time of Ibn ʿAbbās in cash or in kind would not necessarily suit our present time because we do not own slaves/servants or process our transactions in *dirhams* and *dinārs* as during the lifetime of the Prophet, his Companions, and Successors. However, comparing the living costs in both eras would provide a standardized criterion on which to process the assessment, enabling us to determine the satisfactory amount of post-divorce financial support that should be paid by the economically more fortunate husband vis-à-vis the less fortunate one.

In addition to using Ibn ʿAbbās's hadith as supportive evidence, Ibn Kathīr made two important points that represent an important breakthrough in determining post-divorce financial support in kind and in cash, taking into consideration that Ibn Kathīr lived in the seventh century after the Hijrah – 656 years ago – when owning a servant was tantamount to owning a house in our time. Therefore, if Ibn Kathīr believed that a divorced woman whose husband was wealthy was entitled to a servant who would serve her and her dependents for the rest of her life and be inherited by her children after her death, then we can easily deduce that in our modern time a divorced woman whose husband is wealthy should be entitled to no less than a house to shelter her and her dependents for the rest of her life and be inherited by her children after her death.[36]

In the process of determining the level of financial support, one should not ignore the financial contributions of divorced women to the household and their contribution to accumulated assets during the marriage. Women's financial contributions to household expenditures should be taken into consideration, besides their help in a husband's business, care for their husband and children, household work such as cleaning, cooking, laundry, and dishwashing, etc.

The western socio-economical style of life, which Muslim communities residing in the West inevitably imbue an element of as part of the western structural fabric, is based on family cooperation among the adult members of the household. Often, both the husband and wife work fulltime with in some cases, one or both having more than one job and usually a joint bank account. Therefore, they jointly share the expenses of life and equally enjoy the surplus of their earnings. If their marital life ends for any reason, then all the real and personal assets, in principle, should be subjected to a communal division.

This state of affairs in principle, disturbs some Islamic Shariʿah rules, including, but not limited to, the principles of financial independence of the spouses, the Islamic rules of inheritance (where the share of the wife is only one fourth, or one eighth in case of the presence of a child, see Qur'an 4:12), the rules of guardianship (*al-qiwāmah*), and eventually, the rule of one-sided spousal support.

POST-DIVORCE FINANCIAL SUPPORT: REFLECTIONS THROUGH CASE STUDY

Outlined below are two sample case studies concerning issues related to post-divorce financial support and property settlement in Muslim communities in North America to illustrate the serious problems facing Muslim families in the West, and to support the most viable solution based on the Qur'an and Sunnah, both of which call for adherence to fairness and justice. Both cases have been widely publicized among Muslims in America and in the American media: one concerns a Muslim family in Detroit, Michigan, whose case was adjudicated by the Shariʿah Scholar Association of North America (SSANA), and the second concerns a Muslim family in Bethesda,

Maryland, whose case was adjudicated by a courthouse in the State of Maryland.

Case Study #1

This involved a couple who had been married overseas and then emmigrated to the United States, where they lived and raised their children. Both the husband and wife were medical doctors, and had accumulated considerable wealth in cash and real estate, worth millions.

After some time, the husband proposed that his wife quit practicing as a physician and stay at home, to care for him and their children. She accepted the proposal and quit. Some years later, the husband decided to divorce the wife for personal reasons. Once she learned of his intention, she was disturbed and wanted to secure physical custody of their minor children and obtain some post-divorce financial support. She thought of hiring a lawyer to help her in court, but the husband convinced her that resorting to American courts would be against the Islamic Shariʿah and that an alternative solution allowing adjudication of the matter in accordance with the Shariʿah in a way that would satisfy both of them would be better. Both parties willingly appeared before the Shariʿah Scholars Association of North America (SSANA) for an Islamic arbitration. The couple signed a prepared binding arbitration agreement.

The arbitration panel conducted all the prerequisite legal procedures, including family history, the husband's abusive attitude, annual business income, the best interests of the children, and so forth. The panel found the husband guilty of the following:

- Being abusive to his wife and children
- Planning to inflect a despotic divorce against the wife for no justification other than her age
- Deceiving his wife into accepting an Islamic Shariʿah law that would entitle her to three months of post-divorce support, known as the ʿ*iddah* period

The panel rendered its judgment as follows:

- The wife to be granted an Islamic divorce effective from the date of the judgment.
- The wife to be granted one million dollars in cash from the husband's accumulated assets as her post-divorce financial support, including her *ʿiddah* period expenses.
- The wife to be granted one of the two mansions [they owned] with all furniture therein.
- The wife to be granted physical custody of the minor children.
- The wife to be granted child support on a monthly basis.

Upon reading the verdict, the husband crumpled the paper containing the verdict, before the panel, saying, "This is trash, this is not Islam." He immediately called me and asked for my intervention, as I was the chairman of the Islamic Judiciary Council of SSANA. I advised him to settle the case with his wife outside the court through reconciliation, to facilitate my intervention. He rejected the idea and hired two lawyers to fight the case before the state court. He lost the case in Detroit and asked his lawyers to appeal the verdict. While his lawyers pursued a lawsuit against SSANA's judgment and against his wife, he went to Al-Azhar in Egypt and to Saudi Arabia to get a fatwa against the verdict, but failed.

I do not know what answers he obtained from Muslim scholars in Egypt and Saudi Arabia, but he lost the case before the state courts, as the trial court upheld our arbitrational judgment. The plaintiff's lawyers filed at the special Appellate Court of Michigan, but I assume the lawyers advised him of the likelihood that the Appellate Court would uphold the Islamic arbitration ruling. Therefore, before the Appellate Court decided on the case, the plaintiff called me again requesting review of the verdict. I simply reiterated the same recommendation as before. The husband accepted my advice, humbly met his ex-wife and was able to persuade her to enter into a bilateral agreement with him upon which she agreed to withdraw all pending cases, demands or litigations against him.

Case Study #2

This case was widely publicized by the American media in June 2008.

It concerns a family law case where both parties were Muslims from Pakistan. It is one example of an increasing number of cases of this type in the Muslim community across the United States. I entertained some cases of this nature while I was a Shariʿah court judge in Sudan, as well as here in the United States, as an Islamic arbitrator, and have similar cruel divorce cases pending on my desk.

In cases such as these the parties involved are invariably Muslim immigrants from various Muslim countries, of different socio-economic levels and cultural backgrounds. Common factors among them are consistently the following:

- Evasion of post-divorce financial support and property settlement prescribed by the Qur'an and Sunnah in favor of their divorced wives.
- Invocation of family law from back home, erroneously labeling it Shariʿah law, whilst everybody is fully aware of the motive behind their attempts to revoke the marriage at home, rather than in the US, that is to save them money, satisfy their self-image and deprive their divorcees of their due rights unjustly.
- A vindictive attitude of revenge by the husbands against their wives and minor children who are the most vulnerable victims of these cruel divorces. We find husbands divorcing their wives at their country's consulate office, or sending wives back home to their country of origin via a one way ticket, only to a few weeks later send them a letter of divorce, after blocking their access to visas so as not to allow them a way back to the U.S. anymore.

Returning to the issue of the second case study. The parties in question had married in 1980 in Karachi, Pakistan. Shortly after the marriage, the husband moved to the UK, the wife joining him later, where they lived for four years while he completed his studies. They then moved to the United States and began to reside in Maryland while the husband worked at the World Bank. They maintained a residence in the US for twenty years. Eventually the wife filed for divorce in the US and the husband went to the Pakistani Embassy and performed *Ṭalāq*. The parties had two children, both of whom were born and resided in the US. The wife was now a resident of Maryland, holding a green card status.

According to the *Washington Post*, the court of Maryland declined to "afford comity" to the Pakistani divorce (Comity is a legal term relating to international Law that governs various Countries respect to each other's legal system). The alleged Pakistani marriage contract and the Pakistani statutes addressing the division of property upon divorce conflicted with Maryland's public policy and the Maryland courts would not afford comity to such contracts and foreign statutes.

From the *Post*: Farah Alim filed a case suit for a limited divorce from her husband, Irfan Alim in the Circuit Court for Montgomery County. The husband thereafter filed an answer and counterclaim, raising no jurisdictional objections. Without, however, any advance notification to the wife, and while the Montgomery County action was pending (between the filing of the action for a limited divorce and the filing of the amended complaint for an absolute divorce), the husband, a Muslim and a national of Pakistan, went to the Pakistan Embassy in Washington, D.C., and performed divorce (*Ṭalāq*) by executing a written document that stated: "Now this deed witnesses that I the said Irfan Alim, do hereby divorce Farah Alim, daughter of Mahmud Mirza, by pronouncing upon her divorce/*Ṭalāq* three times irrevocably and by severing all connection of husband and wife with her forever and for good."

The petitioner posited that the performance by the husband of *Ṭalāq* under Islamic religious law and under secular Pakistan law, and the existence of a "marriage contract" deprived the Circuit Court for Montgomery County of jurisdiction to litigate the division of the parties' marital property situation in the US. The trial court found that the marriage contract entered into on the day of the parties' marriage in Pakistan specifically did not provide for the division of marital property and thus, for that reason alone, the agreement did not prohibit the Circuit Court for Montgomery County from dividing the parties' marital property under Maryland law.

The court of Special Appeals agreed "thus, the Pakistani marriage contract in the instant matter is not to be equated with a premarital or post-marital agreement that validly relinquished, under Maryland law, rights in marital property" (*Alim v. Alim*, 175 Md. App. 663, 681, 931 A.2d 1123, 1134 (2007)). The court of Special Appeals further stated:

> If the Pakistani marriage contract is silent, Pakistani law does not recognize marital property. If a premarital or post-marital agreement in Maryland is silent with respect to marital property, those rights are recognized by Maryland law. . . . In other words, the 'default' under Pakistani law is that Wife has no rights to property titled in Husband's name, while the 'default' under Maryland law is that the wife has marital property rights in property titled in the husband's name. We hold that this conflict is so substantial that applying Pakistani law in the instant matter would be contrary to Maryland public policy (*Id.* At 681, 931 A.2d at 1134).

The "marital property" as it would be defined under Maryland law included the husband's pension from the World Bank valued at approximately $1,000,000, real property valued at $850,000, personal property valued at approximately $80,000, and two or more vehicles. The primary property focus in the present case was the petitioner's pension, which was titled only in the husband's name. This stark discrepancy highlights the difference in the public policies of the US state and the public policies of Islamic law, in the form adopted as the civil and secular law of countries such as Pakistan.

Under Pakistani law, unless the agreement provides otherwise, upon divorce all property owned by the husband on the date of the divorce remains his property and "the wife has [no] claim thereto." The opposite is also applicable. The husband has no claim on the property of the wife. In other words, upon the dissolution of marriage, the property follows the possessor of its title.

The central issue in the present case concerned the wife's attempt to obtain the husband's pension from the World Bank, which related primarily to his work performed while a resident of the US, declaring it to be "marital property," and to have the other property declared marital property and thus be entitled to half of that pension and property under Maryland law.

"Comity," in the legal sense, is neither a matter of absolute obligation nor of mere courtesy and good will, but is the recognition one nation allows within its territory to the legislative, executive, or judicial acts of another nation, due both to international duty and convenience, and to the rights of its own citizens, or of other persons who are under the protection of its laws. A judgment affecting the status of persons, such as a decree confirming or dissolving a marriage, is recognized as valid in every country, unless contrary to the policy of its own law.

The court found the *Ṭalāq* divorce of countries applying Islamic law, unless substantially modified, to be contrary to the state's public policy. The court declined to give *Ṭalāq*, as presented in this case, any comity. The court found further that Pakistani statutes which regarded division of property upon the dissolution of marriage to be governed by whose name the property was titled in, unless there existed an agreement(s) specifying otherwise, conflicted with state laws where, in the absence of valid agreements otherwise or in the absence of waiver, marital property is subject to fair and equitable division. Thus, the Pakistani statutes were found wholly in conflict with state public policy as expressed in its statutes, and the court afforded no comity to those Pakistani statutes.

Additionally, the husband was found to confer insufficient due process to his wife, by evading a divorce action begun in the state by rushing to the embassy of a country recognizing *Ṭalāq* and, without prior notice to the wife, performing "I divorce you..." three times and thus summarily terminating the marriage and depriving his wife of marital property. Hence, for this additional reason, the courts of Maryland did not recognize the *Ṭalāq* divorce performed.

CONCLUSION: URGENT CALL TO MUSLIM JURISTS

Muslim jurists should take a proactive role in reviving the application of post-divorce support (*mutᶜat al-ṭalāq*) as it has been clearly decided by the Qur'an and the Sunnah. There are numerous reasons for reinforcing the application of post-divorce support, in our modern time. A few are given below:

- It is a command of Allah as reported in a number of verses in the Scripture.

- It has been supported and illustrated by the Sunnah, the Companions of the Prophet, and the Successors.
- It is a manifestation of the profoundly rooted Islamic principle of justice and fairness for all in general and towards women in particular.
- It is in the best interests of minor children, largely the first victims of arbitrary subjective divorces.
- It serves as a means of deterring all kinds of harm that divorced women may fall victim to, women who today are crying out for help, but receiving none.
- Finally it is an implementation of the Prophet's recommendation (*waṣiyyah*) made to his Ummah on the Day of ʿArafah during the Prophet's Ceremonial Declaration known as the farewell Pilgrimage Sermon.[37]

Besides these reasons, Muslim jurists should consider the growing trend of married women working full-time outside the household by the consent of their husbands, while caring for the household, their children and husbands. If men usually work from eight to ten hours a day, then these women work sixteen to twenty hours a day.

According to ongoing practices in Muslim communities, in the case of divorce all properties and accumulated assets go to the husband. Is it fair to deprive these women of their Islamically-prescribed post-divorce support and financial settlement?

In the same vein when a Muslim woman gives up her education or her career/profession in order to marry and look after the husband, the children, and the home, or works for many years in her husband's business, then is it an equitable act upon divorce to kick her out of the house and the business and leave her with no post-divorce financial support and property settlement?

These issues are fundamental and critical, they impact on human lives and have far reaching consequences. As such I urge Muslim jurists to face this emerging challenge fully, to apply the fairness and justice of Islamic Shariʿah law in all matters, and to protect all the rights of women.

REFERENCES

Ahmad, Muhammad Ibn, *Hāshiyat al-Dusūqī ʿAlā al Sharḥ al-Kabīr* (Cairo, Egypt: Dār Iḥyā' al-Kutub al-ʿArabiyyah, n.d.), vol. 2.

Al-Asimi, Abd al-Rahman ibn Qasim, *Ḥāshiyāt al-Rawdh al-Murbiʿ, Sharḥ Zād al-Mustaqniʿ*. 4th edn (n.d.), vol. 6. (The author completed this work on in Ramadan, 1400 AH in Riyadh).

Al-ʿAsqalānī, *Fatḥ al-Bārī ʿalā Saḥīḥ al-Bukhārī, Book of Marriage* (Cairo: Dār al-Rayyān li al-Turāth), vol. 9.

Abu al-Fidā', Ibn Kathīr, *Tafsīr al-Qur'ān al-ʿAẓīm*, 2nd edn. (Damascus: Dār al-Faybah, n.d.), vol. 1.

Ibn Taymiyyah, Taqiyy al-Dīn, *Majmūʿ al-Fatāwā* (Madinah, Saudi Arabia: Majmaʿ al-Malik Fahd li Ṭibāʿat al-Muṣḥaf al-Sharīf, 1995), vol. 37.

Al-Mawsūʿah al-Fiqhiyyah, by Kuwaiti Ministry of al-Awqaf (Endowment), (Kuwait: Dhāt al-Salāsil Press, 1417 AH/1996), vol. 45.

Al-Nās, Ibn Sayyid, *ʿUyūn al-Āthār fī Funūn al-Maghāzī wa al-Shamā'il wa al-Siyar* (Beirut: Dār al-Agād al-Jadīdah, n.d.), vol. 1.

Al-Nawawī, Muḥiyy al-Dīn Abī Zakariyyah Yaḥyā ibn Sharaf, *Minhaj al-Talibin: A Manual of Muhammadan Law According to the School of Shafii*, Translated by E. C. Howard from the French translation of L. W. C. Van Den Berg (London: W. Thacker & Co., 1914).

Al-Qurṭubī, Muḥammad ibn Aḥmad al-Anṣārī, *Al-Jāmiʿ li Aḥkām al-Qur'ān*, 3rd edn. (Beirut: Dār al-Kitāb al-ʿArabī, 1999), vol. 3.

Al-Rāzī, Fakhr al-Dīn, *Tafsīr al-Kabīr* (Beirut: Dār al-Fikr, 1995), vol. 5.

Rida, Rashid, *Tafsīr al-Manār* (Beirut: Dār al-Fikr, n.d.).

Al-Sarkhaṣī, Shams al-Dīn, *Al-Mabsūṭ* (Beirut: Dār al-Maʿārif, 1913), vol. 5.

Shabun, Abdel Karim, *Sharḥ Mudawwanah al-Aḥwāl al-Shakhṣiyyah al-Maghribiyyah* (Rabat: Maktabah al-Maʿārif, 1987), vol. 1.

Al-Ṭabarī, Muḥammad ibn Jarīr, *Jāmiʿ al-Bayān ʿan Ta'wīl āy al-Qur'ān*, Ahmad Shakir, ed. (Beirut: Mu'assassat al-Risālah, 2000), vol. 2.

Al-Wani, Nashwah, *Mawsūʿat Aḥkām al-Mar'ah al-Muslimah* (Damascus: Dār al-Maktabī, 2002), vol. 2.

Al-Zamakhsharī, Abū al-Qāsim Maḥmūd ibn ʿUmar, *Al-Kashshāf ʿan Ḥaqā'iq al-Tanzīl wa ʿUyūn al-Aqāwīl fī Wujūh al-Ta'wīl* (Damascus: Dār al-Fikr, n.d.), vol. 1.

Al-Zuhayli, Wahbah, *Al-Fiqh al-Islāmī wa Adillatuhu* (Damascus: Dār al-Fikr, 1985), vol. 7.

NOTES

1 Abdel Karim Shabun, *Sharḥ Mudawwanah al-Aḥwāl al-Shakhṣiyyah al-Maghribiyyah* (Rabat, Morocco: Maktabath al-Maʿārif: n.d.), vol. 1.

2 Muḥammad ibn Jarīr al-Ṭabarī, *Jāmiʿ al-Bayān ʿan Ta'wīl āy al-Qur'ān*, 1st edn., (Beirut, Lebanon: Resaalah Foundation, 1415 AH, 1994), vol. 2, pp.81-100. Also in al-Qurṭubī, *al-Jāmiʿ li Aḥkām al-Qur'ān*, (Beirut, Lebanon: Dār Iḥyā' al-Turāth al-ʿArabī, 1405 AH, 1985), vol. 3, pp.196-208 and pp.227-229.

3 Muḥammad ibn Jarīr al-Ṭabarī, *Jāmiʿ al-Bayān ʿan Ta'wīl āy al-Qur'ān*, Ahmad Shakir, ed. (Beirut: Mu'assassat al-Risālah, 2000), vol. 2, pp.80-82.

4 Muḥammad ibn Aḥmad al-Anṣārī al-Qurṭubī, (d. 671 AH), *Al-Jāmʿ li Aḥkām al-Qur'ān* (Beirut: Dār al-Kitāb al-ʿArabī, 1387 AH/1967).

5 Muḥammad ibn Aḥmad al-Anṣārī al-Qurṭbī, *Al-Jāmiʿ li Aḥkām al-Qur'ān*, 3rd edn. (Beirut: Dār al-Kitāb al-ʿArabī, 1999), vol. 3, pp.200-201.

6 Abū al-Fidā' Ismāʿīl ibn Kathīr, (d. 774 AH), *Tafsīr al-Qur'ān al-ʿAẓīm* (Damascus: Dār al-Faqīh, n.d.).

7 Fakhr al-Dīn al-Rāzī, (544-604 AH), *Tafsīr al-Kabīr* (Beirut: Dār al-Fikr, 1415 AH, 1995), vol. 3, pp.146 and 174.

8 *Ibid*, vol. 5, pp.150-151.

9 Abū al-Qāsim Maḥmūd ibn ʿUmar al-Zamakhsharī, (467-538 AH).

10 Abū al-Qāsim Maḥmūd ibn ʿUmar al-Zamakhsharī, *Al-Kashshāf ʿan Ḥaqā'iq al-Tanzīl wa ʿUyūn al-Aqāwīl fī Wujūh al-Ta'wīl* (Beirut: Dār al-Fikr, n.d.), vol. 1, p.337.

11 Rashid Rida was a Syrian-Egyptian jurist, 1865-1935.

12 Rashid Rida, *Tafsīr al-Manār* (Beirut: Dār al-Fikr, 1947), vol. 2, pp.430-431.

13 See translation of (2:236) in Abdullah Yusuf Ali's and King Fahad's translations, among others.

14 Ibn Sayyid al-Nās, *ʿUyūn al-Āthār fī Funūn al-Maghāzī wa al-Shamā'il wa al-Siyar*, (Beirut: Dār al-Agād al-Jadīdah, n.d.), vol. 1, p.389.

15 Ibid.

16 See al-Qurṭubī, *Al-Jāmiʿ li Aḥkām al-Qur'ān*, vol. 3, pp.201-203.

17 Imam Abū Ḥanīfah, d. 150 AH.

18 Imam al-Shāfiʿī, born on the day Imam Abū Ḥanīfah passed away.

19 Imam Abū Ḥanīfah (al-Nʿumān ibn Thābit), 80-148 or 150 AH.

20 See *al-Mawsūʿah al-Fiqhiyyah*, by Kuwaiti Ministry of Endowment, 1st ed. (Kuwait: Dār al-Ṣafwah Press, 1417 AH / 1996), vol. 36, pp.94-95.

21 Shams al-Dīn al-Sarkhaṣī, *Al-Mabsūṭ* (Beirut: Dār al-Maʿārif, 1913), vol. 5, p.62.

22 Imam Mālik ibn Anas, (93-179 AH).

23 Al-Qurṭubī, *Al-Jāmiᶜ li Aḥkām al-Qur'ān* (Beirut: Dār Iḥyā' al-Turāth al-ᶜArabī, 1405 AH / 1985), vol. 3, p.200.

24 See his position on post-divorce financial support summarized in *Mudawwanah al Aḥwāl al-Shakhṣiyyah a Maghribiyyah* (Rabat: 1987), pp.248-250

25 See Ibid, and Shabun, Abdel Karim, *Mudawwanah al-Aḥwāl al-Shakhṣiyyah* (Rabat: Maktabat al-Mᶜārif, 1987), vol. 1, pp.249-250.

26 See (4:128).

27 See *Fatḥ al-Bārī ᶜalā Saḥīḥ al-Bukhārī* by al-ᶜAsqalānī, *Book of Marriage* (Cairo: Dār al-Rayyān li al-Turāth), vol. 9, p.312.

28 Imam Aḥmad ibn Ḥanbal, 164-241 AH.

29 See *al-Mawsūᶜah al-Fiqhiyyah*, 1st ed., vol. 36, p.94.

30 Abd al-Rahman ibn Qasim al-Asimi, *Hāshiyāt al-Rawdh al-Murbiᶜ, Sharḥ Zād al-Mustaqniᶜ*, 4th edn (n.d.), vol. 6, p.393.

31 See the collection of Taqiyy al-Dīn ibn Taymiyyah, *Majmūᶜ al-Fatāwā* (Madinah, Saudi Arabia: Majmaᶜ al-Malik Fahd li Ṭabaᶜat al-Muṣḥaf al-Sharīf, 1995), vol. 32, p.27; and Shams-al-Dīn al-Sarkhaṣī, *Al-Mabsūṭ* (Beirut: Dār al-Mᶜarifah, 1406AH/ 1986), pp.61-63.

32 See Ibid, and for Imam Aḥmad's other opinion see Nashwah al-Wani, *Mawsūᶜat Aḥkām al-Mar'ah al-Muslimah* (Damascus: Dār al-Maktabī, 2002), vol. 2, p.837.

33 *Tafsir Ibn Kathir Juz' 2 (Part 2): Al-Baqarah 142 to Al-Baqarah 252*, 2nd Edition. By Muhammad Saed Abdul-Rahman (UK: MSA Publication Ltd, 2009), p.179.

34 See Wahbah al-Zuhayli, *Al-Fiqh al-Islāmī wa Adillatuhu* (Damascus: Dār al-Fikr, 1985), vol. 7, pp.320-321.

35 Ibid., p.321.

36 Abū al-Fidā', Ibn Kathīr, *Tafsīr al-Qur'ān al-ᶜAẓīm*, 2nd ed. (Damascus: Dār al-Fayḥā' Library), vol. 1, p.387.

37 Muḥyi al-Dīn Abī Zakariyyah Yaḥyā ibn Sharaf al-Nawawī, *Minhaj al–Talibin: A Manual of Muhammadan Law According to the School of Shafii*, Translated by E. C. Howard from the French translation of L. W. C. Van Den Berg (London: W. Thacker & Co., 1914).

PART IV

10

A Muslim Approach to Western Studies of Islam

KHALEEL MOHAMMED

SEPTEMBER 11, 2001 ranks undoubtedly as one of the most horrific manifestations of terrorism in the name of religion. That catastrophe has generated a strain of Islamophobia in the West that has affected not only the media and academe but also the personal safety of Muslims. Yet, however, it is not to be assumed that prior to 9/11 there was any semblance of tolerance for Muslims and Islam. The position of the Western world, with its Eurocentric world view, was aptly summarized by an entry in the 1910 *Encyclopaedia Britannica*: "Islam is clearly repugnant to Europeans."[1]

Generations later, Professor Edward Said of Columbia University noted that he was unable to discover any period in European or American history since the Middle Ages in which Islam was discussed without passion, prejudice, or political interests.[2] In his 1997 edition of the same book, he stated: "Malicious generalizations about Islam have become the last acceptable form of denigration of foreign culture in the West; what is said about Muslim mind, or character, or religion, or culture as a whole cannot be said in mainstream discussion about Africans, Jews, other Orientals, or Asians."[3]

One may dismiss the hate literature of popular media on the grounds that such material is not subject to the demanding intellectual standards of the academic milieu. Yet, as two independent researchers have discovered, media coverage indeed affects what happens in academe. In 1995, Professor Khalid Blankenship observed:

> Even from its founding, the area of Islamic studies, which used to be described by the gradually-discredited term "orientalism," was established for the purpose of creating control through knowledge. Today...Muslims are almost never allowed to speak about Islam; rather, non-Muslim "experts" are called in, of Jewish, Christian, secularist or Arab nationalist backgrounds, all of whom are carefully selected from those who will not stray from the framework of acceptable opinions ...Thus, a university instructor is likely to find the students already completely convinced by what appears in the media and unreceptive to alternative views.[4]

Professor Kevin Reinhardt of Dartmouth College echoes the same point, noting:

> What we are confronted with instead are problems with 'pseudo knowledge.' All students who walk into an Islam class, though they profess ignorance, still "know" something about Islam – if only from the news. Every Islamicist is aware that, whether it is in the New York Daily News or on National Public Radio, it is the negative, the violent, the ignorant that characterize the images and voices presented in the media as Muslim. Garbled or dated history, plotted summaries of creeds and practices – all these are framed by distaste, dislike, or outrage. Yet, in the end, this is less a problem of fact than of affect: students arrive with a constellation of terms, mostly negative, that cluster round the notion of Islam, so that words like "terrorist" come naturally and unreflectively when they answer an exam question about, say, the Khārijīs.[5]

Given this calamitous connection between the popular news media and the academic world, in an America that is beset by a zealous nationalism characterized by the most insidious Islamophobia, it is easy to understand the gross generalizations and simplifications about Islam. This situation is exacerbated by the claim of some who see a pro-Islam bias in the academic community. As the Center for Islam and Public Policy (CIPP), a Maryland think tank, discovered, there is an ongoing debate with contradictory claims, with one position that the study of Islam is tainted with anti-Muslim bias, and the other view that the academic establishment of (Middle Eastern and) Islamic Studies in the United States has been pro-Islam.[6]

The proponents of the latter position would have us believe that the Middle Eastern Studies Association (MESA), America's largest membership organization of scholars whose work can be classified as relating to the Middle East, is guilty of "political correctness" and "inattention to radical Islam." Professors Bernard Lewis and Fouad Ajami have founded the Association for the Study of the Middle East and Africa (ASMEA), for, among other things, "studying those elements of Islam and the Middle East that MESA's leaders ignore or downplay."[7]

The CIPP project made several deeply insightful suggestions for solving the situation, including the funding of research and chairs of Islamic positions at American universities.[8] In examining the history of Islamic studies in America, CIPP found that the discipline was primarily set up in the form of area studies programs, to train experts who could assume positions of leadership in government, universities, and corporate sectors, and with focus on modern Islamic developments.[9] The CIPP study, for all its cogency, was somewhat flawed. While it addressed supposed differences between the European and American approaches, it overlooked the fact that the core texts and theories for such studies were largely the product of *Islamwissenschaft* (Islamic studies) – a German formulation that *ab initio* presented Islam as an alien, backward, and anti-Western religion and ideology.

The genesis of *Islamwissenschaft* shows its incipient negativity, and Muslim scholars have contributed to the negative state of affairs by neglecting the study of Western religion theory, terminology, and the study of the other Abrahamic religions. They have therefore allowed for outsiders to make erroneous or dubious comparisons of the Qur'an with other scriptures. By not developing a foundation in religious studies and the ability to structure adequate terminology, they often fall prey to the use of non-Muslim-designed, derogatory, political coinages in a religious setting, thereby reinforcing negative images of Islam. Following are some examples of the problem as it applies to the Qur'an and the idea of its "borrowing." By focusing on narratological analyses, Muslim researchers can refute some of the wrong ideas and play a meaningful role in removing negative images of their religion.

Unlike the situation when Edward Said made his scathing critique in 1981, Muslim professors are now part of religion departments in many universities, and one would expect that their academic training and understanding of their faith would make for a better presentation of Islam. This expectation, however, falls short for the simple reason that there is a vast disconnect between Islamic and religious studies. Islamic studies cover a large swath of topics, including politics, economics, religion, mysticism, and biographies. The end result is that many "islamicists" who are employed in the various departments of religion are not religion specialists, and, as such, they are not generally familiar with religious theory and terminology. Even if the professor has had a background from a department of religion in a Middle Eastern Islamic university, his/her approach to scripture is contrary to the norm of religious studies.[10]

Apart from the foundational issue is the added problem that some Muslim professors are not even trained in Islamic studies; they have become lecturers on the subject either because they are Arabs or claim they can teach Islam. In many instances, they do not even know Arabic, and can therefore misunderstand and misrepresent Islam.[11] One of the most pressing problems is that many Muslim professors bring either their sectarian or faith-based prejudices, and do not objectively approach their subjects. This is a particularly thorny issue since academic protocol at secular institutions requires that a professor teach objectively. Yet, as Yushau Sodiq points out, it is hard for Muslim professors to be detached completely from religious bias.[12] This implies that Muslim professors, apart from their bias regarding their own religion (forgetting the fact that they complain about the bias against Islam from non-Muslim professors), give inadequate consideration to sects to which the majority does not belong, such as Shi'i, Ahmadis, Zaydis, etc.

Clearly there is a great need for improvement in Islamic studies as a discipline within religion, and several studies have been conducted on the issue. Richard Martin wrote *Approaches to Islam in Religious Studies* in 1985, giving the viewpoints of several scholars, both Muslim and non-Muslim.[13] The Saudi-sponsored Institute for Islamic and Arabic Sciences in America (IIASA) held annual symposia on the subject from

1993-5.[14] Professor Brannon Wheeler of Bard College edited a volume that was the result of a MESA research with several distinguished specialists on methods of integrating Islamic studies into the general study of religion.[15]

THE *ISLAMWISSENSCHAFT* APPROACH

The study of religion in post-Enlightenment Germany started as *Religionwissenschaft*, which then spawned sub-disciplines of *Wissenschaft des Judentums* and *Islamwissenschaft*. It would be wrong, however, to think that the only difference between the mentioned sub-disciplines is the religion of focus. While non-Jews did play a role in *Wissenschaft des Judentums*, it was primarily the brainchild of Jews, whereas *Islamwissenschaft* was designed by non-Muslims, with Muslims being denied any role whatsoever. As Professor Amos Funkenstein explained, *Wissenschaft des Judentums* "faithfully reflected the desires and self-image of nineteenth-century Jews craving for emancipation, the mood of the "perplexed of the times."[16]

The most prominent names associated with early *Islamwissenschaft* are non-Muslim, among them Georg Freytag, Antoine Isaac Silvestre de Sacy, Abraham Geiger, Gustav Weil, Theodor Nöldeke, Aloys Sprenger, and Ignaz Goldziher, all of whom were non-Muslims and who applied the then-condescending Orientalist perspective in their examination of Islam. There is no record of any Muslim scholar being substantially associated with the initial formation of these western approaches; Fazlur Rahman in the latter part of the twentieth century was the first outstanding Muslim personality to challenge the prevailing opinions.[17]

One of the most famous early theses on Islam, completed in 1833 at the University of Marburg, was Abraham Geiger's *Was Hat Mohammad aus dem Judenthume aufgenommen?* (What Has Muhammad Taken from Judaism?). The dissertation was developed from Geiger's presentation in a competition sponsored by one of the most noted Islamophobes of the time, Professor Georg Wilhelm Freytag, himself the protégé of the French Arabist, Antoine Isaac Silvestre de Sacy. Later research was to later find several problems in Geiger's formulations.[18] He had operated largely on the idea of Islam's wholesale borrowing from Judaism, not entertaining the idea of common origins and ancient bonds between Hebrews and Arabs – a theory that was advanced by a contemporary, Heinrich Ewald. Geiger, for example, frequently posited Qur'anic borrowings from the Midrash of Pirqe de Rabbi Eliezer, not realizing that the latter document was composed after the advent of Islam.[19] Geiger's views of Islam are indeed problematic when one reflects on some of his views, such as, 'There is hardly a word for 'holy' in the Arabic language."[20] In assessing Muhammad, he seemed to have not fully availed himself of original sources, preferring rather to rely on Aloys Sprenger as "a thorough and competent investigator," and therefore describing Muhammad as having a "devotion with treachery."[21]

Geiger, a rabbi and historian, obviously wrote primarily as a Jew to bring about reform and to counteract prevalent anti-Jewish feelings. In her masterful study of Geiger, Susannah Heschel has noted that, during the Middle Ages, it was a common anti-Semitic practice to blame Judaism for the rise of Islam. Geiger's approach was not to deny any of this, but to skillfully show that in its dependence on Jewish tradition, Islam was totally a human concoction and absolutely unoriginal.[22] Whatever good that lay in Islam came from Judaism and the bad derived from the innate backwardness of Muhammad and his Arabs.[23] Based on Geiger's writings, until the ideas of Christian provenance were propounded by Richard Bell,[24] German scholars christened Islam as *Schmarotzergewächs* (a parasitic growth out of Judaism).[25] By focusing on his stories of Jewish suffering at the hands of Muslims, Geiger hoped to show, that for both Christianity and Judaism, Islam was the common enemy.

Islamwissenschaft developed in this intellectual setting, where the prevalent western academic ideas of Islam were nurtured. While Geiger presented Islam in a negative light, he was as critical of many aspects of Judaism and the traditional practice. Geiger and several other Jewish scholars were able, by their scholarly approach, to redefine in many ways the approaches to the study of Judaism. To be sure, the demonization of Jews and Judaism continued for a long time afterwards, but the contribution of Geiger and his colleagues can today be credited for the state of Jewish studies in western universities.

While the field of religious studies has evolved tremendously, and the overtly critical approach to Islam has largely been abandoned, the most consulted theories and texts in Western studies of Islam are still largely based on the writings of scholars who, knowingly or unknowingly, have coined problematic terminologies. Among such terminologies are words like "fundamentalist," "radical" and "moderate," which are three of the most-used designations in both academic and popular books. No reliable lines of demarcation have been charted to indicate the exact difference among fundamentalists, moderates, radicals, normative, and militants; nonetheless, some have postulated that approximately 10 to 15 percent of the total Muslim population is militant.[26]

Today, "fundamentalist" is an umbrella term denoting everything from the die-hard traditionalist to the militant anti-American extremist. The term is confusing, as its initial coinage arose within a Protestant Christian worldview that opposed liberal, secular viewpoints. Many Muslims, unfamiliar with the genesis of the word in its American usage and its current negativism, would willingly identify with the praiseworthy Arabic equivalent *uṣūlī* that indicates adherence to the Islamic sources, with no overtones of anti-modernity or politics. To use fundamentalism then, in religious and political discourse, and to apply the label indiscriminately equates "movements forged in radically different historical and political contexts, and obscures their doctrinal differences, including the place of violence in religious doctrine."[27]

The terms fundamentalist, radical, and moderate are meant to polarize and establish labels that can be terribly misleading. Ever since President Bush's declared war on terror, with "radical Islam" as the enemy, no right-thinking Muslim would use the term in self-description, but instead, direct it towards identifying an opponent. When Muslims use these divisive and denigrating labels, they close the doors to all forms of meaningful intra-faith discourse. Use of those terms identifies them to those whom they have so disparagingly labeled, albeit sometimes erroneously, as being inimical to their own religion and co-religionists. The identified "fundamentalists" and "radicals" would be correct in stating that the appliers of such labels, while Muslims, are often the products of western orientalist thought.[28]

One does not hear similar descriptions applied by Christians and Jews to their own; instead, one hears terms such as Orthodox, Reform, Reconstructionist, Conservative, and Born-again, none of which are designed to imply a negative image of the other.[29] Being introduced at conferences by non-Muslims as a "moderate" Muslim is a description that deems other Muslims who do not share the same viewpoints as immoderate fanatics.[30]

COMPARATIVE NARRATOLOGY

At present, more than 1,000 undergraduate departments and programs in the study of religion exist in North America.[31] The change in immigration policies in both Canada and the United States changed religious demography, with a proportional demographic shift in universities, to the point where Muslims are a noticeable presence at most universities, both as students and faculty.[32] The presence of Muslim faculty, however, has not, for reasons mentioned earlier, led to any substantial change in the approach to Islam.

Since Islamic studies is not conducted under the aegis of religious studies, the Muslim "specialists" who conduct Qur'anic studies often do so without a knowledge of western concepts (and the attendant vocabulary) of exegesis. Even when Muslim professors approach their subject from the perspective of religion, their presentations tend to focus on the pre-modern period. One hears of the exegeses of al-Ṭabarī, al-Zamakhsharī, and a host of classical scholars, but rarely does one hear of the modern discourse of Muhammad al-Ghazali or Taha al-Alwani. There is not a total eschewal of modern names; unfortunately, however, such modern studies only represent those that can be researched for their fanaticism or animosity towards the United States, typical examples being Yusuf al-Qaradawi, more notorious for his fatwa on suicide bombing than for his groundbreaking book *Al-Ḥalāl wa al Ḥarām*.

Muslim professors might waste time arguing about the Qur'an's divine provenance (a concept that cannot be proven in an academic forum), but they cannot explain the differences between Biblical and Qur'anic narratives except in a way that attributes corruption to the

Biblical version. This of course overlooks the idea of canonization and the fact that such canonization arbitrarily accepted and rejected books. In dealing with Qur'anic stories vis à vis Biblical versions, an Islamicist ought to have a good background in the forming of the Jewish and Christian canons in order to attempt any narratology.

If a professor were to present a particular religion using the terminology and jargon specific to religion, this would lead to better communication with students who are specialists in the field. For many, it seems still a difficult idea to grasp that Muslims can be sociologists and scholars of religion, and can present their own religion objectively. One of the doctrinal hurdles that presents itself for observant Muslims in academe is that western scholarship sees scripture as text and subject therefore to the same criteria of examination as any other written work. As such, they are often at a loss to understand the use of terminologies imported through interdisciplinary studies, or from within religious studies.

Examples of such terms are logocentrism, phallocentrism, reader response criticism, preterism, presentism the affective fallacy, the intentional fallacy, the hermeneutic circle, and the Divine Command theory, just to name a few.[33] Sadly, Muslim scholars, both classical and modern, have discussed most of these ideas, albeit under different terms. When their ideas are presented, however, if the scholar does not know the western term, s/he cannot draw parallels and make the necessary comparisons.

The late medieval Muslim opposition to Isra'iliyaat has continued throughout the centuries, and as such, many scholars chose not to explore the Jewish and Christian testaments, despite what might seem like Qur'anic exhortations.[34] This means that few are therefore adequately equipped to rebut the still prevailing theory of borrowing that gained fame with Abraham Geiger's thesis. This idea assumes that the shared narratives in Abrahamic religions make the supposedly earlier materials normative, and the later derivative. William Sandmel used the term "parallelomania" to describe this concept, defining it as "the extravagance among scholars which first overdoes the supposed similarity in passages and then proceeds to describe source and derivation as if implying literary connection flowing in an inevitable or predestined direction."[35]

States Marilyn Waldman, a good complement to the issue of influence and transmission studies is found in narratology, wherein one may identify the "biblical" material in the Qur'an to clarify not only the relationship of the Bible to the Qur'an, but also the art of the Qur'anic narrative itself.[36]

The borrowing theory is problematic because it does not account for the deviation between the elements of some Qur'anic and Biblical stories, and as such, there has been a rather hasty assumption that the Qur'an's versions were somehow the Prophet's misinterpretations. The story of Mary in the Qur'an illustrates this fallacious reasoning, as some have opined that the author of the Qur'an committed a historical error when having Mary addressed as "sister of Aaron."[37] Said Schwarzbaum, "We should never forget that Muhammad rarely retells exactly what he has heard from his mentors and informants. Most of the scraps of information which he has got orally from his Jewish and Christian informants...have become mixed up in his mind...[38]

The idea of Mary being brought up in the Temple is not found in the canonical gospels, but rather in the Protoevangelium, or Proto-Gospel of James, a mid-second-century work, that names Joachim and Anna as the parents of Mary.[39] While many Muslims might be happy to accept this supposed provenance, under the assumption that it therefore proves that the story is not a Qur'anic concoction, but that it was existent at an early stage, a thorough reading of the document shows several lines of departure from the Qur'anic narrative. Only knowledge of the cognate relationship between the Arabic *nadhartu*[40] and the Hebraic term *nazir*[41] gives a sense of deep meaning to the story, one that is not easily deciphered from the Protoevangelium. In the Qur'an, the mother of Mary consecrates her child to God, and her prayer is answered. Given the purity rites of the time, the mother (Anna) assumes the child will be a male, since a female would, by menstruation, defile the temple, which clarifies her exclaiming that she had given birth to a female to which the response comes in the Qur'anic *ayah*, "And the male is not like the female."[42] Without this understanding, one is forced to see the appropriateness of the *ayah* in context.

In addition, the *ayah* shows that God does not allow for gender discrimination in terms of worship, a theme adumbrated in the

Qur'an.[43] The Protoevangelium does not touch on this aspect of the story, having us believe that even from conception Anna would have welcomed a child of either gender,[44] despite no reported case of a female Nazirite in Biblical history. One sees why the Qur'an's version is significant, and why Mary's birth story would be significant, given the Arab disregard for female children at the time.[45] Even then, the Protoevangelium is provably older than the Qur'an, so attributing provenance of the Qur'anic narrative to the older document is manifestly problematic.[46]

At best, one might argue for a allusive relationship wherein the Qur'an presupposes its readers are somewhat familiar with the Protogospel version (or versions that have, while similar in content, not reached us). Attributing provenance to a written Judeo-Christian document also presupposes that the events depicted in the Bible or non-Arab Judeo-Christian literature are the only and oldest versions from which all others must have been derived. Yet the vocabulary and depiction within the Qur'an seem to refute such an idea: the issue of Arab narratives is clearly evidenced by the Qur'an wherein it describes how some of the Prophet's contemporaries referred to the stories as *asāṭīr al-awwalīn* (tales of the ancients).[47] In his dealing with the matter, Fazlur Rahman has convincingly propounded that the Qur'anic verses evidence a fairly systematic knowledge of what is termed Biblical material.[48]

That the Qur'an should accord a Judeo-Christian figure such honor is a fact often alluded to in interfaith discussions, and certainly sets the Qur'an apart from the older Abrahamic documents in terms of its pluralism and inclusivism. Certainly, modern interfaith participants often draw attention to the fact that Mary is the only woman referred to by name in the Qur'an and that she has a chapter named after her; the more in-depth analysis just discussed however is often missed.

By failing to make themselves familiar with Biblical material and the religion theories pertaining thereto, Muslims are often unable to make the intertextual connections. The story of the destruction of Sodom and Gomorrah is a good example. In the Hebrew Bible, Abraham pleads for Lot's people, presenting his case to the point where in the final verses of Genesis 18, it would seem that if ten good people were present, the city would have been spared divine punishment. If a reader of the Qur'an brings the details of this narrative (not provided in the Qur'an), when contemplating (11:70–4), then Lot's question in (11:78) can be perceived for what it actually is: not simply a plea, but trying to evoke a certain action, in response to a divine promise.

In classes on comparative themes in Abrahamic religions, students have never failed to note the difference they found in studying the Qur'anic verses when taken along with the readings of the relevant Biblical material. The judgmental, strict, litigious God of Islam that has been created in the imagination of Western Orientalists (and to a certain extent in some Muslim perception) is in fact a forgiving, affectionate Lord, certainly far more peaceful than the deity that orders the slaughter of man, woman, and child in some verses of the Bible.

A study of the creation story from both texts clearly shows this: in the Biblical version, Eve is the one who is misguided and then leads Adam astray; they are both cursed and their lot is suffering. By contrast, in the Qur'an both parties are equally blameworthy, and are forgiven. Through such studies, one can further delve into the studies of the evolution of Shariᶜah, and point out that many of the ideas of Shariᶜah are in fact the result of human reasoning, and not of divine edict. The time has come for Muslim professors to shed themselves of the inferiority complex of using texts of famous but dated Orientalist authors, and instead rely on the works of their co-religionist scholars who, trained in religion, are better suited as sources for instructional material.

While it is certainly easy to lay the blame for the sad state of Islamic studies at the feet of Orientalists, only by a new approach to Islamic studies in general, and Qur'anic studies in particular, can Muslims make any meaningful contribution to the field. Fazlur Rahman's identification of the two main problems in Muslim scholarship regarding Islam's scripture still applies: lack of a genuine feel for the relevance of the Qur'an today and a fear that such a presentation might deviate on some points from traditionally received opinions.[49] The problems are interconnected; approaching them from the perspective of Western religious studies offers a solution.

REFERENCES

Bell, Richard, *The Origin of Islam in its Christian Environment.* (London: Cass, 1968).

Blankenship, Khalid, "Islamic Studies at Universities in the United States," *Proceedings of the First Annual Symposium* (Fairfax: Institute of Islamic and Arabic Sciences in America, 1995).

Center for Islam and Public Policy, (CIPP), "Project Executive Summary: the State of Islamic Studies in American Universities: Project Executive Summary," December 2007.

CIPP, "Policy Recommendations" (Working Draft), July 2007.

Eliot, Sir Charles N. E., "Asia: History," *Encyclopaedia Britannica*, 11th edn. (Cambridge: Cambridge University Press, 1910), vol. 2.

Ehrman, Bart, *Lost Scriptures* (Oxford and New York: Oxford University Press, 2003).

Funkenstein, Amos, *Perceptions of Jewish History* (Berkeley/ Los Angeles: University of California Press, 1993).

Geiger, Abraham, *Judaism and its History* (New York: The Bloch Publishing Company, 1911).

Heschel, Susannah, *Abraham Geiger and the Jewish Jesus* (Chicago: University of Chicago Press, 1998), http://www.answeringislam.org.

Lewis, Bernard, "The Roots of Rage," *The Atlantic Monthly*, 1990. http://www.theatlanticmonthly.com/issues/90Sep/rage.htm.

Malik, Iftikhar, *Crescent Between Cross and Star* (London and Karachi: Oxford University Press, 2006).

Mamdani, Mahmoud, *Good Muslim, Bad Muslim* (New York, Pantheon Books 2004).

Martin, Richard, *Approaches to Islam in Religious Studies* (Tucson: University of Arizona Press, 1985).

McAuliffe, Jane Dammen, "Disparity and Context: Teaching Quranic Studies in North America," in *Teaching Islam*, Brannon Wheeler, ed. (Oxford & New York: Oxford University Press, 2003).

Metzger, Bruce and Michael Coogan, eds. *Oxford Companion to the Bible* (Oxford and New York: Oxford University Press, 1995).

Muhammad, Khalil, "The Art of Heeding," *Interfaith Dialogue at the Grass Roots*, Rebecca Kratz Mays, ed. (Philadelphia: The Ecumenical Press, 2008).

Murfin, Ross and Ray, Supriya, *The Bedford Glossary of Critical and Literal Terms* (Boston and New York: Bedford Books, 1997).

Rahman, Fazlur, *Islam* (Chicago: University of Chicago Press, 1979).

______, *Major Themes of the Qur'an* (Minneapolis: Bibliotheca Islamica, 1994).

Reinhardt, Kevin, "On the 'Introduction to Islam,'" *Teaching Islam*, Brannon Wheeler, ed. (Oxford and New York: University Press, 2003).

Said, Edward, *Covering Islam* (New York: Pantheon Books, 1981).

Sandmel, William, "Parallelomania," *Journal of Biblical Literature*, no.81, vol. 1, March 1962.

Schwarzbaum, Haim, *Biblical and Extra-biblical Legends in Islamic Folk-Literature* (Walldorf-Hessen: Verlag für Orientkunde Dr. H. Vorndran, 1982).

Sodiq, Yushau, "Teaching Islamic Studies in American Universities," *Proceedings of the First Annual Symposium* (IIASA Research Center: Fairfax, VA 1993-1995).

Stillman, Norman, "The Story of Cain and Abel in the Qur'an and the Muslim Commentators: Some Observations," *Journal of Semitic Studies*, vol. 19, 1974.

Stillwell, Cinnamon, "Truth about Islam in Academia?" *FrontPage Magazine*, July 2, 2008. http://www.campus-watch.org/article/id/5325.

Waldman, Marilyn, "New Approaches to "Biblical" Materials in the Qur'an," *Studies in Islamic and Judaic Traditions*, William Brinner and Stephen Ricks, eds. (Atlanta, GA: Scholars Press, 1986).

Wheeler, Brannon, "The Jewish Origins of Q 18:65-82: Reexamining Arent Jan Wensinck's Theory," *Journal of the American Oriental Society*, vol. 118, no.2, 1998.

Wheeler, Brannon, Ed., *Teaching Islam* (New York and Oxford: Oxford University Press, 2003).

NOTES

1 See Sir Charles N. E. Eliot (former British diplomat), "Asia: History" in *Encyclopaedia Britannica*, 11th edn. (Cambridge: Cambridge University Press, 1910), vol. 2, pp.749-55.

2 Edward Said, *Covering Islam* (New York: Pantheon Books, 1981), p.23.

3 Ibid., pp.xi-xii.

4 Khalid Blankenship, "Islamic Studies at Universities in the United States," *Proceedings of the First Annual Symposium* (Fairfax, VA: Institute of Islamic and Arabic Sciences in America, 1993), pp.25-29.

5 Kevin Reinhardt, "On the 'Introduction to Islam,'" in *Teaching Islam*, ed. Brannon Wheeler (Oxford and New York: University Press, 2003), pp.22-45.

6 Center for Islam and Public Policy, "Project Executive Summary: the State of Islamic Studies in American Universities: Project Executive Summary," December 2007.

7 Cinnamon Stillwell, "Truth about Islam in Academia?" *FrontPage Magazine*, July 2, 2008. http://www.campus-watch.org/article/id/5325. The term "clash of civilizations" so frequently attributed to Samuel Huntington was actually coined by Bernard Lewis in his 1990 article in "The Roots of Muslim Rage" in *The Atlantic Monthly*. Available at http://www.theatlantic.com/magazine/archive/1990/09/the-roots-of-muslim-rage/4643/4/. In a lecture by Lewis in Philadelphia in 2003, he rejected the concept by arguing that civilizations are not governments, and do not make foreign policies.

8 CIPP, "Policy Recommendations" (Working Draft), July 2007.

9 "Project Executive Summary" in *Proceedings of the First Annual Symposium*, 1993, pp.25-29.

10 For a particularly good analysis of this, see Jane Dammen McAuliffe, "Disparity and Context: Teaching Quranic Studies in North America," in *Teaching Islam*, ed. Brannon Wheeler (Oxford & New York: Oxford University Press, 2003), pp.94-107. In this article, the author analyzes a classroom experience in Jordan with that of western approaches.

11 Yushau Sodiq, "Teaching Islamic Studies in American Universities," *Proceedings of the First Annual Symposium*, 1993, pp.21-24.

12 Ibid.

13 Richard Martin, *Approaches to Islam in Religious Studies* (Tucson: University of Arizona Press, 1985).

14 Published in separate volumes as "Proceedings of the First, Second and Third Annual Symposium" (IIASA Research Center: Fairfax, VA 1993-5).

15 Brannon Wheeler, ed. *Teaching Islam* (New York and Oxford: Oxford University Press, 2003).

16 Amos Funkenstein, *Perceptions of Jewish History* (Berkeley/ Los Angeles: University of California Press, 1993), p.19.

17 See Fazlur Rahman, *Islam* (Chicago: University of Chicago Press, 1979).

18 See Norman Stillman, "The Story of Cain and Abel in the Qur'an and the Muslim Commentators: Some Observations," *Journal of Semitic Studies*, vol. 19, 1974, pp.231-239.

19 Ibid.

20 Abraham Geiger, *Judaism and its History* (New York: The Bloch Publishing Company, 1911), p.250. His summation is rather surprising and raises the question of his depth of Arabic training. The Hebrew Qoddesh is a cognate of the Arabic "Quddus."

21 Ibid., p.254.

22 Susannah Heschel, *Abraham Geiger and the Jewish Jesus* (Chicago: University of Chicago Press, 1998), p.59.

23 Abraham Geiger, *Judaism*, pp.253-255.

24 Richard Bell, *The Origin of Islam in its Christian Environment* (London: Cass, 1968).

25 Susannah Heschel, *Abraham Geiger*, p.59.

26 Iftikhar Malik, referring to Daniel Pipes in *Crescent Between Cross and Star* (London and Karachi: Oxford University Press, 2006), p.134.

27 Mahmoud Mamdani, *Good Muslim, Bad Muslim* (New York, Pantheon Books 2004), pp.34-37.

28 For a critique of this, see Fazlur Rahman, *Islam* (Chicago: University of Chicago Press, 1979), pp.251-252.

29 I am aware of the term fundamentalist in Christian discourse. That term, however, was designed by those wishing to identify themselves as being conservative, and opposed to secularism and liberal thought as earlier pointed out. Today, it is primarily used as a form of 'othering.'

30 See Khaleel Mohammed, "The Art of Heeding," *Interfaith Dialogue at the Grass Roots*, Rebecca Kratz Mays, ed. (Philadelphia: The Ecumenical Press, 2008), pp.75-86.

31 Brannon Wheeler, *Teaching Islam*, preface.

32 See Jane Dammen McAuliffe, "Teaching Qur'anic Studies in North America," *Teaching Islam*, pp.94-107.

33 Many of these terms can be found online or in Ross Murfin and Supriya Ray, *The Bedford Glossary of Critical and Literal Terms* (Boston and New York: Bedford Books, 1997).

34 As in Qur'an (16:43); (21:7).

35 William Sandmel, "Parallelomania," *Journal of Biblical Literature*, no.81, vol. 1, March 1962, p.1-13.

36 See Marilyn Waldman, "New Approaches to "Biblical" Materials in the Qur'an," *Studies in Islamic and Judaic Traditions*, William Brinner and Stephen Ricks, eds. (Atlanta, GA: Scholars Press, 1986), pp.47-64.

37 (19:28).

38 Haim Schwarzbaum, *Biblical and Extra-biblical Legends in Islamic Folk-Literature* (Walldorf-Hessen: Verlag für Orientkunde Dr. H. Vorndran, 1982), p.99. See also http://www.answeringislam.org.

39 Bart Ehrman, *Lost Scriptures* (Oxford and New York: Oxford University Press, 2003), p.63.

40 (3:35).

41 An individual who was dedicated to special sacred service through a vow made by the individual or by a parent. See "Nazirite" in *Oxford Companion to the Bible*, Bruce Metzger and Michael Coogan, eds. (Oxford and New York: Oxford University Press, 1995), p.552.

42 (3:36).

43 Further underlined in (3:195).

44 In *The Protevangelium of James: The Birth of Mary*: 4.

45 (16:58); (81:8).

46 Another excellent article for disproving parallelomania is Brannon Wheeler's "The Jewish Origins of Q 18:65-82? Reexamination of Arent Jan Wensinck's Theory," *Journal of the American Oriental Society*, vol. 118, no.2, 1998. pp.153-171.

47 (27:68).

48 Fazlur Rahman, *Major Themes of the Qur'an* (Minneapolis: Bibliotheca Islamica, 1994), pp.150-161.

49 Ibid., p.xii.

BIBLIOGRAPHY

Ābādī, Al-Fayrūz, *Al-Qāmūs al-Muḥīṭ* (Dār Iḥyā' al-Turāth al-ʿArabī, 2003).

Abū ʿUbayd, Al-Qāsim ibn Salām, *Al-Nāsikh wa al-Mansūkh fī al-Qur'ān al-ʿAzīz* (Riyādh: Maktabah al-Rushd, 1990).

Abū Yūsuf, *al-Radd ʿalā Siyar al-Awzāʿī*, ed. Abu al-Wafa al-Afghani (Cairo: Maktabat Dār al-Hidāyah, 1357 AH).

Addas, Claude, *Ibn 'Arabi, ou, La quete du sourfre rouge* (*Quest for the Red Sulphur: The Life of Ibn ʿArabī*), Peter Kingsley, trans. (Cambridge: Islamic Texts Society, 1993).

Afifi, A. E., "Memorandum by Ibn 'Arabi of His Own Works," Introduction, in *The Bulletin of the Faculty of Arts* (Alexandria University VIII, 1954).

Akkach, Samer, *Cosmology and Architecture in Premodern Islam: An Architectural Reading of Mystical Ideas* (Albany: State University of New York Press, 2005).

Afsaruddin, Asma, "Sunni-Shiʿi Dialectics and the Qur'an," in Khalil Muhammad and Andrew Rippin, *Coming to Terms with the Qur'an* (North Haledon, NJ: Islamic Publications International, 2008).

Aḥmad ibn Ḥanbal, *Al-Musnad Aḥmad ibn Ḥanbal*, ed. Ahmad Muhammad Shakir, edn. 1, 20 vols. (Cairo: Dār al-Ḥadīth, 1995, 1416).

Ahmad, Imad-ad-Dean, *Signs in the Heavens: A Muslim Astronomer's Perspective on Religion and Science*, 2nd edn. (Beltsville: Amana, 2006).

Al-Andalusī, Abū Muḥammad, *Al-Muḥarrir al-Wajīz fī Tafsīr al-Kitāb al-ʿAzīz*, http://www.aljamea.net/services/viewing/Preview_Books.php, (December 2, 2008).

Al-Ashqar, Muhammad, *Muʿjam ʿUlūm al-Lughah al-ʿArabiyyah* (Beirut: Mu'assassat al- Risālah, 1995).

Alkhairo, Wael, *Speaking for Change: A Guide to Making Effective Friday Sermons* (Maryland: Amāna Publications, 1998).

Almond, Ian, "Divine Needs, Divine Illusions: Preliminary Remarks

Toward a Comparative Study of Meister Eckhart and Ibn 'Arabi," *Medieval Philosophy and Theology*, vol. 10, 2001.

Aquinas, Thomas, *Summa Theologia*, 2.2ae.1.2, in John Hick, "Ineffability," *Religious Studies*, 2000, vol. 36, no. 1.

Arslan, Muhammad Shahir, *Al-Qaḍā' wa al-Quḍāt* (Beirut: Dār al-Irshād, 1389 AH/1969 CE).

Al-Asimi, Abd al-Rahman bin Qasim, *Ḥāshiyāt al-Rawdh al-Murbiᶜ, Sharḥ Zād al-Mustaqniᶜ*, 4th edn., vol. 6.

Al-ᶜAsqalānī, Ibn Ḥajar, *Forty Ḥadīth*, trans. into English by Assad Busul, (Chicago: Kazi Publication, 1982).

——, *Fatḥ al-Bārī fī Sharḥ Ṣaḥīḥ al-Bukhārī* (Riyadh, Saudi Arabia: Dār al-Aslam Press, 1997).

——, *Taqrīb al-Tahdhīb* (Beirut: Mu'assat al-Risālah, 1996).

Ates, A., "Ibn ᶜArabi." *The Encyclopedia of Islam*, new edn., Bernard Lewis et al, eds. (Leiden: E. J. Brill, 1971).

Ayoub, Mahmoud, *A Muslim View of Christianity: Essays on Dialogue*, Irfan A. Omar (ed.), (New York: Orbis Books, 2007).

——, *The Qur'an and Its Interpreters vol.* 2, [hereafter M. Ayoub Qur'an] (Albany: State University of New York Press, 1992).

——, "Qur'an As Revelation," IIIT Summer Institute Proceedings, accepted for publication, 2008.

——, "Nearest in Amity: Christians in the Qur'an and Contemporary Exegetical Tradition." *Journal of Islam and Christian-Muslim Relations.* (July, 1997).

——, "Towards an Islamic Christology, Part,1," *The Muslim World*, vol. LXVI (July, 1976) No:3, pp.163-188.

——, Religious Pluralism and The Challenges of Inclusivism, Exclusivism and Globalism: An Islamic Perspective." In Th. Sumartana et. al. (eds.), *Commitment of Faiths: Identity, Plurality and Gender* (Yogyakarta, Indonesia: Institute of DIAN/ Interfidei, 2002).

——, *The Qur'an and its Interpreters: The House of 'Imrān* (State University of New York Press, 1992), vol. 2.

Azami, Muhammad Mustafa, *Studies in Early Ḥadīth Literature* (Al-Maktab al-Islāmī, 1968).

Azmi-al-Badi, Muhammad, "ᶜAyn al-Maᶜbūd Sharḥ Sunan Abī Dāwūd" (Beirut, Lebanon: Dār al-Kutub Al-ᶜIlmiyyah, 1998).

Balbaki, Munir, *Al-Mawrid Arabic-English Dictionary* (Dār al-ᶜIlm li al-Malāyīn, 1998).

Badawi, Jamal, *The Muslim Woman's Dress* (Indiana: MSA, 1980).
Al-Baghawi, *Tafsīr al-Baghawī*. http://www.aljamea.net/services/viewing/Preview_Books.php, (December 2, 2008).
Al-Baghdādī, Abū al-Faḍl, *Rūḥ al-Maʿānī fī Tafsīr al-Qur'ān al-ʿAẓīm wa al-Sabʿ al-Mathānī*, http://www.aljamea.net/services/viewing/ Preview_Books.php, (December 2, 2008).
Balādhurī, Yaḥyā, *Futūḥ al-Buldān*, edited by Radwan Muhammad Radwan, (Beirut: Dār al-Kutub al-ʿIlmiyyah, 1403 AH/1983CE).
Bashir, Salman H., *Ibn al-ʿArabī's Barzakh, the Concept of the Limit and the Relationship between God and the World* (Albany: State University of New York Press, 2004).
Al-Bayḍawī, *Tafsīr al-Bayḍawī*, http://www.aljamea.net/services/viewing/Preview_Books.php, (December 2, 2008).
Bell, Richard, *The Origin of Islam in its Christian Environment* (London: Cass, 1968).
Blankenship, Khalid, "Islamic Studies at Universities in the United States," *Proceedings of the First Annual Symposium* (Fairfax: Institute of Islamic and Arabic Sciences in America, 1995).
Bohm, David, *Wholeness and the Implicate Order* (London: Routledge, 1981).
Brown, Daniel, *Rethinking Tradition in Modern Islamic Thought* (Cambridge University Press, 2003).
Al-Bukhārī, *Ṣaḥīḥ*.
Burton, John, *The Sources of Islamic Law: Islamic Theories of Abrogation* (Edinburgh: University of Edinburgh Press, 1990).
Busul, Assad, *Islam Relationship to Christianity and Judaism* (Chicago: American Islamic Educational Foundation, 1994).
——, *The Wise Judge* (Chicago: The Qur'an Society, 1417 AH/1997 CE).
Center for Islam and Public Policy, "Project Executive Summary: the State of Islamic Studies in American Universities: Project Executive Summary," December 2007.(Chicago Press, 1996).
Chittick, William C., "Belief and Transformation: Sufi Teaching of Ibn al-Arabi," *The American Theosophist*, vol. 74, 1986.
——, *Imaginal Worlds: Ibn al-'Arabī and the Problem of Religious Diversity* (State University of New York Press: 1994).
——, and Sachiko Murata, *The Vision of Islam* (Aragon House: New York, 1994).
Chodkiewiecz, Michel, *An Ocean Without Shore: Ibn 'Arabī, the Book, and the Law* (Albany, NY: State University of New York Press, 1993).

CIPP, "Policy Recommendations" (Working Draft), (July 2007).

Coates, Peter, *Ibn 'Arabī and Modern Thought: The History of Taking Metaphysics Seriously* (Oxford: Anqa Publishing, 2002).

Corbin, Henry, *Creative Imagination in the Sūfīsm of Ibn 'Arabī* (Princeton: Princeton University Press, 1969); or *Alone with the Alone: Creative Imagination in the Sūfīsm of Ibn 'Arabī*, new preface by Harold Bloom, 1998 (*A New Translation of the Creative Imagination*).

Dabashi, H., "Persian Sufism during the Seljuk Period," in Leonard Lewisohn, ed., *The Heritage of Sufism, Classical Persian Sufism: From its Origins to Rumi (700-1300)*, vol. 1. (Oxford: Oneworld, 1999).

Dagli, Caner (trans.), *Fuṣūṣ al-Ḥikam* (Chicago: Kazi Press, 2001).

Dārimī, Abū Muḥammad ʿAbd Allah ibn ʿAbd ar-Raḥamān ibn al-Faḍl ibn Baḥram, *Sunan*, ed. Shaykh Muḥammad Abd al-Aziz al-Khalidi, 1st edn., (Beirut: Dār al-Kutub al-ʿIlmiyyah, 1417 AH/1996 CE), 4 volumes).

Al-Dawadari, Ibn, *Kanz al-Durar wa Jāmiʿ al-Ghurar* (Wiesbaden: Qism al-Dirāsāt al-Islāmiyyah, al-Maʿhad al-ʿIlmī li al-Āthār bi al-Qāhirah, 1960-1982).

Daylamī, Shirawayh ibn Shahradār ibn Shirawayh, *Firdaws al-Akhbār*, ed. Fawwaz Ahmad al-Zamurli and Muhammad al-Mutasim billah al-Baghdadi, 1st edn., (Beirut: Dār al-Kitāb al-ʿArabī, 1407 AH/1987 CE), 5 volumes.

Al-Dhahabī, Shams ad-Dīn Muḥammad ibn Aḥmad ibn ʿUthmān, *Siyar Aʿlām al-Nubalā'*, ed. Shayb al-Arnaut, 8th edn. (Beirut: Mu'assasat al-Risālah), 25 volumes.

Dirks, Jerald F., *The Abrahamic Faiths: Judaism, Christianity, and Islam: Similarities and Contrasts* (Maryland: Amana Publications, 2004).

Doi, A. Rahman, *Hadith: An Introduction* (Kazi Publications, 1980).

——, *Women in Shari'ah* (London: Taha Publishers, 1989).

Ehrman, Bart, *Lost Scriptures* (Oxford and New York: Oxford University Press, 2003).

Eliot, Sir Charles N. E., "Asia: History," *Encyclopaedia Britannica*, 11th edn. (1910), vol. 2.

Elmore, Gerald T., *Islamic Sainthood in the Fullness of Time: Ibn 'Arabī's Book of the Fabulous Gryphon* (Leiden: Brill, 1999).

Ernst, Carl W., *Words of Ecstasy in Sufism* (Albany: State University of New York Press, 1985).

Esack, Farid, *Qur'an Liberation and Pluralism: An Islamic Perspective of Interreligious Solidarity against Oppression* (Oxford: Oneworld, 1997).

Al-Fadl, Khaled Abu, *Speaking in God's Name: Islamic Law, Authority and Women* (Oneworld Publications, 2001).

Al-Fārūqī, Ismā^cīl, *Al-Tawḥīd: Its Implications for Thought and Life* (Herndon, VA: International Institute of Islamic Thought, 1982).

Al-Fasawi, Abū Yūsuf Ya^cqūb ibn Sufyān, *Kitāb al-Ma^crifah wa al-Tārīkh*, ed. Akram Diya al-Umari (Baghdād: Maṭba^cat al-Irshād, 1394 AH/ 1974 CE), 3 volumes.

Fawad al-Barazk, Muhammad, *Ḥijābul Muslimah* (Riyadh: Maktab Aḍwā' al-Salaf, 1995).

Fishbane, Michael, *The Garments of Torah: Essays in Biblical Hermeneutics* (USA: Indiana University Press, 1992).

Funkenstein, Amos, *Perceptions of Jewish History* (Berkeley, Los Angeles: University of California Press, 1993).

Geiger, Abraham, *Judaism and its History* (New York: The Bloch Publishing Company, 1911).

Al-Gharnaṭī, Muḥammad al-Kalbī, *Al-Tahṣīl li ^cUlūm al-Tanzīl.* http://www.aljamea.net/services/viewing/Preview_Books.php, (December 2, 2008).

Al-Ghazālī, Imam Abū Ḥāmid, *Al-Munqiḍ min al-Ḍalāl* (Lahore: Hay'ah al-Awqāf bi-Ḥukūmat al-Bunjāb, 1971).

Al-Ghazālī, The Incoherence of the Philosophers, Michael E. Marmura, trans. Provo (UT: Brigham Young University, 2000).

Al-Ghazali, Muhammad, *A Thematic Commentary on the Qur'an* (Herndon, VA: The International Institute for Islamic Thought, 2000).

——, *Understanding The Life of Prophet Muhammad* (International Islamic Publishing House, 1997).

Gleick, James, *Chaos: Making a New Science* (New York: Viking Penguin, 1987).

Guillaume, A., *The Life of Muhammad* (Oxford, UK: Oxford University Press, 1978).

Haddad, Yvonne, "The Conceptions of the term *Dīn* in the Qur'ān," in *Muslim World*, vol. 74, (April, 1974).

Haithami, Nūr ad-Dīn ^cAlī ibn Abī Bakr, *Majma^c al-Zawā'id wa-Manba^c al-Fawā'id*, 3rd edn. (Beirut: Dār al-Kitāb al-^cArabī, 1402 AH/ 1982 CE), 10 volumes.

Hakim, Souad, "Ibn ʿArabī's Twofold Perception of Woman," *Journal of the Muhyiddin Ibn ʿArabi Society*, vol. 39, 2006.

Halim Abu Shuqah, Abdul, *Taḥrīr al-Mar'ah fī ʿAṣr Risālah* (Kuwait: Dār-al-Qalam, 1990), vol. 4.

Hamid, Ayub A., *Unveiling the Commands: The Truth about Hijaab, Jilbaab and Khimaar* (Ontario: Bayan Communications and Publications, 2004).

Hassab-Elnabi, Mansur, "A New Astronomical Qur'anic Method for the Determination of the Greatest Speed C," May 10, 2001, http://www.55a.net/firas/english/?page=show_det&id=297.

Heschel, Susannah, *Abraham Geiger and the Jewish Jesus* (Chicago: University of Chicago Press, 1998). http://www.answeringislam.org.

Hirtenstein, Stephen, *The Unlimited Merciful, The Spiritual Life and Thought of Ibn 'Arabī* (Oxford: Anqa Publishing, 1999).

Hodgson, Marshall, *The Venture of Islam: Conscience and History in a World Civilization* (Chicago and London: University of Chicago Press, 1974), vol. 1.

Homerin, Emil, "Ibn Arabi in the People's Assembly: Religion, Press, and Politics in Sadat's Egypt," *The Middle East Journal*, vol. 40, 1986.

Hoodbhoy, Pervez, *Islam and Science: Religious Orthodoxy and the Battle for Rationality* (London: Zed, 1991).

Houedard, Dom Sylvester, "Ibn ʿArabi's Contribution to the Wider Ecumenism," *Muhyiddin Ibn 'Arabi. A Commemorative Volume*, Stephen Hirtenstein and Michael Tiernan, eds. (Shaftesbury: Element, 1993).

Ibn ʿAbd al-Barr, Abū ʿUmar Yūsuf ibn ʿAbd Allāh ibn Muḥammad, *ad-Durar fī Ikhtiṣār al-Maghāzī wa al-Siyar*, ed. Dr. Shawqi Dayf (Cairo: Lajnat Ihyā' al-Turāth, 1386 AH/1966 CE).

____, *Bahjat al-Majālis wa al-'Uns al-Mujālis*, ed. Muhammad Mursi al-Khuli (Cairo: al-Dār al-Miṣriyyah li al-Ta'līf wa al-Tarjamah, n.d.), 2 volumes.

Ibn ʿArabī Muḥiyyu al-Dīn, *Tafsīr al-Qur'ān al-Karīm*, Edited by Mustafa Ghalib (Beirut: Dār al-Andalus, 1978), vol. 1.

____, *Al-Diwān al-Akbar* (Būlāq: 1271 AH).

Ibn ʿAsākir, *Mukhtaṣar Tārīkh Dimashq* (See Ibn Manẓūr).

Ibn al-ʿArabī, *Aḥkām al-Qur'ān* (Beirut: Dār al-Maʿrifah, 1982), vol. 4.

Ibn al-Jawzī, ʿAbd al-Raḥmān, *Nawāsikh al-Qur'ān* (Beirut: Dār-al-Kutub al-ʿIlmiyyah, n.d.).

____, *The Attributes of God*, Abdullah bin Hamid Ali, trans. (Amal Press Ltd., 2006).

Ibn al-Ṣalāḥ, al-Shahrazūrī, *An Introduction to the Science of the Ḥadīth* (Reading: Garnet Publishing, 2006).

Ibn Ḥanbal, Aḥmad, *Al-Musnad*, ed. Ahmad Muhammad Shakir and Hamzah Ahmad az-Zayn, 1st edn. (Cairo: Dār al-Ḥadīth, 1416 AH/1995 CE), 20 volumes.

Ibn Ḥazm, *On the Perfect Knowledge of Juridical Bases* (*Al-Iḥkām fī uṣūl al-aḥkām*), 8 books in 2 vols. (Cairo: 1926 – 28).

Ibn Hishām, Muḥammad, *Al-Sīrah al-Nabawiyyah* (Beirut, Lebanon: Dār al-Wifāq, 1955).

Ibn Isḥāq, Muḥammad, *The Life of Muhammad*, translation of Ibn Isḥāq's *Sirat Rasūl Allah*, translator, Alfred Guillaume (Oxford University Press, reprint 1967).

Ibn Kathīr ʿImād al-Dīn Abū al-Fidā' Ismaʿīl, *Tafsīr al-Qur'ān al-ʿAẓīm* (Beirut: Dār al-Fikr, 1970), vol. 1.

——, *Qaṣaṣ al-Anbiyā'*, ed. Mustafa Abd al-Wahid, 2nd edn., (Cairo: Dār al-Kutub al-ḥadīthah, 1398 AH/1978 CE), 2 volumes.

Ibn Mājah, Abū ʿAbd Allāh Muḥammad ibn Yazīd al-Qazwīnī, *Sunan*, ed. Muhammad Fuad Abd al-Baqi (Cairo: ʿĪsā al-Bābi al-Ḥalabī, n.d.), 2 volumes.

Ibn Manẓūr, *Lisān al-ʿArab* (Beirut: Dār al-Ṣādir li Ṭībāʿah wa al-Nashr, 1955).

Ibn Manẓūr, Muḥammad ibn Mukarram, *Mukhtaṣar Tārīkh Dimashq* of Ibn ʿAsākir, 1st edn. (Dimashq: Dār al-Fikr, 1404 AH/1984 CE), 29 volumes.

Ibn Nujaym, *Al-Baḥr al-Rā'iq*, v.1.02, al-Muhaddith Program. 11.36 (CD) available at www.muhaddith.org.

Ibn Qutaybah, Abū Muḥammad ʿAbd Allāh ibn Muslim, *ʿUyūn al-Akhbār*, (Cairo: Wizārat al-Thaqāfah wa al-Irshād al-Qawmī, al-Mu'assasah al-Miṣriyyah al-ʿĀmmah li al-Taʿlīf wa al-Tarjamah wa al-Nashr, a photocopy of Dār al-Kutub edn., 1383 AH/1963 CE, 4 parts in 2 volumes).

Ibn Taymiyyah, Taqiyy al-Dīn Aḥmad, *Al-Siyāsah al-Sharʿiyyah fī Iṣlāḥ al-Rāʿī wa al-Raʿiyyah*, ed. Qusay Muhib al-Din al-Khatib (Cairo: al-Maṭbaʿah al-Salafiyyah, 1387 AH).

——, *Majmūʿ al-Fatāwā*, vol. 37, (Majmaʿ King Fahd: 1995).

Al-ʿImādī, Abū al-Suʿūd, *Irshād al-ʿAql al-Salīm ilā Mazāya al-Qur'ān al-Karīm*, http://www.aljamea.net/services/viewing/Preview_Books.php, (December 2, 2008).

Imām Muḥy al-Dīn Abī Zakariyyah Yaḥyā ibn Sharaf al-Nawawī, al-Dimashqī, *Minhaj et-Talibin: A Manual of Muhammadan Law According to the School of Shafiʿi*. Translated by E. C. Howard from the French translation of L. W. C. Van Den Berg (London: W. Thacker & Co., 1914).

Islahi, Amin Ahsan, *Tadabbur-i-Qur'ān* (Delhi: Taj Company, 1997).

Izutsu, Toshihiko, *Creation and the Timeless Order of Things: Essays in Islamic Mystical Philosophy* (Ashland, Oregon: White Cloud Press, 1994).

——, *God and Man in the Qur'an: Semantics of the Qur'anic Weltanschuug* (Ayer Company Publishers, Inc, 1998).

Jalālyan, Jalāl al-Dīn al-Maḥallī, and Jalāl al-Dīn al-Suyūṭī, *Tafsīr al-Qur'ān al-ʿAẓīm* (Cairo: al-Maktabah al-Tijāriyyah al-Kubrā, n.d.), 2 parts in one volume.

Jaspers, Karl, *Origin and Goal of History* (New Haven: Yale University Press, 1953).

Al-Jaṣṣās, Abū Bakr, *Aḥkām al-Qu'rān* (Beirut: Dār Iḥyā' al-Turāth al-ʿArabī 1985), vol. 5.

Jayyusi, S. K., *The Legacy of Muslim Spain* (Leiden: Brill, 2000), vol. 1.

Al-Jazarī, Majd al-Dīn Abū al-Saʿādah al-Mubārak ibn Muḥammad ibn al-Athīr, *Jāmiʿ al-Uṣūl fī Aḥādīth al-Rasūl*, ed. Abd al-Qadir al-Arnaut, ed. 2, 13 vols. (Beirut: Dār al-Fikr, 1403 AH).

Jomier, Jacques, *The Bible and the Qur'an*, translated by Edward P. Arbez, (Ignatius Press: 1964).

Jeffrey, Arthur, "Ibn 'Arabī's Shajarāt al-Kawn," *Studia Islamica*, vol. 11, 1959.

Kamali, Muhammad Hashim, *A Textbook of Ḥadīth Studies* (Islamic Foundation, 2005).

Al-Kāshānī, ʿAbd al-Razzāq, *Sharḥ al-Kāshānī ʿalā Fuṣūṣ al-Ḥikam* (Cairo: 1321 AH).

Khadduri, Majid, *War and Peace in the Law of Islam* (Baltimore: The John Hopkins Press, 1955).

Khalidi, Tarif, *Arabic Historical Thought in the Classical Period* (Cambridge University Press, 1994).

Khan, Israr Ahmad, *Qur'anic Studies: An Introduction* (Kuala Lumpur: Zaman Islam Media, 2000).

Knysh, Alexander D., "Ibrāhīm al-Kurānī (d. 1101/1690), An Apologist for *wahdat al-wujūd*," *Journal of the Royal Asiatic Society*, 3rd series, vol. 5, 1995, 39-47.

Kuhn, Thomas *The Structure of Scientific Revolutions*, 3rd edn. (USA: University of Chicago Press, 1996).

Kutty, Sheikh Ahmad, http://www.islamonline.net/servlet/Fatwa EAskTheScholar, accessed on October 20, 2007.

Lane, Edward William, *An Arabic–English Lexicon*.

Lanzetta, Beverly J., *Other Side of Nothingness, Toward a Theology of Radical Openness* (Albany: State University of New York Press, 2001).

Lawrence, Bruce, *The Qur'an, A Biography* (New York: Broadway, 2006).

Lewisohn, Leonard, ed., *The Heritage of Sufism, Classical Persian Sufism: From its Origins to Rumi (700-1300)*, (Oxford: Oneworld, 1999), vol. 1.

Lewis, Bernard, "The Roots of Rage," *The Atlantic Monthly*, 1990. http://www.theatlanticmonthly.com/issues/90Sep/rage.htm.

——, *Semites and Anti-Semites* (New York, NY: W.W. Norton & Company, 1986).

Little, John T., "*Al-Insān al-Kāmil*: The Perfect Man According to Ibn al-ʿArabī," *The Muslim World*, vol. 7, 1987.

Mohar Ali, Muhammad, *A Word for Word Meaning of the Qur'an* (Oxford: Jam'iat Ihyaa' Minhaaj al-Sunnah, 2003), vol. 2.

Makdisi, George, "Ibn Taymīya: A Sufi of the Qādirīya Order," *American Journal of Arabic Studies*, vol. 1, 1973, in Muhammad Umar Memon, *Ibn Taymiyya's Struggle Against Popular Religion* (The Hague: Mouton, 1976).

Makkī, Ibn Abī Ṭālib, *Al-'Īḍāḥ li Nāsikh al-Qur'ān wa Mansūkhihi* (Jeddah: Dār al-Manārah, 1986).

Malik, Iftikhar, *Crescent Between Cross and Star* (London and Karachi: Oxford University Press, 2006).

Mamdani, Mahmoud, *Good Muslim, Bad Muslim* (New York: Pantheon Books 2004).

Maqrīzī, Taqiyyu al-Dīn Aḥmad ibn ʿAlī, *Imtāʿ al-Asmāʿ bimā li al-Rasūl mina al-Abnā' wa al-Amwāl wa al-Ḥafadah wa al-Matāʿ*, ed. Mahmoud Muhammad Shakir, 2nd edn., (Qatar: Ministry of Religious Affairs, n.d.).

Martin, Richard, *Approaches to Islam in Religious Studies* (Tucson: University of Arizona Press, 1985).

Maududi, Seyyed, *Tafhīm al-Qur'ān* (Lahore: Idara Tarjuman al-Qur'an, 1997).

McAuliffe, Jane Dammen, "The Prediction and Prefiguration of

Muhammad," *Bible and Qur'an: Essays in Scriptural Intertextuality*, Edited by John C. Reeves (Atlanta: Society of Biblical Literature, 2003).

McAuliffe, Jane Dammen, *Qur'ānic Christians,: An Analysis of Classical and Modern Exegesis* (Cambridge University Press, 1991).

___, "Disparity and Context: Teaching Quranic Studies in North America," in *Teaching Islam*, Brannon Wheeler, ed. (Oxford & New York: Oxford University Press, 2003).

McNeill, William H., *The Rise of the West: A History of the Human Community* (Chicago: University of Chicago Press, 1991).

Metzger, Bruce and Michael Coogan, eds. *Oxford Companion to the Bible* (Oxford and New York: Oxford University Press, 1995).

Mimun, Muhammad Umar, *Ibn Taymiyya's Struggle Against Popular Religion* (The Hague: Mouton, 1976).

Morris, James Winston, "How to Study the *Futūhāt*: Ibn 'Arabi's Own Advice," Stephen Hirtenstein and Michael Tiernan, eds., *Muhyiddin Ibn 'Arabi. A Commemorative Volume* (Shaftesbury, 1993).

Mubarakphuri, Muhammad, *Tuḥfat al-Aḥwathī bi Sharḥ Sunan al-Tirmidhī* (Beirut, Lebanon: Dār Iḥyā' al-Turāth al-ʿArabī, 2000).

Muḥammad ibn Aḥmad, *Ḥāshyat al-Dusūqī ʿAlā al Sharḥ al-Kabīr* (Dār Iḥyā' al-Kutub al-ʿArabiyyah), vol. 2.

Muhammad, Khalil, "The Art of Heeding," *Interfaith Dialogue at the Grass Roots*, Rebecca Kratz Mays, ed. (Philadelphia: The Ecumenical Press, 2008).

Muller, Max, (ed), *Sacred Books of the East, vol. 47 "Pahlavi Texts, vol. 5 of 5. Marvels of Zoroastrianism"* (Oxford: Oxford University Press, 1897).

Mundhirī, ʿAbd al-ʿAẓīm ibn ʿAbd al-Qawī, *Al-Targhīb wa al-Tarhīb min al-Ḥadīth al-Sharīf*, ed. Mustafa Muhammad Amarah, 1st edn. (Beirut: Dār al-Kutub al-ʿIlmiyyah, 1406 AH/1986 CE), 4 volumes.

Murata, Sachico, *The Tao of Islam* (State University of New York Press, 1992).

Murfin, Ross and Supriya Ray, *The Bedford Glossary of Critical and Literal Terms* (Boston and New York: Bedford Books, 1997).

Muslim, Muhammad, *Al-Jāmiʿ al-Ṣaḥīḥ*. Abd al-Hamid Siddiqi, trans. (Lahore, Pakistan: Sh. Muhammad Ashraf Booksellers, 1990).

Mutawalli al-Darsh, Sayyed, *Muslim Women's Dress: Ḥijāb or Niqāb* (Kuala Lumpur: Islamic Book Trust, 1997).

Al-Nasafī, *Tafsīr al-Nasafī*.

http://www.aljamea.net/services/viewing/Preview_Books.php, (December 2, 2008).

Nasr al-Din al-Albani, Muhammad, *Ḥijābul Mar'ah al-Muslimah fī al-Kitāb wa al-Sunnah* (Beirut: Al-Maktab al- Islāmī, 1969).

Nasr, Seyyed Hossein, *Sufi Essays* (London: 1972).

——, *Ideals and Realities of Islam* (Chicago, IL: ABC International Group, 2000).

Al-Nawawi, Muhiyi al-Din, *Sharḥ Ṣaḥiḥ Muslim* (Beirut, Lebanon: Dār al-Maᶜrifah, 1996).

Nicholson, Reynold A., "Lives of 'Umar, Ibnu'l-Farid and Muhiyyu'ddin Ibnu'l-'Arabi, *Journal of the Royal Asiatic Society* (*J.R.A.S.*), 1906.

Nyazi, Imran Ahsan Khan, *Islamic Jurisprudence* (Islamabad: The International Institute of Islamic Thought, 2000).

Palacios, Miguel Asin, *Ibn al-'Arabi, hayatuhu wa-madhhabuh*, tr. al-Isbaniyah 'Abd al-Rahsan Badawi, translation of *El-Islam Christianizado; estudio del "sufismo" a través de las obras de Abenarabi de Murcia* (Cairo: Maktabat al-Anjlu al-Miṣriyyah, 1965).

Plantinga, Alvin, "Pluralism: A Defense of Religious Exclusivism," in *The Philosophical Challenge of Religious Diversity*, K. Meeker and P.Quinn (eds.), (New York: Oxford University Press, 1999).

Ibn ᶜArabī (ᶜAbd al-Razzāq al-Kashānī), *Tafsīr Ibn ᶜArabī*, vol. 1. (Beirut).

Punch, 1915, at http://mathworld.wolfram.com/YoungGirl-Old WomanIllusion.html.

Quḍāᶜī, Abū ᶜAbd Allāh Muḥammad ibn Salāmah al-, *Musnad al-Shihāb*, ed. Hamdi Abd al-Majid al-Salafi, 1st edn. (Beirut: Mu'assasat al-Risālah, 1405 AH/1985 CE), 2 volumes.

Al-Qummī, Abū al-Ḥasan ᶜAlī ibn Ibrāhīm, *Tafsīr al-Qummī*, edited by al-Sayyid Tayyib al-Musawi al-Jaza'iri (Najaf: Maṭbaᶜat al-Najaf, 1967), vol. 1.

Al-Qurṭubī, Abū ᶜAbd Allāh Muḥammad ibn Aḥmad al-Anṣārī, *Al-Jāmiᶜ li Aḥkām al-Qur'ān* (Cairo: Dār al-Kitāb al-ᶜArabī, 1967), vol. 1.

Qutb, Sayyid, *Fī Ẓilāl al-Qur'ān* (Beirut: Dār Iḥyā' al-Turāth, 1971).

Rahman, Fazlur, "Pre-Foundation of Muslim Community in Mecca," *Studia Islamica*, No 43, (1976).

Rahman, Fazlur, *Islam and Modernity: Transformation of an Intellectual Tradition* (Chicago: University of Chicago Press, 1984).

———, *Major Themes of the Qur'an*, ed. 2 (Minneapolis: Bibliothica Islamica, 1994).
Al-Rāzī, Fakhr al-Dīn, *Tafsīr al-Kabīr* (Dār-al-Fikr: 1995).
Reinhardt, Kevin, "On the 'Introduction to Islam," *Teaching Islam*, Brannon Wheeler, ed. (Oxford and New York: University Press, 2003).
Rida, Rashid, *Tafsīr al-Manār* (Dār al-Fikr, 1947), vol. 2.
Said, Edward, *Covering Islam* (New York: Pantheon Books, 1981).
Sabiq, As-Sayyed, *Fiqh al-Sunnah* (American Trust Publications, 1996).
Sachedina, Abdul-Aziz, *The Islamic Roots of Democratic Pluralism* (Oxford: Oxford University Press,2001).
———, "The Nature of Scriptural Reasoning in Islam," in *The Journal of Scriptural Reasoning*, Number 5.1 (April 2005).
Ṣafadī, Cf. Khalīl ibn Aybak al-, *al-Wāfī bi al-Wafayāt* (Weisbaden: 1966), vol. 4.
Safi, Louay, *The Qur'anic Narrative: The Journey of Life as Told in the Qur'an* (Westport, CT: Praeger, 2008).
Sakhāwī, Shams ad-Dīn Muḥammad al-, *Al-Qanāʿah fī mā Yaḥsun al-Iḥaṭah min Ashrāṭ al-Sāʿah*, ed. Muhammad ibn Abd ar-Rahman al-Uqayl, (Riyadh: Aḍwā' al-Salaf, 1st edn., 1422 AH/2002 CE).
Salih, Subhi, *Mabāḥith fī ʿUlūm al-Qur'ān* (Beirut: Dār al-ʿIlm li al-Malāyīn, 2000).
Sandmel, William, "Parallelomania," *Journal of Biblical Literature*, no.81, vol. 1, March 1962.
Schwarzbaum, Haim, *Biblical and Extra-biblical Legends in Islamic Folk-Literature* (Walldorf, Hessen: Verlag für Orientkunde Dr. H. Vorndran, 1982).
Scriptures in Dialogue: Christians and Muslims Studying The Bible and The Qur'an Together, Edited by Michael Ipgrave (London: Church House Publishing, 2004).
Sells, Michael Anthony, *Mystical Languages of Unsaying* (Chicago: University of Chicago Press, 1994).
Shabun, Abdel Karim, *Sharḥ Mudawwanah al-Aḥwāl al-Shakhṣiyyah al-Maghribiyyah* (Rabat, Morocco: Maktabat al-Maʿārif), vol. 1.
Shah-Kazemi, Reza, *Paths to Transcendence: According to Shankara, Ibn Arabī, and Meister Eckhart* (Bloomington: World Wisdom, 2006).
Shahrur, Muhammad, *Al-Kitāb wa al-Qur'ān: Qirā'ah Muʿāṣirah*.
Shams al-Dīn al-Sarkhasī, *Al-Mabsūṭ* (Beirut: Dār al-Maʿarif: 1331 AH), vol. 5.

Al-Sharani, Abd al-Wahhab, *Al-Ṭabaqāt al-Kubrā* (Cairo: 1954), vol. 1.

Siddiqi, Muhammad Zubayr, *Ḥadīth Literature: Its Origin, Development and Special Features* (Islamic Texts Society, 2003).

Al-Sindi, Abu Hassan, *Sharḥ Sunan Ibn Mājah* (Beirut, Lebanon: Dār al-Maᶜrifah, 1996).

Smith, Wilfred Cantwell, *The Meaning and End of Religion* (New York: 1963).

Sodiq, Yushau, "Teaching Islamic Studies in American Universities," *Proceedings of the First Annual Symposium*. IIASA Research Center: (Fairfax, VA 1993-1995).

Stillman, Norman, "The Story of Cain and Abel in the Qur'an and the Muslim Commentators: Some Observations," *Journal of Semitic Studies*, vol. 19, 1974.

Stillwell, Cinnamon, "Truth about Islam in Academia?" *FrontPage Magazine*, July 2, 2008. http://www.campus-watch.org/article/ id/5325. *Studies* 36, (Cambridge University Press, 2000).

Al-Suyūṭī, Jalāl al-Dīn, *Al-Itqān fī ᶜUlūm al-Qur'ān* (Beirut: Dār al-Kutub al-ᶜIlmiyyah, 2000).

——, *Sharḥ Sunan al-Nasā'ī* (Beirut, Lebanon: Dār-al-Maᶜrifah, 1992).

——, *Al-Durr al-Manthūr fī al-Tafsīr al-Ma'thūr*, 1st edn. (Beirut: Dār al-Kutub al-ᶜIlmiyyah, 1411 AH/1990 CE), 10 volumes.

——, *Jāmiᶜ al-Ahādīth*, ed. Abbas Ahmad Saqr and Ahmad Abd al-Jawad (Beirut: Dār al-Fikr, 1414 AH/1994 CE), 21 volumes.

Al-Ṭabarī, Abū Jaᶜfar Muḥammad ibn Jarīr, *Jāmiᶜ al-Bayān ᶜan Ta'wīl Āy al-Qur'ān* (Cairo: Dār al-Maᶜārif, 1969), vol. 6.

Al-Ṭabarānī, Sulaymān, *Al-Muᶜjam al-Kabīr* ("al-Mu'jam" CD, Third Edition, 2001).

Al-Ṭabarānī, *Al-Muᶜjam al-Awsaṭ*, ed. Dr. Mahmoud al-Tahhan, 1st edn., (Riyadh: Maktabat al-Maᶜārif, 1407 AH/1987 CE), 10 volumes.

Tabatabaei Sayyid Muhammad Husayn, *Al-Mīzān fī Tafsīr al-Qur'ān* (Mu'assasāt al-Aᶜlamī li al-Matbūᶜāt, 1974), vol. 3.

Al-Tābiᶜī, Mujāhid ibn Jabr al-Makhzūmī, *Tafsīr Mujāhid* (Exegesis of Mujāhid), http://www.aljamea.net/services/viewing/Preview_Books.php, (December 2, 2008).

Tabrizi, Muhammad ibn Abd Allah, *Mishkāt al-Maṣābiḥ*, ed. Nasr ad-Din al-Albani, 3rd edn. (Beirut: Al-Maktab al-Islamī, 1405 AH/1985 CE), 3 volumes.

Tahmaz, Abdul Hamid, *Al-Fiqh Al-Ḥanafī* (Damascus: Dār al-Qalam, 1998).

Tahrali, Mustafa, "The Polarity of Expression in The Fuṣūṣ al-Ḥikam," in Hirtenstein and Tiernan, eds., *Muhyiddin Ibn 'Arabi. A Commemorative Volume* (Shaftesbury, Dorset; Rockport, MA: Element, 1993).

Takeshita, Masataka, *Ibn 'Arabī's Theory of the Perfect Man and Its Place in the History of Islamic Thought* (Tokyo: 1987). (*Studia culturae islamicae*, v. 32).

Ṭayālisī, Sulaymān ibn Dāwūd al-Jārūd, *Al-Musnad* (Beirut: Dār al-Maʿrifah [1406 AH]. This edition is a photocopy of Haidarabad al-Dakan, India, edition, 1321 AH).

Tottoli, Roberto, *Biblical Prophets in the Qur'ān and Muslim Literature*, (Curzon Press, 2002).

Wahbah al-Zuhayli, *Al-Fiqh al-Islāmī wa Adillatuhu* (Damascus, Dār-al-Fikr: 1985), vol. 7.

Wāḥidī, Abū al-Ḥasan ʿAlī ibn Aḥmad, *Asbāb Nuzūl al-Qur'ān*, ed. Sayyid Ahmad Saqr, 1st edn. (Cairo: Dār al-Kitāb al-Jadīd, 1389 AH/1969 CE).

Waldman, Marilyn, "New Approaches to "Biblical" Materials in the Qur'an," *Studies in Islamic and Judaic Traditions*, William Brinner and Stephen Ricks, eds. (Atlanta, GA: Scholars Press, 1986).

Walī Allāh, Shāh, *Al-Fawz al-Kabīr*, Khurshid Anwar, Urdu trans. (Deoband, India: Kutub Khana Husayniyah, n.d.).

Al-Wany, Nashwah, *Mausūʿat Aḥkām al-Mar'ah al-Muslimah* (Damascus, Syria: Dār al-Maktabī, 2002), vol. 2.

Watt, William Montgomery, *Muslim Intellectual: A Study of al-Ghazali* (University of Edinburgh Press).

Wehr, Hans, and Ed. Cowan, Milton, *A Dictionary of Modern Written Arabic*, 3rd Edn. (Beirut, Lebanon: Librarairi Du Liban, 1980).

Wheeler, Brannon, "The Jewish Origins of Q 18:65-82? Reexamination of Arent Jan Wensinck's Theory," *Journal of the American Oriental Society*, vol. 118, no.2, 1998.

____, Ed., *Teaching Islam* (New York and Oxford, 2003).

Winkel, Erick, "Ibn 'Arabi's *Fiqh*: Three Cases from the *Futūhāt*," *Journal of the Muhiyyidin Ibn 'Arabi Society*, vol. 13, 1993, 54–74.

Winter, Michael, *Society and Religion in Early Ottoman Egypt* (New Brunswick, NJ).

Wright, W., *A Grammar of the Arabic Language* (Beirut: Librairie du Liban, 1996).
Al-Zamakhsharī, Abū al-Qāsim Jār Allāh Maḥmūdibn ʿUmar, *Al-Kashshāf ʿan Ḥaqā'iq al-Tanzīl wa ʿUyūn al-Aqāwīl fī Wujūh al-Tafsīr* (Cairo: Muṣṭafā al-Bābī al-Ḥalabī, 1966).
Al-Zamakhsharī, *Al-Kashāf ʿan Ḥaqā'iq al-Tanzīl wa ʿUyūn al-aQāwīl fī Wujūh al-Ta'wīl* (Dār al-Fikr: n.d.), vol. 1.
Zarabozo, Jamal Aldin, *The Friday Prayer* (Islamic Assembly of North America, 1994).
Al-Zarkashi, *Al-Burhān fī ʿUlūm al-Qur'ān* (Beirut: Dār-al-Maʿrifah, 1994).
Al-Zurqani, Muhammad Abd, *Manāhil al-ʿIrfān fī ʿUlūm al-Qur'ān* (Beirut: Dār Iḥyā' al-ʿArabī, 1998).